Zagreb

the Bradt City Guide

Piers Letcher
Sarah Parkes

www.bradtguides.com

Bradt Travel Guides Ltd, UK
The Globe Pequot Press Inc, USA

edition
1

St Mark's and the Zagreb coat of arms (PL) page 187

Croatian National Theatre (PL) page 147

Dolac market (SP) page 139

Tkalčićeva – the perfect place to unwind (PL) page 129

The Fisherman, by Simeon Roksandić (VJK) page 164

Bogovićeva's cafés by night (PL) page 173

Fernkorn's golden angels, Kaptol (RM) page 168

Statue of King Tomislav and Zagreb's main railway station (BB) page 171

Mirogoj Cemetery (PL) page 218

Lighting votive candles, Stone Gate
(PL) page 184

The Medvednica bear marking the entry to the Nature Park (PL) page 22

The Plešivica wine region (PL) page 263

Nesting storks south of Zagreb (PL) page 278

Authors

Piers Letcher Born and educated in the UK, Piers has lived in France for the past 25 years. As an independent writer and photographer he has published 16 books, more than 1,000 newspaper and magazine articles and hundreds of photographs. From the mid 1990s he spent several years as a speechwriter at the United Nations in Geneva, before returning to his freelance career in 2002. He is the author of *Eccentric France*, *Croatia: The Bradt Travel Guide* and *Dubrovnik: The Bradt City Guide*, and contributes irregularly to the *Guardian Unlimited*. *Zagreb: The Bradt City Guide* is his eighth guidebook.

Sarah Parkes began her career as a journalist, and was an editor at Lonely Planet travel guides in Australia before moving to France in 1995. A highly successful freelance writer whose work has regularly appeared in leading publications in the UK, US and Australia, Sarah also works intermittently as a consultant with the United Nations in Geneva, most recently as Chief of Media Relations for the UN World Summit on the Information Society. *Zagreb: The Bradt City Guide* is her first guidebook.

First published April 2007

Bradt Travel Guides Ltd
23 High Street, Chalfont St Peter, Bucks SL9 9QE, England; www.bradtguides.com
Published in the US by The Globe Pequot Press Inc, 246 Goose Lane, PO Box 480,
Guilford, Connecticut 06437-0480

A catalogue record for this book is available from the British Library

ISBN-10: 1 84162 189 7   ISBN-13: 978 1 84162 189 0

Photographers Bojan Bonifačić/www.photocroatia.com (BB), Vlatko Juric-Kokic/www.photocroatia.com
(VJK), Piers Letcher (PL), Robin McKelvie (RM), Sarah Parkes (SP)
Cover Sunset over Zagreb's main shopping street, Ilica (Dražen Stojčić/www.photocroatia.com)
Title page St Mark's Church (PL), Fernkorn's golden angels (RM)
Maps Steve Munns   **Illustrations** Carole Vincer

Typeset from the authors' disk by Wakewing   Printed and bound in Spain by Grafo SA, Bilbao

Contents

FEEDBACK REQUEST

At Bradt Travel Guides we're well aware that guidebooks start to go out of date on the day they're published – and that you, our readers, are out there in the field, doing research of your own. You'll find out before us when a fine new family-run hotel opens or a favourite restaurant changes hands and goes downhill. So why not write to us and tell us about your experiences? We'll happily include you in the acknowledgments of the next edition of the guide if we use your feedback – so write to us: we'll look forward to hearing from you!

Piers Letcher and Sarah Parkes **e** bradtcroatia@yahoo.co.uk

Acknowledgements

First and sincerest thanks must go to Dubravka Mičić, at the Zagreb Tourist Board, who did wonders in helping to make busy research trips in 2006 a whole lot easier than they might have been – and we're grateful also to Amelia Tomašević and Iva Čaleta in the same office.

Thanks too, to Lidija Mišćin and Vlatka Marić at the Zagreb County Tourist Board; Ingrid Lovrić and Krešo Jakubak at the Medvednica Nature Park; Krešimir Režek and Želko Škiljan in Plešivica; Dina Begić, Anđelka Mađar and Dubravka Lapčić in Karlovac; Branka Tropp, Tanja Bunjevac and Elizabeta Dolenc in Varaždin; Sandra Bojić in Krapina; Kristijan Kovačić and Rudi Gruba in the Međimurje; Stuart Panes, Gary Jarvis and Renata, and Pat and Vince Carson in Zagreb; Paul Newman, Trudy Smith, Jonathan Hemus, Susannah Little and Pete Wilson in Berlin; and Darinka Širola at www.bicikl.hr. For showing us around museums and dealing patiently with our idiot questions, we're grateful to Ivana Čukvina Nikolić at the Mimara Museum; Ivana Rončević at the Modern Gallery; Sanjin Mihelić at the Archaeological Museum; Borivoj Popovčak at the Strossmayer Gallery; Mirjana Randić at the Ethnographic Museum; Vladimir Crnković at the Naïve Art Gallery; Deana Kovačec at the State Archives; Mario Mirković at the Technical Museum; Petra Tramiščak at the Klovićevi

Dvori; Vesna Vrabec at the Bela and Miroslav Krleža House; Silvija Berković at the Gvozdanović Collection; Duda Dravica Modriča at the Museum of the Turopolje; and last but not least Jakov Radovčić and David Frayer (Krapina men both!) and Edo Kletečki at the Natural History Museum.

Individual thanks also to Vladimir Fumić who rented us the bicycles which made the research possible, and Sanda Sokol at the Regent Esplanade, who made us welcome and proved her point about the *štrukli*.

We'd also like to express our gratitude to all the good people at Bradt Travel Guides, whose hard work make these guides the best in the field, and of course, a heartfelt thank you to all the people whose names we never caught, who offered help, hospitality and kindness along the way.

Finally, we'd like to thank the people at OnAir, SITA and TCF (among others) for helping keep a roof over our heads, and Brice and Alec, who do a great deal, in the best possible sense (we're sure), to distract us.

DEDICATION

To our parents – Peter, Virginia, Fred and Shirley – and to all those who make Zagreb the wonderful place it is.

Introduction

Piers and Sarah have been travelling together around Croatia for most of the present century, and Piers has a relationship with the country going back 25 years, since he first inter-railed round Europe in 1982, and got off at the wrong train station in Zagreb on his arrival.

They've both worked on *Croatia: The Bradt Travel Guide* (now in its third edition) and *Dubrovnik: The Bradt City Guide* (first published in 2005; new edition in 2007) but have been champing at their collective bit to write about Zagreb for years: it's quite possibly their favourite European city. As a result, they hope you'll find, between these covers, the most useful, interesting, up-to-date and (dare they say it) comprehensive guide to the city you could possibly hope for.

How to Use this Book

Most museums close at least one day a week – usually Monday. They're mostly open by 10.00 and close sometime between 13.00–18.00. Policies vary around national holidays so do check beforehand. Pre-booked groups can usually arrange for museums to be opened specially for them.

EMAIL ADDRESSES Where one is given, assume that correspondence in English is fine.

WEBSITES Where websites are listed, there's usually an English text available somewhere on the site. A few restaurants publish menus online.

MAP REFERENCES (eg: [2 G1]) relate to the colour map section at the end of the guide.

HOTEL PRICES These can fluctuate according to the booking agency used, and the day of the week. Take those listed here as a good indication of what you'll pay as an individual traveller; and try bargaining for reductions at weekends.

x

RESTAURANT PRICES These always include VAT (PDV) and service; rounding up to the nearest 10kn or so is standard practice. Prices are usually the same for lunch and dinner.

OPENING HOURS Cafés and bars open up from breakfast-time onwards, and most stay open until 23.00–midnight. Restaurants open at 11.30 and some will stay open through the afternoon. Closing time is usually around 22.00–23.00, though some places stay open later, especially in summer; check the closing time if you have a particular favourite, and bear in mind that many places take one day off a week. Where bookings are necessary, we say so in the text.

ZAGREB AT A GLANCE

Location In northern Croatia, 20km from the Slovenian border, 100km from Hungary. Longitude: 15°59', latitude: 45°49'

Climate Continental; hot summers, cold winters

Population 780,000 (2001 census). 1.2 million in greater Zagreb

Language Croatian

Religion Roman Catholic (87%); agnostic and non-believers (8%); Muslim (2%); Orthodox Christian (2%)

Currency kuna: £1 = 10.8kn; € 1 = 7.4kn; US$1 = 5.7kn

Time CET (GMT +1)

Telephone code 01 (+385 1 from abroad)

Electricity/plugs Electricity comes in the European standard size and shape, at 220V and 50Hz, via standard European twin round-pinned sockets.

Public holidays 1 January; Easter Monday; 1 May; Corpus Christi; 22 June; 25 June; 5 August; 15 August; 8 October; 1 November; 16 November (Day of the City of Zagreb); 25 December; 26 December (see page 25 for further details)

| Contexts

INTRODUCTION TO THE CITY

Rebecca West sized up Croatia's capital nicely when she was here in 1937:

> Zagreb makes from its featureless handsomeness something that pleases like a
> Schubert song, a delight that begins quietly and never definitely ends. It has the
> endearing characteristic noticeable in many French towns of remaining a small town
> when it is in fact quite large.

Indeed, today, with a population of a million, Zagreb is easily Croatia's largest and
most cosmopolitan city, though the centre is still agreeably manageable on foot.

Zagreb's heart is a fine, clean example of solid Habsburg architecture, tending
towards palatial elegance, and large squares from which to view it – though if you
move away from the city centre you'll find sprawling suburbs and high rises, thrown
up to accommodate waves of incoming workers over the past 60 years.

For more than six months of the year Zagreb is a lively outdoor city, with café
tables spilling out across the pavements and flowers everywhere. In winter it can be
cold and a bit oppressive, with snow on the ground for an average of over 50 days
annually and the streets of the lower town seeming too large for their occupants –

WHAT'S IN A NAME?

There are several conflicting theories about why Zagreb should be so called, but everyone agrees that the name was first recorded in 1094, when Hungary's King Ladislav founded the bishopric here.

The most logical hypothesis is that 'Zagreb' means 'in the ditch', because of its geographic situation – a theory backed up by the old German name for the city being 'Agram', a contraction of '*am Graben*', meaning 'the same thing'. Another supposition is that the city was named after efforts to scrape and dig away the soil in search of water here – though we're sceptical about how much water that theory can hold, with the great River Sava a stone's throw away.

The name could also – if the word is Slavonian, which is itself doubtful – come from '*za grebom*', meaning 'behind the tomb', though *which* tomb also seems to be a well-shrouded mystery.

Our favourite explanation, however, is that 'Zagreb' is a corruption of '*za breg*', meaning 'behind the hill'. Quite apart from anything else, it reflects an elegantly Austro-Hungarian centric view of the world; anyone else would describe Zagreb as being 'in front of the hill'.

but with a big university and heaps of bars, clubs and nightlife on offer, the locals certainly know how to have a good time. The city is also particularly strong on classical culture, with regular opera, ballet, theatre and musical performances of international standard.

HISTORY

Judging by the remains found in the Veternica Cave (see page 225) on Medvednica, people have been living in the Zagreb area for at least 35,000 years. Modern history here doesn't begin until much, much more recently, however – around the 4th century BC – when Celtic tribes poured in from the north, only to be swiftly mopped up by Romans arriving from the south.

The Romans created several settlements in the area, which was important then, as now, as a crossroads on east–west and north–south trade routes. After the decline of the empire, the region faded back into obscurity, however, until the year AD879, when it became part of the first Croatian state, which reached its apotheosis in 925 under King Tomislav – the guy on the big horse in front of Zagreb's main train station.

At the end of the 11th century, a lack of heirs saw the Croatian crown pass to Hungary, paving the way for the creation of the Zagreb diocese in 1094. It was nonetheless the rival communities of Kaptol (with the cathedral) and Gradec (today's old town) which made the running for several centuries thereafter.

FEUDS AND FORTIFICATIONS The first cathedral was built in 1217, only to be trashed – along with everything else – by rampaging Tartars 25 years later. As a

3

consequence, Bela IV, the Hungarian king, authorised the construction of fortifications for Gradec (it was home to the Hungarian garrison, after all) in 1242, and gave the settlement 'Free City' status for its part in hiding him from the enemy.

Solid ramparts and walls were built around Gradec by 1266, though today the only signs you'll see are the Lotrščak Tower (where the noonday cannon is fired from – see page 183) and the Stone Gate (Porta Lapidea, see page 184), one of the original entrances to the old town, though the current version is 18th century. Up above the city, on Medvednica, meanwhile, work started in 1254 on what would eventually become the imposing Medvedgrad Fortress – though from the 16th century to its pricey restoration in the 1990s, there wasn't much more to it than a few ruins.

Kaptol, for its part, was only allowed to fortify in the 15th century, with the Turks practically on the doorstep. In 1469, the Sultan's army got as far as the Sava River, where they were miraculously scared off by a single cannon shot from the Lotrščak Tower. No, of course they weren't – but that's the legend behind the cannon still fired towards the Sava every day. What actually repulsed the Turks was the Sava conveniently and spectacularly bursting its banks (something that would happen regularly, and catastrophically, until the current dykes were built in 1971).

The Ottomans went on being uppity for another century, though even their great victory of 1525, which led Croatia to seek Habsburg protection, didn't see Zagreb directly invaded, and the Turks were finally routed definitively in 1593 at Sisak, 50km southeast of the city.

With no common enemy to divert them, Gradec and Kaptol were now free to continue their rivalrous relationship across the Medveščak creek dividing them (now Tkalčićeva). The painted wooden bridge across the brook was the scene of frequent and violent conflicts – most famously in 1667, when drunken soldiers loyal to the powerful Zrinski family were persuaded by Kaptol to attack Gradec, with bloody results on both sides. Although today neither creek nor bridge remains, the short street where the bridge once stood still bears the name 'Krvavi Most' – literally 'Blood Bridge'.

THE CREATION OF A HABSBURG CAPITAL It was only in the 19th century that the ancient rivalry between Gradec and Kaptol began to ease, with common interests finally prevailing – Zagreb was, after all, an important regional staging post on the routes from Vienna and Budapest to the sea. They were also brought together by the resurgence of Croatian nationalism, driven in large part by Ljudevit Gaj, who oversaw the publication of the first Croatian newspapers in 1835. New institutions flourished, with the founding of the Music Society in 1826, Croatian (originally Illyrian) Heritage in 1839, the Academy of Arts and Sciences in 1866, and the University in 1874.

Key to this burgeoning scene was Josip Jelačić, the guy on the big horse in Zagreb's eponymously named main square. Jelačić was made 'ban' (viceroy) of Croatia in 1848, and swiftly made his mark, confirming Croatian as the new parliamentary language (it was formerly Latin), recapturing the Međimurje (the part

5

of Croatia north of Varaždin) from Hungary, and abolishing serfdom – and all before the year was out.

Two years later, Franz Josef I, the Habsburg emperor, proclaimed Zagreb as a single city, and ushered in a whole new architectural era – particularly after 1857, when new building regulations came in stipulating streets at least 13m wide intersecting at right angles, and prescribing the heights and shapes of all new buildings (Habsburg, basically).

Everything was going swimmingly for Zagreb until 9 November 1880, when a devastating earthquake almost totally destroyed the city. The massive rebuilding programme which followed explains the uniform late 19th-century architecture which characterises Zagreb today, and was particularly noteworthy for the achievements of two men, the architect Hermann Bollé, and the urban planner Milan Lenuci. Bollé was responsible for the new neo-Gothic façade on the cathedral, the lovely Mirogoj Cemetery north of the city and the solid elegance of the Arts and Crafts Museum, while Lenuci designed the so-called 'Green Horseshoe', a series of grand, green squares which dominate the lower town between the train station and the central square.

INTO THE 20TH CENTURY Zagreb remained annexed to the Austro-Hungarian Empire until the end of World War I, when it became part of the newly created Kingdom of Serbs, Croats and Slovenes – first under the Crown of King Petar I, and then three years later under his son, King Aleksandar I. The idea of an independent Croatia was still fiercely held onto by many Croats, including Croatian firebrand

Stjepan Radić and his Croatian Peasants' Party (CPP). After a decade of vigorous debating, the issue was resolved spectacularly when Radić and several other CPP delegates were shot in Belgrade's parliament on 20 June 1928.

Radić died of his wounds a few weeks later, and was given a huge funeral in Zagreb. The ongoing unrest proved so intense that at the beginning of 1929, Aleksandar 'reluctantly' suspended parliament and established a dictatorship. He did manage to put diplomats and letter writers out of their misery, however, by changing the country's name to the much more manageable Yugoslavia – the country of the South Slavs – before himself being assassinated in Marseille in 1934.

Behind the plot was the Ustaše, a fascist party founded by Ante Pavelić, who had apparently been known as an extremist even in his youth, and who had been condemned to death in absentia by Belgrade for organising anti-Serb demonstrations in exile. Yugoslavia, meanwhile, was struggling under the stewardship of Aleksandar's son, who was only 11 when he came to the throne – and World War II was just around the corner.

Amazingly, Yugoslavia managed to remain neutral for the first 18 months of the war, but it fell promptly when Germany attacked in April 1941, and within days the Ustaše declared the Independent State of Croatia (*Nezavisna Drzava Hrvatska*, NDH), with Pavelić at the helm. The NDH conducted an organised extermination campaign against Serbs, Jews, Gypsies and communists, and stayed in power until the end of World War II, when it finally succumbed to the Partisans, the army of the Communist Party, led by Josip Broz 'Tito'.

Franjo Tuđman was born in 1922 and at the age of 19 joined Tito's Partisans, becoming a decorated hero by the end of World War II. His youngest brother was killed in 1943, and his depressed father is said to have shot himself and his second wife in 1946 – though Tuđman himself claimed first that they were victims of the Ustaše and later that they were victims of the communists. (As a curious parallel, both of Milošević's parents died before their time too, both committing suicide.)

After the war, Tuđman stayed in the army until 1961, when he retired at the age of 38. During the 1960s, as a historian, he gradually began to fall out of favour with the communists, and in 1971, following the suppression of the 'Croatian Spring', he was jailed for a short time, escaping a longer sentence only through the intervention with Tito of the respected Croatian writer Miroslav Krleža (see page 207).

A decade later and more strongly nationalist than ever, Tuđman was given a three-year sentence and banned from all public activity for his dissident/revisionist views on history

AFTER WORLD WAR II Post-war elections gave Tito's communists 90% of the vote – with separate ballot boxes provided for those who cared to vote against Tito – and the freedom to rule on the lines adopted by Stalinist Russia. After Yugoslavia's disastrous experiment with collectivisation, the day was fortunately saved by the launch of mass tourism in the 1960s, and the country did remarkably well until Tito's death.

and for advocating a pluralist democracy. He served about half of this before being released because of failing health.

In 1987, having finally got his passport back after 17 years, he travelled widely in the West, promoting the cause of Croatian independence, and in 1989 he founded the Croatian Democratic Union (HDZ), which became the dominant political force in the first multi-party parliamentary election in the spring of 1990. The tenor of the campaign can be measured by Tuđman reportedly having said 'Thank God my wife is neither a Serb nor a Jew.'

In spite of the strong words, Tuđman nonetheless found time for a secret meeting with Milošević in March 1991, to discuss how Croatia and Serbia might carve up Bosnia and Herzegovina for themselves. Nonetheless, Tuđman was hugely popular, as the first person since the Middle Ages to gain international recognition for Croatia as an independent state. At his funeral, in December 1999, thousands filed past his coffin – but only his death may have saved him from being indicted, like Milošević, by the Hague Tribunal.

Croatia, as the autonomous republic bringing most of the tourist Deutschmarks into Yugoslavia's state coffers, was still champing at the bit, however, and in 1967 a new wave of dissent started in Zagreb with calls for decentralisation of the economy and improved civil rights for Croatians. This didn't sit well with the communist government, which feared – rightly, as it turned out – instability and the break-up of the country, and in 1971 the 'Croatian Spring' was suppressed, with the arrest of prominent activists. Among their number was Croatia's future first president, Franjo Tuđman (see box, page 8). In 1974, however, a new federal constitution was adopted which gave each republic the official right to secede – which they've now all done, leaving lonely Serbia behind.

For all Tito's strengths, he left behind a weak succession on his death in 1980. Each of the republics would, in theory, get a year as head man, but without Tito's personal charisma and unifying muscle it was never going to work well. It wasn't long before the old problems of nationalism, unfair distribution of wealth between the republics, and corruption in government resurfaced.

Onto the scene stepped Slobodan Milošević, who rapidly gained popularity in Serbia after defending Serb protestors against mostly ethnic Albanian police in Kosovo in 1987. Two years later, on 28 June 1989 (the 700th anniversary of the great Serbian defeat by the Turks at Kosovo Polje), Milošević addressed a million Serbs at the fateful field, and was elected President of Serbia in the autumn.

It was the beginning of the end for a united Yugoslavia. Milošević's bluster about an ethnically pure Greater Serbia was never going to sit well with Croats – or indeed Slovenes, Bosnians, Macedonians and Kosovars.

WAR AND CROATIAN INDEPENDENCE The 1989 collapse of the Soviet Union and the fall of communist governments across Europe encouraged several Yugoslav republics, led by Slovenia and Croatia, to try and change the country's political structure. In 1990, the Croatian Democratic Union (HDZ), led by Franjo Tuđman, won elections. Once in power, the HDZ pushed parliament to drop the word 'Socialist' from the Croatian republic's name, and the red star was quietly removed from public symbols.

The HDZ also put Croatia's 600,000 Serbs on the defensive by changing their status from 'constituent nation' in Croatia to 'national minority', and many Serbs in government lost their jobs. The HDZ didn't improve matters by making itself an easy target for Serb propaganda – party members playing straight into Serb hands by attempting to rehabilitate the Ustaše.

During the summer of 1990, encouraged by Belgrade into fearing real danger, Croatia's Serbs (armed by the Yugoslav People's Army, the JNA) declared an autonomous region around Knin, 200km south of Zagreb. Croatian police helicopters, sent in to sort out the trouble, were soon scuttled by Yugoslav air force MiGs. Tension continued to mount until March 1991, when Knin paramilitaries took control of the Plitvice Lakes, resulting in the first casualties of the conflict.

Slovenia, meanwhile, had unilaterally decided to declare independence on 25 June 1991, so Croatia declared independence on the same day. Milošević sent tanks into Ljubljana, Slovenia's capital, and to the Italian and Austrian borders. The world sat up and took notice, and the EU introduced sanctions; within a week the war in Slovenia was over, and within a month the JNA had left the country – though it only retreated as far as Croatia, and later distributed many weapons to the local Serb population.

Croatia, with a significant Serb minority, wasn't as fortunate as Slovenia. As soon as it proclaimed independence, the Serbs countered by proclaiming the independent state of Republika Srpska Krajina (RSK) within Croatia, declaring loyalty to Belgrade and Milošević (the commander of the army), and choosing Knin as its capital.

In six months at the end of 1991 – with the help of the JNA, and heavy fighting, bombardments and air strikes – the Serbs ethnically 'cleansed' nearly a third of Croatia, re-awakening memories of the brutality of the 1940s. Thousands of Croats were forced to leave their homes and many were killed by the JNA or loosely associated paramilitary forces. The tourist trade – one of Croatia's main sources of foreign earnings – came to a complete halt.

Zagreb itself was fortunate in largely avoiding direct conflict during the war, though in the autumn of 1991 the Ban's Palace (the official president's residence) was successfully targeted by a rogue rocket attack (you can see a reconstruction in the City Museum of what happened – see page 190), and in the spring of 1995, seven people lost their lives during the last shellings of the city.

The city was spared, but the people of Zagreb were scarred, and from 1993 a touching raw brick monument to lost and missing soldiers and civilians was built by their mothers and relatives around the UN Peace Mission headquarters (on the corner of Ilica and Selska) – with each brick representing a dead or missing person. The monument is being replaced by a new formal memorial in Mirogoj Cemetery, though relatives are upset that the original bricks won't be visible.

PENKALA THE INVENTOR

Largely forgotten now, but enormously influential at the time, was a man called Eduard Slavoljub Penkala (1871–1922). An inveterate inventor, he was forever looking for ways to improve day-to-day life. In 1906, he patented the world's first 'mechanical pencil', the pioneer in a whole range of writing devices which actually worked, and from 1914 to 1926, as a direct result, Zagreb became the European capital for the production of writing instruments.

Penkala himself never gave up his job at the Ministry of Finance (where he was Royal Technical Controller), but seems to have had plenty of time to work on his inventions, leaving him free to become Croatia's first aviator, in 1909, and the inventor of its first two-seater aircraft the following year. He also patented a hovercraft design in 1908, half a century ahead of Christopher Cockerell's antics on the Isle of Wight, and a rotating toothbrush the same year, when dental hygiene was still barely a blip on the horizon.

In a short life – he died of pneumonia, aged only 50 – Penkala came up with hundreds of inventions and registered over 70 patents.

In 1994, while the war was still on, Pope John Paul II visited Zagreb as part of the city's 900th anniversary celebrations, and a million people turned out to see him. A decade later, in 2004, Croatia became an official EU candidate country.

KEY DATES IN THE HISTORY OF ZAGREB

1094   King Ladislav founds the Archbishopric of Zagreb.

1217   Completion of Zagreb's first cathedral.

1242   King Bela IV gives Golden Bull to Gradec, proclaiming it a free city.

1469   Turkish army scared off by a single cannon shot from the Lotrščak Tower.

1517   Completion of Kaptol fortifications.

1641   Creation of a new main square (now Trg Jelačića).

1835   Publication in Zagreb of the first newspaper in the Croatian language.

1848   Ban Jelačić confirms Croatian as official parliamentary language, abolishes serfdom and gets back Međimurje for Croatia.

1850   Franz Josef proclaims Zagreb as a single city.

1880   Huge earthquake destroys most of Zagreb.

1918   Zagreb becomes part of the Kingdom of Serbs, Croats and Slovenes (from 1929 Yugoslavia).

1928   Stjepan Radić shot in Belgrade's parliament.

1941   Zagreb becomes part of the fascist NDH.

1945   Zagreb becomes part of Yugoslavia.

1971   Suppression of the 'Croatian Spring'.

1987   Zagreb hosts the World Student Games (and gets a major facelift).

1990   First multi-party elections held and first session of the Croatian parliament (Sabor).

1992 Croatia receives formal recognition of nationhood from the international community.
1994 Pope's visit to Zagreb coincides with city's 900th anniversary.
1996 Peace treaty with Serbia.
2004 Croatia becomes an official EU candidate country.

POLITICS

Independence brought Croatia a new constitution and a new political system which – as the Ministry of Foreign Affairs says on its website (*www.mvp.hr*) – is now 'democratic and based on a respect for human rights, law, national equality, social justice and multiple political parties'. The last part is certainly true, with a bewildering array of three- and four-letter acronyms to deal with. The really important one to remember is the HDZ, the nationalist Croatian Democratic Union, which was founded by the new nation's first president, Franjo Tuđman (see box on page 8).

After Tuđman's death in 1999, the HDZ was trounced in parliamentary elections, and Stipe Mesić was elected president in 2000. The popular centrist was elected to a second five-year term in 2005, having used his personal friend Charlie's bar (see page 133) as an electoral stump. Even today, the president continues to live at his private house on Ilica, rather than up in the official residence in the old town, and you can see him often enough having a drink at one of his favourite watering holes in town – surely unique among modern political leaders.

In the most recent parliamentary elections, held at the end of 2003, the HDZ saw a return to form, winning 66 of the 151 seats available in the Sabor (parliament), and able to form a government via an informal coalition with other smaller parties. Both the president and the prime minister, Ivo Sanader, are keen to join NATO and the EU – although hopes that this might happen sooner rather than later may be overly optimistic.

In Zagreb itself, the other really important political figure is the controversial, larger-than-life mayor, Milan Bandić, who has bounced back and is now serving a third term after resigning in 2002, following a drink-driving traffic accident. Bandić has been doing a great deal of populist work in smartening up the city – notably, recently cleaning up and reopening the Bundek lakes and parks south of the river. With Zagreb said to be responsible for three-quarters of Croatian GDP, and a city budget of close to seven billion kuna, Bandić is widely considered the third most important politician in the country, after President Mesić and Prime Minister Sanader. News that Bandić may run for president in 2010 is already causing consternation in political circles.

ECONOMY

Progress towards economic reform after the war in the 1990s was hampered by coalition politics and resistance on the street, mainly from trade unions, but the government is now keen to achieve EU membership, and the economy is looking in better shape than it has for years.

WESTERN TIES

Most businessmen dressing for work in the morning don't spare a thought for Croatia – which is a pity, as the ubiquitous necktie they put on not just originated there but is named after the country.

The origins of one of fashion's most durable accessories date back to the Thirty Years War in Europe, which ran from 1618 to 1648. The story goes that Croatian mercenaries of the period wore a colourful silk scarf tied around the neck. Some of their number were stationed in Paris, and were presented to the court (whether that of Louis XIII, who died in 1643, or Louis XIV, who succeeded him, is debatable), triggering off a copycat craze for *cravates* – the word coming from dressing *à la Croat* (or *Hrvat*, in Croatian).

During the dandyish reign of Louis XIV, the wearing of *cravates* by Frenchmen became widespread, and the new fashion soon spread right across Europe – indeed the French word '*cravate*' exists in one form or another in almost every European language, from '*gravata*' in Greek to '*krawatte*' in German.

Today, businessmen and politicians worldwide consider the tie as a basic part of their wardrobe – though for the most part they probably aren't wearing the enormously expensive long, floppy silk scarves favoured by Croatian soldiers, but the rather more sober ties which first appeared in England at the end of the 19th century.

17

Inflation was 3.3% in 2005, and GDP grew by 4.3% during the year. Nonetheless, Croatian GDP per capita, at US$12,300 PPP, (Purchasing Power Parity) was still under half that in the UK or France. Average gross salary had risen to 6,248kn per month (around €860), however, and unemployment was down to 12.3% – and just 10% in Zagreb.

Zagreb is said to be responsible for three-quarters of Croatian GDP, and it shows in the number of expensive restaurants and hotels, as well as in the price of real estate across the city.

TOURISM Visitor numbers to Zagreb are increasing steadily, with a 16% rise between 2003 and 2005, and numbers are now well in excess of their pre-war levels. In 2006, daily low-cost flights started from London, which should push up numbers considerably. The city's central European location, manageable size and modern exhibition and congress centres are also making it an increasingly popular convention venue.

Nonetheless, in terms of absolute numbers, Zagreb sees relatively few visitors for its size – 550,000 in 2005, compared with 910,000 for the Dubrovnik region and 2.5 million for Istria – meaning that tourism doesn't have as much impact on the capital as it does on the coast and islands.

The vast majority of visitors (over 85%) to Croatia are other Europeans, the most numerous among them in 2005 being Germans (1.6 million) and Italians (1.3 million). The UK comes some way down the list, with 256,000 visitors in 2005 – though that's a figure up 66% on the 2003 numbers.

PEOPLE

In spite of the large displacement of people – both Serbs and Croats – during the war of the 1990s, Croatia's total population has remained fairly stable (at around 4.4 million) over the past 20 years.

Ethnic demographics have changed, however. In the 1991 census around three-quarters of people considered themselves Croats, while 12.2% said they were Serbs. A decade later, the 2001 census showed that almost 90% of people thought of themselves as Croats, while Serbs accounted for only 3.3% of the population. There are a number of quite complex reasons for the decline in Serb numbers, including changes in the census methodology, changes in the registration of expatriates of Croatian origin, and of course the exodus of Serbs from Croatia after the war.

Around a quarter of all Croats live in Zagreb – the most recent census (2001) puts the number at 780,000, but it's widely agreed that the real figure is now well over a million. The city has grown steadily over the past century: the population in 1900 was just 58,000; by 1919 it was 100,000; and by 1939 it was 200,000.

However they identify themselves, the majority of people in Zagreb are warm, hospitable and generous. Those you're most likely to come into contact with are also sociable, with-it and well educated – and most young people now speak English.

Zagreb people are proud of their city and those of its natives who go on to achieve world fame; so expect at least to be able to name local sporting celebrities.

Clue: former AC Milan player Zvonimir Boban owns a restaurant here, and skiing star Janica Kostelić, who came home with three golds and a silver from the 2002 Winter Olympics, is fêted wherever she goes.

CULTURAL ETIQUETTE

All visitors have an effect not just on the place they're visiting but on its people too. There are numerous arguments for and against this which don't need to be enumerated here – suffice it to say that it's worth considering both the environmental and sociological effects of your visit.

ENVIRONMENT Zagreb's environment is in pretty good shape (see *Environmental issues*, page 28), so don't spoil it – preserving it is in everyone's interests. In town, the city streets are kept remarkably spotless, and littering is much frowned upon, though of course like anywhere you'll come across a certain amount of graffiti. Out of town, where stuff won't necessarily be picked up by the authorities, the issue is even more important. Paper tissues take months to deteriorate, orange peel positively glows, and tin cans always look horrible. So be responsible and take your litter with you – and if you collect any you find along the way, you can feel suitably saintly about yourself. If you're in the wilds, and you can't find a toilet, do at least bury your doings – there are few sights (or sensations) more unpleasant than coming across someone else's.

GAY/LESBIAN Homosexuality may have been legalised a generation ago in Croatia, but there's still a grudging acceptance, particularly among the older members of the population. Zagreb's first ever gay parade wasn't held until 2002, and only a few hundred people took part – heavily protected from hecklers by a slew of riot police.

Same-sex couples (men in particular) can still raise eyebrows (or even hackles) when checking into hotels. How you handle this will of course be up to you – some may be happy with a plausible cover story, while others might find this stance too hypocritical.

That said, the situation is slowly changing, and Zagreb does now boast some good gay clubs, bars, video stores and saunas (see pages 152–3 for more details), and some hotels – notably the Arcotel and the Regent Esplanade – have earned a reputation for being gay-friendly. As everywhere, younger people tend to be more tolerant than their elders.

DRUGS Illegal drugs are best avoided. They're available, but the penalties are stiff, and harsher still for smuggling – and don't for heaven's sake be tempted or tricked into carrying anything across borders.

INTERACTING WITH LOCAL PEOPLE/GIVING SOMETHING BACK Unlike its sister cities on the coast, Zagreb remained largely unaffected by tourism through the second half of the 20th century, but is now seeing increasing numbers, with around 550,000 visitors in 2005, and more expected with the arrival of direct low-cost flights from cities like London and Berlin in 2006 and beyond. As a result, the city is changing, and mostly for the better.

With English now widely spoken, it can be rewarding to chat to staff in restaurants, bars and hotels, or to share a coffee or drink with chance acquaintances. It's not a great idea to discuss the recent war, however; while you'll find people in Zagreb much less touchy about the subject than those living in areas that saw significant action, it's still something of a minefield – and the last thing you'd want to do is to step on a conversational landmine. The only really safe thing you can say, if you're asked directly, is that you're pleased it's all now over, and that peace is clearly bringing prosperity.

After travelling to Zagreb (and possibly even before you go) you may also want to do something for the community. After asking around when we were in town and extensive searches on the internet, however, we're sorry to have to say that we were unable to find any voluntary programmes operating in the area – but if you know of any please drop us a line. I also drew a surprising blank with charities; again, if you hear of any, please pass on the news for the next edition.

BUSINESS/TIME

Most offices officially operate from 08.30–16.30, Monday to Friday. If you're calling ahead of your visit – or having people call you in Zagreb – remember that the city's on Central European Time (CET). That's one hour ahead of GMT, six hours ahead of New York and Washington, nine hours ahead of California, and eight hours behind Sydney and Melbourne (ten during the European winter). Summertime operates in Zagreb at the same time as most of the rest of Europe, with the clocks going forward one hour in spring, and back an hour in autumn.

The working environment – dress, culture, etc – is similar to most European countries, but if you're doing business don't be surprised if you're expected to cement deals or friendships with a shot (or several) of *rakija* or *travarica* (see page 117). If you don't drink out of choice, you need to invent a good reason why – the culture isn't particularly tolerant of non-drinkers.

RELIGION

Zagreb is marginally more secular than the rest of the country, but even so only 7.6% of the population is registered as agnostic or non-believers, compared with 87.1% Catholic, 2.1% Muslim, 2.0% Orthodox Christian and 0.04% Jewish.

With Catholicism long having been tied to Croatian national identity, it's as much a statement against Tito's brand of socialism or Serbia's Orthodox Church as it's a credo in itself. As a result, church attendance was hugely popular in the first years of Croatian independence, but has tailed off somewhat in recent years. Nonetheless, you'll still find people worshipping privately outside of church service times, or just popping in for a quick dab at the holy water; either way you should respect their quiet and privacy. The most popular places for impromptu veneration in Zagreb are the Stone Gate (see page 184) and the cathedral (see page 176).

Smaller churches – and even some of the bigger ones, like St Blaise – are often closed outside the periods immediately before and after mass.

CULTURE AND FESTIVALS

While Zagreb has a wonderful cultural heritage, its locally famous artists, sculptors and writers are little known outside Croatia – with the possible exception of Ivan Meštrović, whose studio in the old town is well worth a visit (see page 182).

As the capital, Zagreb does get more than its fair share of cultural happenings, however, ranging from excellent ballet, opera and theatre (notably at the National Theatre, see page 147) to an entire summer schedule chock-full of local and international performances – everything from classical to jazz to rock and beyond.

As in Dubrovnik, there's also a major summer festival, which runs for two weeks from the end of July. This features some of Croatia's best folk performances, and remains one of your best opportunities to see genuine folk dancing with the traditional costumes being worn. Zagreb also hosts several other festivals, one of the biggest being Animafest (*www.animafest.hr*), the world festival of animated films, which has a week of short films in even-numbered years (usually June) and full-length features in odd-numbered years (usually October). Odd-numbered years also see modern music celebrated at the Music Biennial.

You'll find a lot going on, too, around religious festivals and political holidays, with masses, processions and music aplenty. Festivals start with the February Carnival, followed by the Easter celebrations, and Corpus Christi two months later – which effectively kicks off the summer concert and gigging seasons, which run pretty much uninterrupted into September. Things quieten down a little until All Saints' Day, which is followed by Zagreb's 'City Day' on 16 November, and then Christmas – which is much as you'd expect, though a big fish rather than a turkey tends to take pride of place at the main celebration, on Christmas Eve.

More details on all of the above can be found in *Chapter 7, Entertainment and nightlife*, page 143.

PUBLIC HOLIDAYS Croatia has the usual European mix of religious and secular public holidays. Banks and most shops will close on these days:

New Year's Day	1 January
Easter Sunday and Monday	8–9 April in 2007, 23–24 March in 2008 and 12–13 April in 2009
Labour Day	1 May
Corpus Christi	7 June in 2007, 15 June in 2008 and 11 June in 2009; 60 days after Easter Sunday, and taken seriously in Croatia, with processions and lots of first communions.

Day of Antifascist Struggle	22 June
Statehood Day	25 June
Homeland Thanksgiving Day	5 August
Assumption of the Virgin Mary	15 August
Independence Day	8 October
All Saints' Day	1 November
Zagreb City Day	16 November
Christmas	25 and 26 December

GEOGRAPHY AND CLIMATE

GEOGRAPHY Zagreb is situated in northern Croatia, just 20km southeast as the crow flies from the Slovenian border and 100km southwest of the Hungarian border. The city is at longitude 15°59', latitude 45°49', and lies 122m above sea level.

The great hulk of Mount Medvednica, rising up to the peak of Sljeme, at 1,030m, dominates the northern side of the city, while to the south and east are the great fertile plains of the River Sava, which separates 19th-century Zagreb in the north from the modern high-rise suburbs of Novi Zagreb in the south.

Southeast of the city are the farmlands of the Turopolje, leading to the stork nests and floodplains of the Lonjsko Polje, while southwest of Zagreb you'll find the lovely rolling hills of the Žumberak, home to the delightful little town of Samobor and the Plešivica wine-making region. Heading north of Medvednica, meanwhile, will take you to the hills and castles of the Zagorje region, stretching up to Varaždin, briefly Croatia's capital and a charming, compact Baroque town, and further north still to the Međimurje region tucked right up against the Hungarian border.

CLIMATE Zagreb has a moderate continental climate, which essentially means cold winters and hot summers – though the influence of both is tempered somewhat by the presence of Mount Medvednica behind the city.

Annual rainfall is around 950mm a year, almost halfway between London's 600mm and Scotland's average of 1,400mm. It rains, however, a bit harder and faster here, leaving room for plenty of sunny spells – Zagreb has 133 rainy days to London's 145, and benefits from 1,600 annual hours of sunshine.

Winters are calm, cold and often cloudy, and there's snow on the ground for an average of 54 days a year. But once spring comes the temperature quickly softens, and the precipitation comes in short thundershowers rather than continuous rain – meaning that from early in the season to late autumn there are abundant opportunities for alfresco drinking and dining. Summer in Zagreb is great. It's hot, but not excessively so, with the highest temperature ever recorded being 37°C.

NATURAL HISTORY

Few people come to Zagreb with natural history in mind, and from the point of view of **fauna** you're likely to see little more here than sparrows and whatever meat or fish of the day happens to be served up on your lunch plate. That said, venture up onto Medvednica or out into the country and you can find everything from obscure species of bat (see page 225), to wild boar and deer on the hoof (see page 221), to several species of butterflies you won't find in Britain. There's also a surprisingly well stocked, if rather old-fashioned natural history museum in town (see page 203) if you really want to find what's endemic to the area, and there's a truly excellent zoo (see page 220) in Maksimir Park which puts the likes of London's to shame.

You might also be rather unimpressed with Zagreb's **flora**, which is pretty much limited to some good solid trees in the big squares leading up to the centre of town, and whatever oleanders and geraniums people have used to decorate their terraces and balconies. But there's also a pleasant botanical garden (see page 171) near the main train station, and lots of bigger green spaces within reach of the city centre, including the vast Maksimir Park (see page 220), and of course Mount Medvednica (see page 221), where you can get a whole lot closer to nature.

ENVIRONMENTAL ISSUES Zagreb's a big city, and obviously pays the consequences of that in terms of a certain amount of pollution and noise. But it's also a green city, with easy access to designated nature parks, such as Mount Medvednica, or the Žumberak, and has two important national parks within 60km of the capital, in the shape of Risnjak, to the southwest, and Lonjsko Polje to the southeast.

For centuries, Zagreb's biggest problem was the great River Sava, which would flood regularly and often catastrophically. This happened most recently in 1964, prompting the building of the huge earthen dykes you can see today, and which have useful walking/cycling trails along their tops.

2 Planning

ZAGREB – A PRACTICAL OVERVIEW

As the capital, Zagreb hosts conferences and business events aplenty, meaning hotels are generally busy year round, and especially during the week. That means the best deals are often had by travellers who booked packages well ahead of time, and there are few if any special offers to be found on arrival. Indeed, there's a noticeable shortage of budget accommodation, even with the recent opening of a number of smaller, family-run hotels.

The city is easy to navigate your way around, and most sights are reachable on foot. Equally, there's an excellent network of trams and buses if you want to cut out most of the legwork, and the airport and main train and bus stations are well connected both to the city and to each other (see *Chapter 4*, page 85, for full details of local transport).

Museums are closed one day a week (usually Monday), and have variable opening times (see page x for details), and if visiting any particular museum is essential to your trip then check within the text before you go, to avoid disappointment. Churches are always open before and after services, but often closed otherwise – with the obvious exception being the cathedral.

Finally, don't worry too much about what you need to bring with you. As a fully paid-up member of the Western world, Croatia has pretty much everything on sale which you might have forgotten to pack; possible exceptions would include eclectic literature in English, or non-Croatian wine.

WHEN TO VISIT

Summer – broadly speaking from mid May to mid September – is absolutely the best time to visit Zagreb, as that's when the weather's finest, the café culture is at its most vibrant and the street entertainment is at its most happening. In July and August it can get pretty hot, but you also have the advantage as a visitor – especially if you happen to have a car with you – that a good proportion of the locals will themselves be down on the coast on holiday, freeing up parking spaces and places to sit and watch the world go by.

Spring and autumn are also great times to be here, with frequent sunshine and cloudbursts more likely than continuous rainfall – but there's no denying there won't quite be the same levels of live music and alfresco sitting around as you'll get in summer. Winter, too, has its appeal, though don't fool yourself into thinking that everything on the street won't have moved indoors. That said, Zagreb's one of the few cities in the world where you could visit a couple of top-notch museums in the morning, pack in a decent half-day's skiing in the afternoon, and still go to the opera in the evening.

HIGHLIGHTS

A PERSONAL (BAKER'S) DOZEN ... In no particular order, here are the 13 things we love most about Zagreb ...

Dolac market (see page 139 [4 E3/4]) Every morning, seven days a week, Zagreb's thriving and colourful main food market plays host to locals who've come in from the countryside with whatever's good this week: upstairs in the open air there's fruit, vegetables and flowers, with an indoor fish market off to one side; downstairs in the food hall you can buy anything from fresh bread to obscure cheese to the best air-dried ham.

Café culture (see page 129) It's what Zagreb's all about. Indeed, a look at the packed terraces on the pedestrian streets southwest of the main square or along Tkalčićeva, on a summer's day, would make you wonder whether anyone (other than the waiting staff) even had a job to go to.

The roof of St Mark's Church (see page 187 [4 D3]) Up in the old town, the fantastically gaudily tiled roof shows off the coats of arms of the Kingdom of Croatia, Slavonia and Dalmatia to the left, and the City of Zagreb to the right.

The National Theatre (see page 147 [6 C6]) Hosting excellent performances of ballet, opera and theatre almost nightly, the theatre is an architectural treat inside and out, and – by most standards – endearingly affordable.

Jelačić Square (see page 175 [4 E4]) Zagreb's oversized pedestrianised main square, crossed by clunking trams, and home to some of the bigger, smarter café terraces – not to mention Ban Jelačić himself, magnificent on his horse. The starting or ending place for just about anything that happens in the city.

Street entertainment (see page 143) Throughout the summer months you'll find impromptu live music, street carnivals, folk dancing and beer festivals happening on the street, along with five-a-side football, rallying events and any number of popular happenings. It's wonderful.

Mirogoj Cemetery (see page 218 [1 C3]) A fabulous neo-Gothic oasis of calm north of the city centre, all fading memorials, touching tributes and well-tended pathways; and non-denominational to boot.

The Stone Gate (see page 184 [4 D3]) The last of the old city gates – with a cobbled street curving up through it – shelters a votive memorial, complete with flickering candles and numerous marble thank-you plaques for answered prayers.

Ice cream (see page 138) Croatians love ice cream, year round, and Zagreb has lots of places which sell outstanding Italian-style *gelati*. You'd be mad not to try it.

Maksimir Park (see page 220 [1 D3]) A great big tree- and folly-filled park within easy reach of the city; also home to Zagreb's first-rate zoo.

The Mimara Museum (see page 177 [6 B6]) Zagreb's most extraordinary museum; a vast collection, comprising everything from Greek and Roman antiquities to religious art, and Chinese porcelain to rare Impressionists, reflecting the eclectic, hedonistic collecting style of its larger-than-life founder, Ante Topić Mimara.

The noonday cannon (see page 183 [4 D3]) Fired daily from the Lotršćak Tower, at the top of Zagreb's diminutive city-centre funicular, the noonday cannon can be heard all over town. And you can set your watch by it.

Mount Medvednica (see page 221 [1 B1]) Walking, hiking, biking, skiing, or just a chance to ride the cable car up to the top of Sljeme, the 1,030m peak of Mount Medvednica; it's a delight, and easy to get to. As if that weren't enough, there's an old mine, a Neolithic bat-cave, and a restored castle too.

WHAT TO SEE IN A SINGLE DAY It would be pretty ambitious trying to tackle any capital city in just one day, and Zagreb's no exception – but if a day is all you have you can still get a great sense of the flavour of the place.

With so many of the city's charms being on the street, aim to start with a walking tour (see page 163) which takes in Kaptol and the old town – that way you'll also get to see the cathedral (page 176), Dolac market (page 139), the Stone Gate (page 184) and the view from the Lotršćak Tower (page 183), after which you'll be more than ready for an ice cream (see page 138) or to break for lunch at one of the many restaurant terraces on Tkalčićeva (see page 119). If you have the stamina for just one museum, make it the Mimara (page 177); and if you're here for the evening, a visit to the National Theatre (page 147) is always rewarding, with wonderful ballet and opera performances. Spare time, too, for one of Zagreb's numerous happening bars and cafés (page 129).

TWO OR THREE DAYS With two or three days, you can see a lot more; but leave time too for extra hours sampling the atmosphere and soaking up the sunshine.

Shoppers will want to venture along Ilica, and the streets on either side, but it's also well worth visiting a couple of the museums in the old town, including the Meštrović Atelier (page 182), home to Croatia's most famous sculptor, and the marvellous City Museum (page 190) – or even the more specialist Naïve Art Museum (page 214). If you're in the old town, then drop into St Catherine's (page 188) and St Mark's (page 187) churches, the former finest Baroque, and the latter gloomy 1930s layered-on neo-Gothic.

If you're travelling with children then the zoo at Maksimir Park (page 220) is a must – and even if you're not, it's an especially fine example of the species. Mirogoj Cemetery (page 218) is also a personal favourite, and much less morbid than most burial grounds. Mount Medvednica (page 221), for its part, is easily accessible by cable car and offers great views out over the city, and a genuine sense of being up in the mountains.

Finally, train buffs – or anyone with a taste for the luxurious – should pass by the Esplanade Hotel (page 101), which was built in the 1920s as a swanky stopover for the

Orient Express. It's still a swanky stopover today, but even if you're not staying, it's worth splashing out on a drink at the bar or a portion of their famous *štrukli* (see page 113).

FOUR DAYS OR MORE If you have more time, you should definitely consider a day trip out of town, as Zagreb also has plenty to see and do in the near vicinity. Top destinations would include Samobor (page 254), Varaždin (page 234), Karlovac (page 265) or the Plešivica Wine Road (page 263), all of which are within an hour's drive or so and have great accommodation options too.

In town, there's also a wealth of other outstanding museums, including the comprehensive Archaeological Museum (page 191), the newly restored Museum of Modern Art (page 209), the old masters at the Strossmayer Gallery (page 212), and – especially if you're with the family – the terrific Technical Museum (page 194), as well as the magnificent State Archives (page 200), a Jugendstil triumph.

A WEEK OR LONGER You'd think that was enough, wouldn't you, but Zagreb has heaps more to offer if you have the time. In the city there are still dozens of worthy museums you haven't visited – notably the Arts and Crafts Museum (page 202) and the Ethnographic Museum (page 197) – while out of town there are the rolling hills of the Žumberak (page 258) to explore, as well as the woods and castles of the Zagorje (page 242), north of Mount Medvednica; the fertile lands and vineyards of the Međimurje (page 242) up against the Hungarian border; and the old wooden churches of the Turopolje (page 276), southeast of the city. Further southeast still are the wonderful floodlands of the Lonjsko Polje (page 278), one of Europe's best places for stork watching – and the world-famous Plitvice Lakes (page 271). And of course Slovenia and Hungary are both within easy range too, if you're still short of ideas.

TOUR OPERATORS

IN THE UK There's a long history of package tourism as well as independent travel from the UK to Croatia, though Zagreb as a destination in its own right is a much more recent addition to tour operators' menus; with the advent of low-cost flights and an upsurge in city breaks, however, it's already a great deal more popular than it used to be. In terms of choice, beyond those operators listed below, it's also worth seeing what your local travel agent has to offer, as well as dropping in on www.visit-croatia.co.uk/touroperators or www.tourist-offices.org.uk.

Bond Tours 2 Upper High St, Epsom, Surrey KT17 4QJ; ☏ 01372 745300; f 01372 749111; e info@bondtours.com; www.bondtours.com. Highly recommended. Offers city breaks as well as packages to the most popular coastal resorts.

Bosmere Travel ☏ 01473 834094; e info@bosmeretravel.co.uk; www.bosmeretravel.co.uk. Smaller operator able to organise tailor-made holidays, with group travel & tours a speciality.

Cosmos Tourama Ground Floor, Dale Hse, Tiviot Dale, Stockport, Cheshire SK1 1TB; ☏ 0871 622 4344; e touramaadmin@tourama.co.uk; www.cosmostourama.co.uk. Well-established coach tour operator based in the south of England; offers Zagreb as part of extensive tours of Croatia, Bosnia & Slovenia.

Cresta Holidays Holiday Hse, Sandbrook Pk, Sandbrook Way, Rochdale, Lancashire OL11 1SA; ☎ 0870 238 7711; e websales@bcttravelgroup.co.uk; www.crestaholidays.co.uk. Specialist in city breaks to Zagreb from Birmingham, Edinburgh, London & Manchester, year round.

Croatia For Travellers 63 Theberton St, London N1 0QY; ☎ 020 7226 4460; e croatiafortravel@btclick.com; www.croatiafortravellers.co.uk. Aimed squarely at independent travellers. Zagreb city breaks along with more extensive coach tours that also include major places of interest inland & on the coast. Will also tailor holidays to your precise requirements. Good website.

Hidden Croatia 160 Brompton Rd, Knightsbridge, London SW3 1HW; ☎ 0871 208 0075 (within UK); ☎ +44 207 594 0600 (outside UK); e info@hiddencroatia.com; www.hiddencroatia.com. Offers an extensive range of holiday itineraries – including gourmet, sailing, culture, adventure, city breaks, cruise & family-oriented packages – along with tailor-made trips. Flights from London & Manchester.

Mercian Travel 109 Worcester Rd, West Hagley, West Midlands DY9 0NG; ☎ 0870 036 8372; e jdowning@ merciantravel.co.uk; www.merciantravel.co.uk. Specialises in bridge & bowling holidays to Zagreb year round, & also offers hotel & private accommodation booking in the city.

Regent Holidays 15 John St, Bristol BS1 2HR; ☎ 0870 499 0439; e regent@regent-holidays.co.uk; www.regent-holidays.co.uk. A pioneer of UK travel to central & eastern Europe, Russia & central Asia, this operator of 35 years' standing offers 3-day packages from London Heathrow.

Saga Holidays The Saga Building, Enbrook Pk, Folkestone, Kent CT20 3SE; ☎ 0800 096 0074 (within UK); ☎ +44 1303 771 111 (outside UK); e reservations@saga.co.uk; www.saga.co.uk. With a loyal following among the over 50s, Saga offers flights from the UK, accommodation in Zagreb & tours that combine Zagreb with sights further afield. Calling might be simpler than trying to navigate their complex website.

Vamos Travel 2 Styles Cl, Royal Leamington Spa, Warwickshire CV31 1LS; ☎ 0870 762 4017;

e info@vamostravel.com; www.vamostravel.com. A central & eastern Europe specialist offering a wide range of city breaks, opera & ballet holidays, stag weekends, adventure holidays, active family break holiday packages, etc, with flights from London.

IN NORTH AMERICA A growing number of North American operators now include Zagreb in package tours of *Mitteleuropean* capitals, including those listed below. You can also contact the New York office of the Croatia National Tourist Board (✎ +1 212 279 8672; f +1 212 279 8683) – though a quicker route to a Croatian holiday is often to simply contact one of the UK operators listed above. It's also a good idea to check what's available at your local travel agent, since new tour itineraries are being developed all the time to meet evolving demand. With Croatia voted *National Geographic* 'Adventure Destination of the Year 2006', expect plenty more US operators to start including the country in their European packages.

Friendly Planet Travel ✎ +1 800 555 5765; f +1 215 572 9803; e questions@friendlyplanet.com; www.friendlyplanet.com. Efficient family-run Philadelphia-based operator with an emphasis on upper-end hotels & luxury coach touring. Zagreb forms a key part of a Balkan tour that includes Slovenia, the Plitvice Lakes, the Adriatic & Montenegro.

Homeric Tours ✎ +1 800 223 5570 (within US), ✎ +1 212 753 1100 (outside US); f +1 212 753 0319; e info@homerictours.com; www.homerictours.com. A Mediterranean-focused operator founded in 1969 which offers Zagreb as part of an extensive coach tour of Croatia featuring highlights inland & on the coast.

Picasso Tours ☎ +1 800 995 7997/+1 310 645 7527; **f** +1 310 645 1071; **e** info@picassotours.com; www.picassotours.com. A Washington DC-based boutique operator that includes Zagreb as part of a comprehensive itinerary covering the coast, the Plitvice Lakes & Ljubljana.

Trafalgar Tours ☎ + 1 866 544 4434; **e** contactus@trafalgartours.com; www.trafalgar.com. One of the world's largest & best-known tour operators. Zagreb features in its extensive 'Treasures of Europe' coach tour spanning 9 European countries from Italy & Germany to Hungary, Austria & the Czech Republic.

Virgin Vacations ☎ +1 888 937 8474; **e** res@virgin-vacations.com; www.virgin-vacations.com. Part of the Virgin airline & travel group offering escorted fly-coach tours of the Balkans, including Zagreb.

i TOURIST INFORMATION

You can get a great deal of information before you leave home from the local Zagreb Tourist Board (*www.zagreb-touristinfo.hr*) and the Zagreb Country Tourist Office (*www.tzzz.hr*) – both publish a range of brochures, accommodation details and maps. If you don't have easy access to the internet, contact one of the following offices for more information.

Zagreb Tourist Board Information Centre Trg Jelačića 11; ☎ 481 4051/2/3; **f** 481 4056; **e** info@zagreb-touristinfo.hr. *Open Mon–Fri 08.30–20.00, Sat 09.00–17.00, Sun 10.00–14.00.*

Zagreb Tourist Board head office Kaptol 5; ☎ 489 8555; **f** 481 4340

Zagreb Country Tourist Board Preradovićeva 42; ☎ 487 3665; **f** 487 3670; **e** info@tzzz.hr. *Open Mon–Fri 08.00–16.00.*

You can also contact the local or international offices of the **Croatian National Tourist Board** – particularly useful if you're combining your Zagreb visit with a trip to the coast or islands. The main English-speaking offices are listed below, and you can find the full list of 20-odd international offices listed under the 'About Us' section at www.croatia.hr.

Head office Croatian National Tourist Board, Iblerov Trg 10/IV, Zagreb; ☎ 455 6455; f 469 9333; e info@htz.hr
UK office Croatian National Tourist Office, 162–164 Fulham Palace Rd, London W6 9ER; ☎ +44 208 563 7979; f +44 208 563 2616; e info@cnto.freeserve.co.uk; http://gb.croatia.hr
USA office Croatian National Tourist Office, Inc, 350 Fifth Av, Suite 4003, New York 10118; ☎ +1 212 279 8672/4; f +1 212 279 8683; e cntony@earthlink.net; http://us.croatia.hr

For details about tourist information in Zagreb itself see page 68.

MAPS There are about half a dozen different Zagreb maps in circulation, mostly with the old town on one side and the surrounding city on the other. Given the modest size and scale of the place, any of these should be more than adequate, despite the frequent lack of helpful information like scale, footpaths, bike tracks and so on.

If you're into cycling or walking, and planning to take a trip out of town, get hold of the Zagreb County Tourist Board's excellent maps, which show biking and walking trails along with suggested touring itineraries that take you through some of the county's prettiest countryside on smaller, mostly traffic-free roads.

PASSPORTS AND VISAS Nationals of most English-speaking (UK, Ireland, USA, Canada, Australia and New Zealand) and EU countries need only a valid passport to visit Croatia for up to three months; if you want to stay for longer it's far easier to leave the country and come back in again than it is to get an extension. If you don't need a visa for Croatia you shouldn't need one for hops across the border to neighbouring Bosnia and Herzegovina or Montenegro, which now apply the same three-month visa exemption for tourists as Croatia.

Full details of who does and doesn't need a visa for Croatia, as well as up-to-date addresses and phone numbers of all the Croatian diplomatic missions worldwide – and foreign diplomatic missions in Croatia – can be found on the Ministry of Foreign Affairs' website at www.mvp.hr.

POLICE REGISTRATION All visitors to Croatia are expected to register with the police within 24 hours of arrival. If you're staying in a hotel, hostel or campsite, or in a private room arranged through an agency, don't worry – this will be done for you automatically.

If you're in a private room you've found for yourself, however, or staying with friends, they're supposed to register you. This doesn't always happen – but unless you're picked up by the police, it shouldn't be a problem. Even if you are questioned, if it's clear you're just a tourist the police will generally just tick you off and make sure they know where you're staying. But if you've been unregistered for a long while, you could be in more serious trouble – and even deported.

CUSTOMS There are no restrictions on the personal belongings you can bring into Croatia, though the government recommends you declare big-ticket items to be sure of being able to re-export them hassle-free. Crossing into or out of Croatia in your own non-Balkan registered vehicle, it's incredibly rare to be stopped or seriously questioned for any length of time, however.

Standard customs allowances apply for duty-free – 200 cigarettes, one litre of spirits, two litres of table wine and 250ml of perfume per person – and large amounts of some products, such as coffee and non-alcoholic drinks, also attract a special tax and should be declared. If you're taking your pets then make sure they have an international veterinary certificate showing that it's been at least two weeks but not more than six months since they've had their rabies shot.

You can take as much foreign currency as you want in and out of the country (though you're expected to declare amounts larger than 40,000kn), but you can't export more than 15,000kn worth of local currency. For goods purchased in Croatia costing over 500kn, you can claim a VAT refund on the way out of the country on presentation of the PDV-P tax cheque the merchant will have given you for this purpose – but it can be a giddyingly long procedure. Any questions you have can be answered by the helpful staff at the Customs Administration in Zagreb (↘ *800 1222 (general information) or* ↘ *610 2333 (main office); www.carina.hr*).

CROATIAN DIPLOMATIC MISSIONS ABROAD

The following are Croatia's major diplomatic missions overseas:

Australia (embassy) 14 Jindalee Crescent, O'Malley Act, 2606, Canberra; ☎ +61 2 6286 6988; f +61 2 6286 3544. Also covers New Zealand.
Canada (embassy) 229 Chapel St, Ottawa, Ontario K1N 7Y6; ☎ +1 613 562 7820; f +1 613 562 7821; www.croatiaemb.net
Ireland (diplomatic mission/consulate) Adelaide Chambers, Peter St, Dublin 8; ☎ +353 1 4767 181/2; f +353 1 4676 188
New Zealand (Consulate General) 131 Lincoln Rd, Henderson, PO Box 83200, Edmonton, Auckland; ☎ +64 9 836 5581; f +64 9 836 5481
UK (embassy) 21 Conway St, London W1T 6BN; ☎ +44 207 387 1144; f +44 207 387 0936; e croemb.london@mvp.hr. Also covers Croatian representation for Gambia, Ghana, Liberia, Nigeria, Uganda, Sierra Leone. *Open Mon–Thu 11.00–14.00, Fri 10.00–12.00.*
US (embassy) 2343 Massachusetts Av, NW, Washington DC, 20008; ☎ +1 202 588 5899; f +1 202 588 8936/7

GETTING THERE AND AWAY

As the capital, Zagreb is well served by both international and domestic transport routes, and has an international airport, as well and major rail and bus terminals.

✈ **BY AIR** Croatia Airlines (*www.croatiaairlines.hr*) and Wizz (*www.wizzair.com*) both fly to Zagreb daily from London, and many of Europe's major carriers also offer regular flights to Zagreb from other major European cities. While the advertising sometimes tells a different story, return tickets from London start at around €70, once you've added the various taxes to those under-€10 deals. As more airlines adopt modern pricing models, the later you book, the more expensive your ticket is likely to be; short-notice return tickets can sell for upwards of €500, so book early if possible.

Another option, of course, is to fly to Zagreb via another European city; if you don't mind adding a couple of hours to your travel time and shopping around a bit online, you can sometimes uncover a real bargain. Check out the passenger information section of the Zagreb Airport website (*www.zagreb-airport.hr*) for an up-to-date list of the carriers serving the city. Finally, while charter options abound for the coastal resorts, there are currently no charters direct to Zagreb.

If you're coming from further afield – Australia, Canada, New Zealand or the US – you'll be routed through a European hub, usually in conjunction with Croatia Airlines. Prices from New York to Zagreb start at around US$1,000, but can rise to over US$2,000 depending on the time of year and your choice of airline. From Australia and New Zealand, standard tickets are US$2,500+, but with some judicious searching you can usually get a much better deal by choosing to route your Europe-bound flight through one of the hubs served by low-cost carriers such as German Wings (*www.germanwings.com*) or Wizz.

If you're having trouble finding a reasonably priced flight through the usual channels (newspapers, travel agents, etc) there are several alternatives. One is to take a package tour – see the list of travel agents on page 37. Even if you want to sort out your own accommodation, some operators will be happy to arrange a 'flights-only' package for you. When this isn't the case, it can sometimes still work out cheaper to book yourself on a package and then not use the entire accommodation segment – though if you do this you should check the conditions carefully to ensure you still have a return flight home.

The internet is also a great place to shop around for flights. UK sites such as www.cheapflights.co.uk, www.lastminute.co.uk or www.travelocity.co.uk, or US sites like www.expedia.com or www.farebeater.com will give you a quick idea about what's really available and how much it costs. But don't imagine that just because it's on the internet it's necessarily the cheapest – you may find the fare in your local travel agent's window is still better. Note, too, that the sites listed immediately above don't include fares from low-cost carriers or charter operators.

For information on Zagreb Airport, and travel to and from the city, see page 85.

BY RAIL International trains come into Zagreb at least once a day from each of Austria, Bosnia and Herzegovina, Germany, Hungary, Italy, Macedonia, Slovenia and Yugoslavia – for more details about frequency and international journey times check out www.hznet.hr, where you'll find excellent information in English, as well as domestic timetables online. If you're training it from London, expect the journey to take around 24 hours, with several changes involved.

Long-distance domestic trains run east to Osijek (five daily, 3–5 hours), southwest to Rijeka (five daily, 3.5–4.5 hours), south to Split (five daily, 5.5–8 hours) and Šibenik (once daily, 7.5 hours) and north to Varaždin (13 daily, 2–3 hours). Local trains make up the rest of the traffic, but whilst these are picturesque, they're also slow and not especially punctual.

Finally, make sure when you do arrive in Zagreb that you get off the train at the central station, **Zagreb Glavni Kolodvor** [6 E/F8] – there are two other stations which trains may stop at (but which you don't want): Zagreb Klara and Zagreb Zapadni Kolodvor.

For more detailed information about facilities at the train station, see page 86.

BY BUS Even more international buses service Zagreb than international trains, with at least one direct service coming in daily from major cities in neighbouring countries and good connections through from most big European destinations. Bear in mind it's a long journey, however – count on 30+ hours from London, for example – and not especially cheap, with fares starting at around £95, unless you can get a student or other discount. From the UK, National Express is the principal operator (*www.nationalexpress.com*).

There are also around 200 arrivals a day from Croatian destinations, including a dozen or so from each of Split (5–9 hours), Pula (5–6 hours), Zadar (5 hours), Rijeka

(2.5–3 hours), Plitvice (2–2.5 hours) and Varaždin (1.5 hours); at least six a day from Dubrovnik (11 hours), Rovinj (5 hours), Poreč (4.5 hours) and Osijek (4–6 hours); and two or more a day from practically every other destination in the country.

If you're planning a long-distance bus journey in Croatia, then reckon on hourly speeds coming in at about 45km/h and fares costing from 30–40kn per 100km. Long-distance buses stop every two hours or so for a *pausa*, and the driver shouts out the duration of this above the din: *pet, deset, petnaest* and *dvadeset minuta* are the commonest break lengths (5, 10, 15 or 20 minutes). These invariably occur where you can grab a quick drink/snack/meal. Watch the driver and you won't go far wrong, but be warned that the bus will go without you if you've made a mistake.

For full timetable and price details, click through to the Zagreb bus station's website at www.akz.hr (the button for English is slightly confusingly located on the right-hand side, mid screen). Be warned, however, that if your computer doesn't support Croatian accents, the database won't always find your requested destination – the best way to avoid frustration is simply to type in the first two or three letters, and then use the drop-down menu of possibilities, from which you can quickly select your destination (though this doesn't work for places which start with accented letters, like Šibenik). For more information, and ticket pricing, there's also an information hotline (✆ 611 2789), and if you're staying in Zagreb, you can arrange to have your tickets delivered to your door by calling the premium-rate number (✆ 060 313 333) – though the operators' level of English has been known to frustrate putative users of the service.

If you're leaving Zagreb by bus, it's worth buying your ticket as early as possible, since long-distance buses tend to be booked out ahead of time, especially in summer.

For more information on facilities at the bus station and Zagreb's local trams and buses see page 88.

BY CAR While Zagreb is well served by a constantly improving motorway network, it's not a great city to come to by car. As with most capitals, not only is driving in town a bit of a nightmare, but parking is hell – for more information on parking specifically and managing generally with your car in Zagreb, see page 92.

If you are driving in Croatia, the most important thing to remember is to stay within the law. You may find local drivers rather ambitious – to the extent that blind corners and oncoming traffic aren't seen as a natural impediment to overtaking – but don't be competitive; the omnipresent (and omnipotent) traffic police are quick to keep drivers in line through steep fines (and worse).

Speed limits – 50km/h in built-up areas; 90km/h out of town (locally highly variable; keep your eyes peeled) – are also strictly enforced, and there are an astonishing number of speed traps. Foreigners, rightly or wrongly, attract police attention. If you are stopped for a traffic violation, you may find the police ready to negotiate a lower penalty with you – a heavier fine for speeding, for example, may be traded down to a lower fine (payable in cash) for not wearing your seatbelt.

Most importantly, there's a zero blood alcohol limit for drivers. Checks are pretty frequent, and violations are taken very seriously indeed – so if you're planning on drinking, don't plan on driving. And remember that it's also illegal for drunks, as well as children under 12, to sit in the front of the car.

In the event of an accident or breakdown, you can call the Croatian Automobile Club's hotline (↘ 987) – and if you see someone *else* in need of assistance you're legally obliged to stop and help.

To source car parts or fix mechanical problems, your first port of call should be a petrol station (usually open from dawn until dusk; at the time of writing, fuel was around 8kn per litre). Like anywhere on holiday, repairs can be expensive and time consuming, so it's well worth making sure your car's in good shape before leaving home.

✚ HEALTH, INSURANCE AND SAFETY

For emergency contact numbers, see page 78.

HEALTH There is no reciprocal health-care agreement between Croatia and EU countries and so make sure you have proper health insurance for major emergencies. Normally hospital treatment and some other medical and dental treatments are free, and if you are travelling from the UK then you will need to show your passport; if you are a UK resident but not a UK national then you will need a certificate of insurance from HM Customs Centre for Non-Residents. In practice, however, you may well be told that the service you need (and that should be free) isn't available, and that you can obtain it only privately. Another reason for that all-important health insurance!

If you have a pre-existing medical condition, are pregnant or are travelling with children then you would be wise to establish health-care facilities before arriving in Zagreb. Larger hotels and tour company representatives are often able to assist, but failing that then contact the nearest British embassy or consulate for advice. A list of clinics is also provided by the International Society of Travel Medicine and can be found on their website (*www.istm.org*).

For minor treatment, a visit to a pharmacy (*ljekarna*) should sort you out – Croatian pharmacists are highly trained, and there's very often someone who speaks some English. Prescribed medicines are not free and are often no cheaper than they would be at home. For more serious problems get yourself to the hospital (*bolnica*) – more details can be found in the next chapter on page 82.

There are no official vaccine requirements for Croatia, although it is sensible to be up to date with tetanus, diphtheria and polio. There is no problem at all with drinking the water in Zagreb and the surrounds.

If you use needles for any reason you should bring a doctor's note explaining why, and if you wear contact lenses or glasses, bring spares; repairs and replacements aren't a problem, but can take time. If you're coming for any length of time it also does no harm to have a doctor's and dentist's check-up before you go – far easier at home than abroad.

Common problems You can be more vulnerable to disease abroad, so make sure your diet contains enough vitamins – and take supplements if you're not sure. Do drink bottled water if you think the source is suspect – though publicly supplied water in Zagreb is absolutely fine. In summer, especially, make sure you consume plenty of (non-alcoholic) liquids; it's easy to get dehydrated wandering around a city that's usually hot and sunny.

You may also want to bring with you a mild laxative and something for diarrhoea, although both problems can normally be remedied with a change in diet (soft fruit for the first; dry-skinned fruits for the second). If you are afflicted with diarrhoea your biggest danger is dehydration, so make sure you drink plenty – soft drinks are good.

It's also handy to bring along a small supply of sticking plasters (Band-Aids), antiseptic cream and mild painkillers (aspirin or paracetamol) – if needed, you can easily top up your medical supplies at any pharmacy; and for everything except medicine itself you can also pick up what you need at the large DM outlets dotted around the city.

From May onwards you should also think about protecting yourself against mosquitoes. All you really need is a gizmo which plugs into a wall socket at night – you can buy these easily enough whenever mosquitoes are about. Using an insect repellent when you are out and about will also help to avoid being bitten.

If you intend to visit more rural areas from late spring to early autumn then you should be aware of a disease spread by ticks (tick-borne encephalitis). It may be worth seeking immunisation before travel, though it is not readily available in the UK, or at least use a repellent and keep skin covered with long-sleeved clothing, trousers tucked into boots and not forgetting a hat. Always check yourself – or preferably get someone to do it for you – if you have walked through forested areas or through long grass. If you are travelling with small children remember to check their heads and in particular behind the ears – a body part that is easily forgotten.

Finally, don't hesitate to see a pharmacist or doctor if you're even slightly unsure about a diagnosis or cure. And know your source if you need a blood transfusion – HIV/AIDS is less prevalent in Croatia than in many countries, but you can't be too careful. Occasionally immigrants or long-term expatriates may be asked for proof that they are free from HIV infection. Check if you need this when applying for visas or work permits.

INSURANCE Even on a weekend break, travel/health insurance is a good idea – it's reassuring to know you can be flown home if necessary. Read your policy's fine print and make sure it covers what you'll be doing. A general policy covering health, theft and third party insurance is usually cheaper and less hassle than multiple policies, though you may find you're already covered for some or all of the risks by existing insurance (such as private health care, which sometimes includes foreign travel, or insurance which is sometimes automatic if you hold credit cards).

If you need to claim, you'll have to provide supporting evidence in the form of medical bills, in the case of health, or a police statement, in the case of theft.

Obtaining the latter can be tediously hard work, but essential if you're hoping for reimbursement.

Travel policies are issued by banks, travel agents and others, and it's worth shopping around amongst reputable providers, as the price varies considerably. Arrange for the insurance to cover your full journey time, and keep the policy safe with your other travel documents.

TRAVEL CLINICS AND HEALTH INFORMATION A full list of current travel clinic websites worldwide is available on www.istm.org. For other journey preparation information, consult www.tripprep.com. Information about various medications may be found on www.emedicine.com/wild/topiclist.htm.

SAFETY Zagreb is one of the few European capitals that still has a reassuringly safe feel, even late at night. Indeed, the whole of Croatia is generally safer and freer of crime than most places in the EU, though it's common sense here as elsewhere not to be showy with money, jewellery or flashy possessions, and to keep your valuables close to you and separate from the rest of your luggage.

You'll see lots of police around, and they have rather fearsome powers – freedom of dissent shouldn't be taken for granted. The police carry out occasional spot checks on locals and foreigners alike for identification, so make sure you have your passport or identity card with you at all times. Otherwise you'll find the police friendly and helpful – and these days most officers speak some English.

If you do get arrested, stay courteous, even (especially) when it's difficult to do so. Stand, rather than sit, if you can (it puts you on an even footing), and establish eye contact – if you can do so without being brazen or offensive about it. Some people recommend shaking hands with officialdom, but it depends very much on the circumstances. If language is a problem, wait until an interpreter arrives (or anyone who understands you clearly) rather than taking the risk of being misunderstood. And remember that you can be held at a police station for up to 24 hours without being charged. Your consulate will be informed of your arrest, normally within the first day.

SEXUAL HARASSMENT Zagreb is a very safe city for women travellers; in the unlikely event of being subjected to unwanted male attention on the streets or in clubs or bars, speaking firmly – in any language – should make your lack of interest clear. Aggression is extremely rare – and even young males engaging in what they might see as a bit of playful banter are normally quick to respect your wishes if you make it clear you want to be left alone.

Croatians are keen followers of fashion and are quick to embrace the latest trends, so there's nothing to worry about as far as dressing modestly is concerned. The exception is, of course, churches, where wandering about in skimpy clothing is frowned upon.

SMOKING Non-smokers beware: with more than a million smokers (and one of Europe's highest rates of lung cancer), Croatia is one of the last bastions of the 40-

a-day habit, and very few places offer non-smoking facilities. Unfortunately, Croatians' love affair with the cigarette applies as much to the young as to the older segment of the population, and internet cafés and hip places are often literally thick with smoke. Indeed, the one non-smoking café which opened on Tkalčićeva soon shut down for lack of punters.

That said, most of the upper-end hotels do offer non-smoking rooms, and even non-smoking floors, so it's worth asking when you make your booking. Likewise, the bars and restaurants in these hotels – and some of the city's other more upmarket establishments – do have smoke-free sections, though you're still inevitably going to get some exposure to the smoke drifting over from the main area. In summer, the simplest solution is simply to drink or dine alfresco; in winter, that's not an option, and you may have to pick and choose your venues carefully. With smoking very much the norm, it's not really acceptable to ask local people to refrain.

While the government is aware of the problem, a proposal in mid 2006 to introduce a new bill against smoking in public places, including bars and cafés, caused an uproar, and was quickly withdrawn. As the country slowly edges its way towards EU admission, however, current attitudes – and laws – seem certain to change in favour of a cleaner air policy.

DISABLED TRAVEL As a capital city, Zagreb is pretty disabled-friendly, with active government programmes in place concerning access, toilets, lowered public phones, etc. An ongoing curb-lowering initiative makes the pavements more wheelchair-friendly, and most street crossings are equipped with pedestrian tracks and sound signals for the visually impaired. City public transport is free for the disabled, and a good number of the city's trams and buses, as well as the funicular up to the old town, are wheelchair-friendly. Trams are equipped with displays for the deaf and spoken announcements for the blind – though these are in Croatian only.

There are ramps and lifts in all buildings with public access – including the airport, train and bus stations, and museums, etc – and most have disabled toilets. Most of the better hotels and restaurants are also equipped for the disabled.

WHAT TO TAKE

The best way of packing for anywhere – and Zagreb's no exception – is to set out all the things you think you'll need and then take only about a third. How much you eventually end up taking will depend to a large extent on how long you're going for and whether you have your own transport (everyone takes more in their own car). But be realistic, especially if you're going to have to carry all your own stuff.

Check weather forecasts before you leave – Zagreb's continental climate makes for hot summers, but cold winters. Summer evenings can sometimes be cool, but rarely cold, so a light sweater should suffice. If you're coming in winter, bring a heavy coat, warm clothes, sturdy shoes (there's often snow on the ground) and a waterproof.

Don't forget the usual range of documents you'll need – passport, tickets, travellers' cheques, cash, insurance papers, credit card, driving licence – and something to carry them in. A belt-bag or pouch is practical, but also draws attention to where you're keeping your valuables; we prefer a zipped pocket for the essentials, whether that's in a day pack or trousers, but it's a personal choice. Bring any books you want to read – though you can also pick up papers and magazines in English at the city's larger news stands.

You may also find it handy to have a tube of travel detergent with you for rinsing out your smalls, and a travel alarm for those early starts. And last but not least, if you're bringing any electrical appliances – even just a hairdryer or a phone charger – remember to pack an adaptor. Croatian sockets are the same round two-pinned variety you find all across Europe.

CAMPING It sounds obvious, but if you're camping, take a tent that's easy to pitch (and practice at home before you leave – trying to assemble an unfamiliar model on a windy and rainy night is suffering itself. We know: we've been there). Bring tent sealant and repair material; both are pretty hard to find in Zagreb.

What you have in the way of a sleeping bag and sleeping mat will define the shape of your nights – and again it's worth testing these before you leave home. Buy a down-filled bag if you can afford it.

It can be worth dispensing with cooking materials, eating utensils and pre-packed food altogether. It's a personal choice, but the business of finding fuel, the weight and bulk, and the overriding affordability and cheerfulness of local cafés and restaurants might make you question whether you really want to self-cater after all.

Indeed, with only one campsite in the vicinity – and that neither well located nor especially cheap – you might question whether you really want to camp at all.

PHOTOGRAPHY Digital photography is ever-more popular – but bear in mind the usual limitations of memory size, battery life, etc, and know your camera well. If you're using a film camera it's worth noting that while print film is easily available (if a bit more expensive than at home), slide film is relatively hard to find – especially if you have a particular brand preference. If you are buying film, check the use-by date; some rolls for sale are way past their prime. Finally, take film home for processing, unless you absolutely have to have the prints or slides while you're away.

Zagreb is a cosmopolitan capital city, so its people are unlikely to present problems in terms of photography – they are used to it – but that doesn't mean you shouldn't apply the usual ethical standards. Respect privacy, don't take pictures you know will offend, and especially don't take pictures when you're asked not to.

$ MONEY

Since May 1994, Croatia's currency has been the kuna – literally a marten, named after the trade in marten skins in Roman times, and first struck as a Croatian coin in AD1256. It's one of the few currencies in the world still officially named after an animal (the American *buck* was never legal tender – even if the slang expression is still in fashion an awful long time since trading in deer skins was a measure of anything in the US).

The kuna (generally abbreviated to kn, though HRK is the international three-letter code) is divided into 100 lipa (literally lime tree, or linden). There are 1, 2, 5, 10, 20 and 50 lipa coins, 1, 2 and 5 kuna coins, and 5, 10, 20, 50, 100, 200, 500 and 1,000 kuna banknotes. There's also a 25 kuna coin, but chances are you'll never see one. On the whole, people aren't comfortable with the two largest notes, and you may have trouble breaking them – ask for 100s and 200s when you're changing money.

The euro has also increasingly been used as a semi-parallel currency – the vast majority of Zagreb's visitors switched to the euro in 2002. Most people are comfortable with euro pricing, and you can usually pay with euro if you need to – but don't necessarily expect the right (or complete) change. You're much better off changing enough money for a couple of days at a time and getting used to the kuna. The kuna is pretty stable, averaging around 7.40 to the euro and 10.80 to the pound.

Finding a place to buy kuna is a doddle. All banks, exchange offices and post offices, and most travel agencies and hotels will happily let you turn in your money – though you're better off trying to change euro or sterling than US dollars (as there are so many forged dollar notes in circulation). Exchange rates are (remarkably) almost the same wherever you choose to change your money – fractionally worse at hotels, perhaps, but the difference is minimal.

Major credit cards (notably Visa, Eurocard/MasterCard and American Express) are accepted by most big hotels, restaurants and shops, though if you're staying in private rooms (see page 106) you'll find cash is king (kuna or euro will both do nicely). Credit cards can also be used for raiding Zagreb's ubiquitous cash dispensers.

For long trips, money is safest brought in the form of travellers' cheques, which are worth the small commission you pay for the peace of mind. You lose about the same percentage of your money as with using a credit card, but it's easier to keep track of cheques. American Express cheques are still the most widely used, easily recognised and most quickly refunded in case of loss or theft, and your local bank back home should be able to issue them to you (though you may have to insist).

Finally, have enough money/resources with you. While most post offices can accept transfers through Western Union, getting money wired from home is generally expensive and time consuming. You can get information on Western Union rates, along with a list of the post office branches offering the service, at www.posta.hr.

BUDGETING How much you'll spend will depend mostly on what level of luxury you're looking for. Camping or hostelling and using public transport is going to cost far less than staying in swanky hotels and cabbing it around town. That said, Zagreb is neither particularly cheap nor phenomenally expensive – while prices certainly aren't on a par with London, broadly speaking you should expect to pay about the same as you would in most cities in western Europe. Hotel accommodation and restaurants are on average cheaper than in the UK, but about the same as in France. Supermarket prices are a shade higher than you might expect in other European cities.

After the cost of getting to Croatia, your biggest single expense will be accommodation. Expect to pay from €40 per night for a double room in private accommodation, while doubles in hotels start at around €60 and go right up to €300 (room prices are usually quoted in euro, though paid in kuna). Single rooms are relatively scarce, but when available go for about 70% of the cost of a double. At weekends some hotels will discount by up to 20%.

For a couple, daily food and drink costs from around 250kn for picnic food bought in supermarkets and maybe one meal without wine each day in a cheap restaurant or pizzeria, to 750kn for breakfast in a café and lunch and dinner with wine in slightly more upmarket restaurants. An average grill-type restaurant meal for two, with salad, skewers of meat, and wine, averages around 100kn a head. A decent fish dinner or upmarket Italian on the other hand can easily set two of you back 750kn or more.

Public transport is inexpensive by EU standards, with a single-zone one-and-a-half-hour bus or tram ticket going for 8kn, and the 72-hour Zagreb Card offering unlimited public transport around the city for 90kn. If you're travelling with under-sixes, they ride free of charge.

If you're really eking out the cash (camping, picnic food) you could probably get away with a budget of 150kn per person per day. Double that amount would get you into private rooms and cheap restaurants, while 450kn would buy you a nice holiday, as long as you don't want to eat fish every day. For that, and upper-end hotels, you'd need to count on at least 1,000kn per person per day – and of course you can always spend much more.

Entry fees for attractions are on the whole inexpensive; while prices were correct at the time of writing (late 2006), they may have changed slightly, but are unlikely to be significantly higher.

TIPPING A service charge isn't included in your restaurant bill, so – assuming the service has been good – it's appropriate to round up the bill to the nearest 10kn or so. Don't be afraid not to tip if you think the service was terrible, but equally don't be too extravagant or too stingy – waiting staff in Zagreb appreciate a little extra, since they're generally less well off than their customers, but leaving a huge tip can tend to rub it in (as well as spoiling things for future diners). Taxi drivers the world over expect fares to be rounded up, and those in Zagreb are no exception.

OPENING TIMES

From the look of Zagreb's crowded street cafés in summer, you might wonder if anyone does any work at all. In fact, however, Croats are industrious and hard working, but like to knock off early and enjoy the evening – particularly in summer. So while you'll find many offices and shops open from 07.30 or even 07.00, you may well find some businesses and even tourist facilities closed from as early as 16.00. Bakeries, supermarkets and pharmacies are the exception and tend to be open all day, while smaller shops may close for an extended lunch hour.

Museums are almost always closed at least one day a week – see individual listings for details – and tend to have strange opening hours. Restaurants generally serve lunch from 12.00–15.00, and dinner from 18.00–22.00, though cheaper places like pizzerias and some of the more relaxed places in Tkalčićeva will happily serve all through the day. On weekends, too, dining hours are more flexible – on Sundays, it's not unheard of for groups to turn up for lunch mid or even late afternoon.

Some churches are opened only for services, and some of Zagreb's more niche museums are open only by appointment. If there's something you absolutely must see which you know will be closed while you're in town, it's definitely worth contacting the tourist office ahead of time to see whether they can make special arrangements for you.

3   Practicalities

THE CITY – ORIENTATION

Zagreb is 'pleasantly situated between the north bank of the Sava and the mountains which culminate in Sljeme' (according to my trusty 1911 *Encyclopaedia Britannica*) – and the mountain and the river are the two principal landmarks you'll still find on the larger city maps today, along with the railway line which separates the main city centre and old town to the north from the suburbs to the south.

The vast main square, **Trg Bana Jelačića**, sits on the northern side of the city centre, and is the main rendezvous point in town – for decades the exact spot was under the tail of Jelačić's horse, but people now seem to prefer meeting under the modern clock, about 50m away.

A series of great leafy squares run south to the main **train station**, and these form the eastern arm of the so-called 'green horseshoe' – which then continues west from the station to the Esplanade Hotel and the Botanical Gardens, before turning north for another three blocks.

North of Jelačić Square you'll find **Dolac**, the city's huge daily market, with fruit, vegetables and flowers upstairs, and meat, cheese and all the rest downstairs. To the northeast stands the twin-spired, permanently scaffolding-clad cathedral, at the

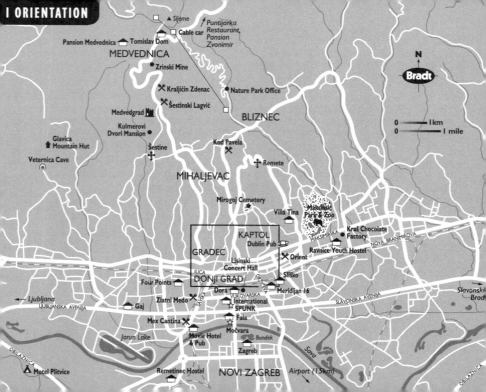

I ORIENTATION

▲ Sljeme

Cable car

↗ Puntijarka
Restaurant,
Pansion
Zvonimir

Pansion Medvednica ⌂ Tomislav Dom

MEDVEDNICA

● Zrinski Mine

✕ Kraljičin Zdenac

● Nature Park Office

✕ Šestinski Lagvić

N

Bradt

Medvedgrad

Kulmerovi
Dvori Mansion

BLIZNEC

0 ——— 1km
0 ——— 1 mile

Šestine

✕ Kod Pavela

Glavica
▲ Mountain Hut

Veternica Cave

MIHALJEVAC

✝ Remete

Mirogoj Cemetery

Villa Tina

Makšimir
Park & Zoo

KAPTOL

MAKSIMIRSKA

✕ Kraš Chocolate
Factory

Dublin Pub

GRADEC

Lisinski
Concert Hall

● Orient

Ravnice Youth Hostel

NOVA BRANIMIROVA

Four Points

DONJI GRAD

Sliško

✕ Dora

ILICA

Meridijan 16

Ljubljana
LJUBLJANSKA AVENIJA

Zlatni Medo

Vukovarska
International

SPUNK

Fala

SLAVONSKA AVENIJA

Slavonski
Brod

Gaj

Mex Cantina ✕

Močvara

Jarun Lake

Movie Hotel
& Pub

Bundek

Zagreb

Sava

OBILAZNICA

▲ Motel Plitvice

Remetinec Hostel

NOVI ZAGREB

Airport (15km)

OBILAZNICA

heart of **Kaptol**, which was formerly a separate religious centre, while to the northwest is the old town, **Gradec**, home to the president's palace and the parliament building (Sabor), along with several of the city's museums. Kaptol and Gradec are separated by **Tkalčićeva**, a café- and restaurant-filled pedestrian street running north, and **Radićeva**, a cobbled street parallel to and above it.

Running west from Jelačić Square is **Ilica**, Zagreb's main shopping area (along with the streets running off it), while to the south and southwest are the regular blocks and streets of **Donji Grad**, the lower town, where you'll find most of the remaining museums and other sights, and which was made possible by the construction of the railway embankment in 1860.

South of the railway are the suburbs built between the two world wars, while across the River Sava is **Novi Zagreb**, the residential area which sprang up in the 1950s and 1960s to house incoming labour. Just south of the railway line, a kilometre or so east of the main train station is the main **bus station**, which is where the shuttle comes in from **Pleso Airport**, itself 15km further southeast.

The bus station, train station and Jelačić Square – and indeed the whole city centre – are well connected by a regular and efficient tram network (see *Chapter 4*, page 85 for more details).

Zagreb's weekend playgrounds – beyond the obvious bulk of Mount Medvednica to the north – are the **Jarun Lake**, to the southwest, with its summer beaches, and the enormous forested **Maksimir Park** (where you'll also find the zoo) to the northeast.

It won't take sharp-eyed readers long to notice that what's written on Zagreb's street signs isn't quite the same as what we've used in this guide, both in the text and on the maps. That's because mapmakers and guidebook writers always use the spoken form of street names rather than the written form, which varies because of the subtleties of the Croatian language. The names we use here are best for obtaining any kind of directions, or what you'd ask a taxi or tram driver.

As a result, if you want the square which is in reality Trg Svetog Marka, you'll be directed to Markov Trg, while if you're walking down Ulica Pavla Radića, it's Radićeva you'll see on the map – and that late-night drink will be on Tkalčićeva, not Ulica Ivana Tkalčića. If that's not confusing enough, a couple of important squares have their own colloquial names – Trg Petra Preradovićeva is generally known as Cvjetni Trg (Flower Square), while the place universally referred to as Zrinjevac is officially Trg Nikole Šubića Zrinskog.

ℹ TOURIST INFORMATION

Zagreb has excellent tourist information, with a number of good free guides and maps available along with an information-packed website (*www.zagreb-touristinfo.hr*).

Heading north from the railway station towards the town centre, the first tourist office you'll come to is on the left-hand side, just past the Strossmayer Gallery, at Zrinjevac 14 [6 E6] (☎ 492 1645; open Mon–Fri 09.00–17.00). The main Information Office (☎ 481 4051/2/4), less than five minutes further on at Trg Jelačića 11 [4 E4], has longer opening hours (Mon–Fri 08.30–20.00, Sat 09.00–17.00 and Sun 10.00–14.00). You can also get information by email at e info@zagreb-touristinfo.hr.

Ask the friendly staff at either of these offices for a city map, and the *City Walks* and monthly *Events and Performances* brochures. They'll also be able give you advice on (but not – officially, anyway – help in) finding accommodation, and can sell you the 72-hour Zagreb Card. This is tremendous value at 90kn, with unlimited city transport for the duration, half-price entry to the city's museums, 20% off most theatre tickets, and discounts on a huge range of goods and services, from restaurants and hotels to medical, dental and beauty treatments – ask for the Zagreb Card Guide for full details, or visit www.zagrebcard.fivestars.hr. The tourist offices also have a good walking map of Mount Medvednica for sale, and, if you're here for more than half a day, the bi-monthly *Zagreb: In Your Pocket* guide is a superb resource easily worth the 20kn cover charge.

For information on sights immediately outside the Zagreb metropolitan area, you'll need to contact the Zagreb County Tourist Office (Turistička Zajednica Zagrebačke Županije), which is at Preradovićeva 42 [6 D6] (☎ 487 3665; f 487 3670; www.tzzz.hr; open Mon–Fri 08.00–16.00). The office has friendly, English-speaking staff, as well as everything you need to know about local attractions such as the picturesque town of Samobor, local wineries, rural accommodation and country restaurants, as well as a comprehensive set of free cycling and walking maps for those keen to enjoy the great outdoors.

For information beyond Zagreb County, you'll need to contact the local tourist offices in each destination – you'll find more details in the relevant pages of this guide.

LOCAL TOUR OPERATORS AND TRAVEL AGENCIES There's a host of local tour operators and travel agencies in Zagreb; of these the following are the best known and longest established. Most can organise entire holidays for you, including travel to and from your home country, as well as excursions and accommodation. You can also book air tickets by phone through the Croatia Airlines office, listed below.

Atlas Cira Carica 3; ✆ 422 222; f 411 100; www.atlas-croatia.com. *Open Mon–Fri 08.00–20.00, Sat 08.00–14.00.* Dubrovnik-based company established in 1923 offering a wide range of coast-focused services, from flights & coach tours to accommodation, & also the Croatian representative for American Express.

Croatia Airlines Savska Cesta 41; ✆ 481 2727; online booking at www.croatiaairlines.hr. Croatia's national airline, offering great-value domestic flights if you reserve & pay for them within Croatia – the catch being that you need to do so a long way ahead. Now a Star Alliance regional member. *Open Mon–Fri 08.00–20.00, Sat 08.00–16.00.*

Croatia Express Teslina 4; ✆ 481 1836/42; f 481 1920, & Tomislav Trg 17; ✆ 492 2237; f 492 2230; www.zug.hr. Specialising in rail, bus, ferry & airline bookings, as well as luxury coach charter & excursions.

Croatian Youth Hostel Association (HFHS) Dežmanova 9; ✆ 484 7474; f 484 7472; www.hfhs.hr. Advance bookings for Croatia's (few) youth hostels. You can also get an ISIC student card here (proof of student status required).

Dalmacijaturist Zrinjevac 16; ☎ 487 3073; f 487 3075; www.dalmacijaturist.com. Focuses, as you'd expect, on accommodation & holidays on the Dalmatian coast. *Open Mon–Fri 08.00–20.00, Sat 08.00–12.00.*

Generalturist Praška 5; ☎ 480 5653, Ilica 1; ☎ 481 2993 & Zrinjevac 18; ☎ 487 3121; www.generalturist.com. A Croatian specialist of 80 years' standing, now owned by Diners Club, offering boat tours, charters & sailing schools, accommodation, coach tours & charters, skiing holidays & wellness programmes, along with Budget Rent-a-Car bookings. *Open Mon–Fri 08.00–20.00, Sat 09.00–14.00.*

Jadrolinija Marko Polo Travel, Masarykova 24; ☎ 481 5216; f 483 0473; www.jadrolinija.hr. Croatia's national ferry operator, with more than 400 departures a day to coastal destinations during the summer months.

Kompas Zrinjevac 14; ☎ 487 8750; f 487 8759; www.kompas.hr. Day excursions, bus tours, accommodation in Zagreb & on the coast, & a range of outdoor activities. *Open Mon–Fri 08.00–20.00, Sat 09.00–13.30.*

Plitvice Lakes National Park Tomislava 19; ☎ 461 3586/492 2274/487 0111; f 492 2270; www.np-plitvicka-jezera.hr. The park office can arrange excursions & accommodation to the national park. *Open Mon–Fri 08.00–16.00.*

STA Zagreb Krvavi Most 3 (1st floor); ☎ 488 6340; f 488 6345; www.sta-zagreb.com. Part of the STA Travel group; specialises in student & discount travel. *Open Mon–Fri 09.00–13.00 & 14.00–17.00.*

$ BANKS

Zagreb has dozens of different banks, and ATMs abound – locally based Zagrebačka Banka has more than 150 dotted around the city, including 11 on Ilica alone, accepting MasterCard, Maestro, Visa, Visa Electron and Diners. Note that in Croatia (as in much of mainland Europe) cash machines spit out your card *before* dishing out your cash.

ATMs generally offer good exchange rates for foreign-currency withdrawals – though bear in mind you'll be charged interest from the day of withdrawal for credit cards, and may also have to pay a fee to your local issuing bank back home. You can also use ATMs to buy recharge vouchers for T-Mobil Simpa and VIP pre-paid mobile phones.

Most bank branches also offer a pretty efficient foreign-exchange service – rates are set daily and vary little between banks, so it's not worth losing time shopping around. You can also exchange foreign currency at post offices, many hotels and some travel agents – and again, rates, even at large business hotels, tend to be pretty competitive.

MEDIA AND COMMUNICATIONS

Croatia has a surprisingly vigorous and wide-ranging press – though it's only relatively recently that the main newspapers, TV and radio stations have been anything other than a mouthpiece for the state.

Communications also suffered from the heritage of state communism, but rapid uptake of mobile telephony and the internet means Croatia now has services worthy of its status as an EU supplicant. Broadband internet connectivity is available in some of the larger business hotels, and there are several moderately priced internet cafés in town (see below). Electricity comes in the European standard size and shape, at 220V and 50Hz, via standard European twin round-pinned sockets.

MEDIA Croatian independence in 1991 did little to bring freedom to the media, and it's only since the election of Stjepan Mesić (in 2000) that any real efforts have been made to liberate editors and journalists from half a century of government puppet-hood. Since then the president himself has spoken out in favour of keeping the media free from politics, and has encouraged journalists to practise their profession independently, as public servants rather than government acolytes.

The dominant media player is Croatian Radio and Television, HRT, which attracts an audience in excess of two million a day to its three television channels and its national and local radio stations. HRT 1 & 2 produce the usual mix of news, documentaries, entertainment and game shows, while HRT 3 is dedicated almost exclusively to sport. The good news for English speakers is that most films and some other programmes are sourced from the US or the UK, and are broadcast in their original English with Croatian subtitles. HRT's website (*www.hrt.hr*) also has an English-language site-map which will help you find the various web-streamed audio services on offer – useful if you're trying to learn Croatian.

The most important daily newspaper is *Večernji List* (online at *www.vecernji-list.hr*), an eclectic mix of local and international news, politics, human interest and lifestyle pieces, and the best source for daily cinema listings. On a lighter note, the Split-based weekly *Feral Tribune*, which uses a cod *Herald Tribune* masthead (*see www.feral.hr*) is a satirical newspaper in the spirit of Britain's *Private Eye*, and in older times was a regular thorn in the side of the Tuđman government.

For news in English, you can tune in to the BBC World Service on a short-wave radio, or – if you're lucky – catch one of the intermittent English-language news bulletins on HRT radio. The *International Herald Tribune* is sold in larger newsagents, where you'll usually also find some of the main English and European dailies – generally one day out of date. Otherwise the internet's your best bet, either by going through one of the big Croatian news portals, such as www.hic.hr (Croatian and English) or www.t-portal.hr (Croatian language only), or by logging on to the BBC or another English-language news provider (*www.bbc.co.uk, www.cnn.com, etc*).

✉ **POST** Mail out of the former Yugoslavia used to take anything from two weeks to three months and, frankly, post out of 21st-century Croatia isn't all that much better – postcards within Europe tend to drift home in around two to three weeks, while airmail letters are quicker, but not enormously so. Just occasionally, something slips through a hole in the space–time continuum – a letter once arrived home in three days, and a card sent to Australia got there in eight – but you should reckon on post being fairly slow unless you pay for a premium, guaranteed-delivery service.

Zagreb has two vast main post offices (pošta, or HPT), one on Branimirova, right next to the train station, and the other a block east of Jelačić square on Jurišićeva. For general postal information: ☏ 9832; www.posta.hr.

Post offices have long opening hours (see below). Parcels are reasonably cheap to send, but don't seal them until you've given the cashier time to check you're not posting bombs or contraband. If you send anything valuable you may have to pay duty on it when you get home.

If you want mail sent to you, have it addressed to Poste Restante, Pošta, 10000 Zagreb (the main post office by the station) or Poste Restante, Pošta, 10101 Zagreb (the branch at Jurišićeva). Remember that you'll need photo ID, such as a passport, to recover your mail. If your family name is underlined and/or in capitals your mail is more likely to be filed correctly – but if there's nothing for you, it's always worth asking them to look under your first name as well. Incoming post takes around ten days from most European destinations and about two weeks from North America – but can be quicker, or indeed slower.

Stamps (*marke*) are also sold at newsstands, tobacconists and anywhere you can buy postcards, which can save you queuing at the post office. In 2006, it cost 3.50kn to send a postcard or 5kn to send a letter to Europe, and 7.50kn to send a postcard to the USA, Australia or New Zealand.

24-hour Post Office Branimirova 4; ✆ 498 1300 [7 G7/8] Send letters weighing less than 5g from lines 9–11, packages less than 3kg from the parcel area on the east side of the building, & heavier items from the HPT office 50m further east of the main entrance. Local & international phone calls can be made from the 1st floor – get a phonecard from reception, & pay for the time used after you've made your call. *Open 24/7.*
Central Post Office Jurišićeva 13; ✆ 481 1090 [5 F4] *Open Mon–Fri 07.00–21.00, Sat 07.30–14.00; closed Sun.*

If you're based south of the railway line or arriving or departing by bus, there's also a convenient post office at the main bus station (Autobusni Kolodvor), at Avenija

Marina Držića 4 (↘ *611 9077;* f *611 8977; open Mon–Fri 08.00–19.30, Sat 07.30–14.00; closed Sun*).

𝓒 **PHONE** Croatia's phone network has vastly improved in the last 15 years, and you'll no longer be faced with multiple attempts to get access to the outside world. The international access code is 00, so for international calls simply dial 00 (or +) followed by your country code (+44 for the UK, +1 for the USA and Canada, +61 for Australia, +64 for New Zealand, etc) followed by the local phone number (without the leading zero in most cases, but not in Italy or Russia, for example).

The international code for calls into Croatia is +385 and the area code for Zagreb and the nearby surrounds is 01. For other towns further afield, see the relevant sections of this guide (we've included the area code with the phone numbers).

Partial privatisation of the former state-owned operator Hrvatski Telekom (HT) has seen the company rebranded as T-Com/T-Mobile by majority shareholder Deustche Telekom (*www.t-com.hr*). Phone boxes are plentiful, and operated by 25- to 500-unit phonecards, with the 25-unit card costing 15kn and the 100-unit card costing 40kn. Local calls normally cost one unit, with long-distance calls being quite a bit more expensive, especially at peak time (*Mon–Sat 07.00–10.00*). International calls can also be made from the main post offices at Jurišićeva 13 and Branimirova 4.

The people of Zagreb, like most Europeans, have gone mobile-mad, and I've yet to meet anyone in Zagreb who doesn't have a mobile phone. There are three mobile

WRONG NUMBER?

There's nothing worse than buying a guidebook and then finding out some of the phone numbers are wrong – but the sad truth is that (even though every single number is checked before going to print) numbers do change. So what to do? Your best option when we fail you (our apologies) is to log on to **www.tportal.hr/imenik/default.asp?lang=en**, Croatia's outstanding online phone directory. It's fast, efficient, and up to date, and there are even links to other online directories worldwide. Another option is to call the tourist office – assuming their number hasn't changed in the meantime.

operators: T-Mobile, Tele-2, and VIP – though with limited geographical coverage and obscure international charges, Tele-2 isn't yet really a viable option for visitors. The network is comprehensive and the two main local operators have roaming agreements with their foreign counterparts, so you should find your own mobile works – as long as you're on GSM. If you're using your own mobile, however, remember that roaming rates will make international calls expensive and local ones even more so.

If you're going to be glued to the phone, one option is to buy a local pre-paid subscription – easily done in just a few minutes at the T-Mobile or VIP shops – and then top up your sim card as needed (recharges available from news stands, post offices, ATMs and, of course, T-Mobile and VIP). Not only is a local pre-paid number convenient and cheaper for your outgoing calls, but it also means you can easily be called by friends and family if necessary. Pre-paid vouchers last six months, and the subscription remains valid (and able to accept incoming calls) for a further six months. Mobile calls to other European countries cost 5–10kn per minute.

T-Mobile Shops dotted throughout the city, the most convenient of which is the one next to the church at Preradovićeva 3, near the corner with Bogovićeva. In 2006, a pre-paid subscription cost 120kn, including 20kn worth of calls.

VIP Centar Located right opposite the Dubrovnik Hotel, at Gajeva 2b, near the corner with Jelačić Square. In 2006, a pre-paid subscription cost 100kn, including 100kn worth of calls.

One final word about phones – like everywhere else in the world, you should aim to avoid calling long distance or international from your hotel room. Tariffs for fixed and mobile calls may have fallen, but hotel rates certainly haven't. The cost of a 15-minute call home from a decent hotel room can spoil your entire trip.

Useful telephone numbers
Emergencies

Police	☏ 92
Fire	☏ 93
Ambulance	☏ 94

Zagreb emergency hospital	☎ 461 0011
Public emergency centre	☎ 985
Roadside assistance	☎ 987

General

Croatia Airlines flight information	☎ 487 2727
Croatia Airlines reservations	☎ 481 9633
Pleso Airport	☎ 626 5222
Central bus station	☎ 603 13333
ZET (public transport)	☎ 365 1555
Jadrolinija Ferries (Marko Polo Travel)	☎ 481 5216
Weather forecast (in Croatian)	☎ 060 520 520
Road conditions (in Croatian)	☎ 464 0800
Lost and found	☎ 633 3439
Taxis	☎ 668 2505/2558

Telecoms

International operator	☎ 901
International directory enquiries	☎ 902
General information	☎ 981
Local operator	☎ 988
Long-distance operator	☎ 989

e INTERNET Internet uptake has been rapid throughout Croatia, and there's an enormous amount of information available online (see *Chapter 14, Web resources,* page 299).

As you'd expect in the capital, most of Zagreb's larger hotels now offer some form of internet access, either in the room or through a central – usually minuscule – shared business centre. Be sure to check prices before you connect – while some hotels offer internet access as part of the room rate, others levy a hefty per-minute charge, particularly for dial-up access, which can add up to an unpleasant shock when you check out. Internet access details for specific hotels are listed in *Chapter 5, Accommodation.*

There are also several conveniently located internet cafés, with hourly fees coming in at anything from 15–40kn.

Art Net Club Preradovićeva 25; ☏ 455 8471; www.haa.hr [6 D5] *Open Mon–Fri 09.00–22.00, Sat 11.00–18.00; closed Sun.*
VIP Centar Iblerov Trg 10; 📱 091 209 1091 [5 H4] Located on the upper floor of the Importanne Galleria shopping centre; fast, pay-as-you-go coin-operated access – but eye-wateringly smoky at times. *Open Mon–Sat 08.00–23.00, Sun 09.00–23.00.*
Charlie's Gajeva 4; ☏ 488 0233 [6 E5] Conveniently situated just a few metres south of the Dubrovnik Hotel, across the street. *Open Mon–Sat 08.00–22.00, Sun 11.00–21.00.*
Net Kulturni Klub Mama Preradovićeva 18 (in courtyard); ☏ 485 6400; www.mi2.hr [6 D5] *Open daily noon–midnight.*

VIP Preradovićeva 5; ☏ 483 0089; www.vipnet.hr [4 D4] *Open Mon–Sat 08.00–23.00, Sun 09.00–23.00.*

If you're travelling with your laptop, you'll also be able to take advantage of the city's growing number of WiFi hotspots with a fast wireless connection, courtesy of T-Com or VIP. Payment can be made via pre-paid voucher or online via credit card. Here's a sprinkling of hotspots around the city:

Arcotel Allegra Branimirova 29; ☏ 469 6000
Bulldog Pub Bogovićeva 6; ☏ 481 7393
Hotel Dubrovnik Gajeva 1; ☏ 487 3555
Sheraton Hotel Kneza Borne 2; ☏ 455 3535
Sheraton Four Points Hotel Sportova Trg 9; ☏ 365 8333
Škola lounge bar Bogovićeva 7 (upstairs); ☏ 482 8196
Tantra lounge bar Gajeva 2b (upstairs); ☏ 492 2888
T-Centar Iblerov Trg 7; ☏ 462 1650
T-Mobile Petra Preradovićeva Trg 3; ☏ 498 4760
T-Mobile Vukovarska 23; ☏ 498 4126
VIP Iblerov Trg 10; m 091 209 109
VIP Avenija Dubrovnik 15; ☏ 652 7103
VIP Gajeva 2b; ☏ 481 5480
Westin Hotel Kršnjavoga 1; ☏ 489 2000

E FOREIGN DIPLOMATIC MISSIONS IN ZAGREB

Most English-speaking countries have embassies or consulates in the capital, Zagreb:

Australia Nova Ves 11/III (Kaptol Centar); ☎ 489 1200; f 489 1216. Visa section: ☎ 489 1209; f 489 1230; www.auembassy.hr. *Open Mon–Fri 08.30–16.30.*

Canada Prilaz Dure Dezelica 4; ☎ 488 1200; f 488 1230; e zagrb@international.gc.ca. *Open Mon–Fri 10.00–12.00 & 13.00–15.00; during summer (1 May–30 Sep) open Mon–Thu 10.00–12.00 & 13.00–15.00, Fri 10.00–13.00.*

Ireland Miramarska 23; ☎ 631 0025; e irish.consulate.zg@inet.hr

New Zealand (c/o the Croatian Homeland Foundation), Trg Stjepana Radića 3; ☎ 615 1382

UK Ivana Lučića 4; ☎ 600 9100; f 600 9111; e british.embassyzagreb@fco.gov.uk. *Open Mon–Thu 08.30–17.00, Fri 08.30–14.00.* Note that the visa section is at Alexandera von Humboldta 4; ☎ 600 9122. *Open Mon–Fri 09.00–11.00.*

US Thomasa Jeffersona 2, Buzin; ☎ 661 2200; f 661 2373, www.usembassy.hr. Out of town, towards the airport; good directions available on the embassy website. *Visa section open Mon, Wed, Fri 08.00–10.00.*

For a comprehensive click-through list of all embassies and consulates in the Croatian capital, go to www.zagreb-touristinfo.hr, and select 'Foreign Institutions' from the sidebar menu.

✚ HOSPITAL AND PHARMACIES

Zagreb's main **hospital** (*opča bolnica;* ☎ *461 0011, for emergencies* ☎ *94*) is located at Draškovićeva 19 [7 G6], on the corner with Boškovićeva near the

Sheraton Hotel, and as you'd expect the accident and emergency service works 24/7. There are dozens of pharmacies (*ljekarne*) spread around Zagreb. Opening hours are usually Monday–Friday 07.00–20.00, Saturday 07.00–14.00 but those listed below operate non-stop, 24/7.

Gradska Ljekarna Zagreb Trg Jelačića 3; ☎ 481 6159
Gradska Ljekarna Zagreb Ilica 301; ☎ 375 0321
Gradska Ljekarna Zagreb Ozaljska 1; ☎ 309 7586

RELIGIOUS SERVICES

Anglican-Episcopal St Joseph's Chapel, Jesuit Seminary, Jordanovac 110; ☎ 309 6620 [1 C3] Services in English, 18.00, second & fourth Sundays of every month.
Catholic Third floor, St Joseph's Chapel, Jesuit Seminary, Jordanovac 110; ☎ 235 4104 [1 C3] Mass in English, Sunday, 10.30.
Zagreb Islamic Community Gavellina 40; ☎ 613 7162 [1 D4]
Zagreb Jewish Community Palmotićeva 16; ☎ 492 2692 [7 F5]

CULTURAL INSTITUTES

British Council Ilica 12/I; ☎ 489 9500; www.britishcouncil.hr [4 D4] *Open Mon–Fri 11.00–17.00, Tue–Thu 13.30–19.30, Sat 10.00–14.00.*

French Institute Preradovićeva 35; ☎ 485 5222; www.ambafrance.hr [6 D5] Mediathèque: *open Mon–Fri 12.00–20.00, Sat 12.00–14.00 (not summer)*; main office: *open Mon–Fri 09.00–17.00.*
Goethe Institute Vukovarska 64; ☎ 619 5000; www.goethe.de/ins/hr/zag/deindex.htm [1 C4] *Open Mon & Wed 09.30–19.00, Tue & Thu 09.30–13.00.*
Italian Institute Preobraženska 4; ☎ 483 0208; www.iiczagabria.esteri.it/IIC_Zagabria [4 D4] *Open Mon, Tue, Thu 09.00–13.00 & 13.30–16.00, Wed 09.00–13.00 & 13.30–19.00, Fri 09.00–14.00.*

4 Local Transport

You're most likely to arrive at Pleso Airport, the main train station or the main bus station, so transfers to and from these are covered first in this chapter, followed by sections on local trams and buses; taxis; cars; and finally bicycles.

AIRPORT TRANSFER

Zagreb's diminutive Pleso Airport is 17km southeast of the city centre. As soon as you come out of International Arrivals you'll see the airport bus stop – shuttles to the main bus station in Zagreb run hourly or half-hourly (depending on the time of day) from 07.00 to 20.00, seven days a week. Outside the standard times, buses will also run whenever new flights arrive.

The trip takes about 25 minutes, and costs 30kn. If you're going to need to make frequent trips to the airport, it might be worth investing in a monthly ticket for 300kn, or a book of 20 tickets for 350kn. For full schedule information, check with **Pleso Transport Company** (✆ 633 1999; www.plesoprijevoz.hr) – they have an easy-to-follow English-language website and you can also get ticket and schedule information over the phone.

Airport shuttles from the main bus station back to the airport run from 05.00 to 20.30 (or from 04.00 to 21.00, depending on the day), seven days a week, as well as two hours before any international flight and 90 minutes before domestic departures. Buses leave from their own small terminal (rather than main long-distance bus departure gates), which is located on the ground-floor level on the north side of the bus station. Buses are marked Zračna Luka Zagreb/Zagreb Airport, seating is first come, first served, and you buy your ticket on board. Don't worry if the driver isn't around when you get on – you can get your ticket when he or she does a round of the bus, just before departing. With such an efficient bus service you're unlikely to need a taxi, but if you do, the stand's right next to the airport bus stop. Zagreb taxi drivers have a good reputation, but it does no harm to make sure the meter's switched on when you set off. Expect to pay upwards of 150–200kn to the main Zagreb hotels, bearing in mind you'll also pay a few kuna extra per piece of luggage, and that there's a 20% surcharge at night, as well as on Sundays and public holidays.

More information on the airport, including real-time flight arrival and departure times (look under 'Timetable' on the home page), can be found at www.zagreb-airport.hr.

MAIN TRAIN STATION

The railway originally linked Zagreb to its Habsburg rulers to the north, before assuming a more glamorous international role as one of the stops on the Simplon *Orient Express* line from Paris to Istanbul in the 1920s.

The station itself – Glavni Kolodvor – is an imposing neoclassical edifice completed in 1891 by the Hungarian architect Ferenc Pfaff (who presumably had to endure a lifetime of wags telling him to stop faffing about). It's also known as Željeznički Kolodvor, just meaning 'railway station', but as it's a bit of a mouthful you're safer sticking with 'Glavni', meaning 'main'. It's located at the southern end of the city, a straight kilometre down from Zagreb's main square, Trg Bana Jelačića – trams #5 and #6 connect the two, or it's a ten-minute walk. From the train station it's a rather dreary 1.5km east to the main bus station, which can be comfortably shortened by four stops on tram #2 or #6.

The station has good facilities, including large Arrival (*Dolazak*) and Departure (*Odlazak*) boards in the main hall, and a terrific new website in English providing comprehensive information on timetables, ticket prices, journey duration, train types and configuration and more – see www.hznet.hr. For trains to and from Zagreb, select Zagreb Gl kol as your departure or arrival station from the drop-down menu.

Lockers are available at 15kn per 24 hours, with extra-large ones for 20kn per 24 hours, making this a cheaper and more convenient place to store your stuff than the main bus station (see below). Coins for the lockers and information on timetables are available at the Croatia Express office (↘ *457 3253*), which also has a foreign-exchange service.

The kiosks in the central hall offer a limited selection of foreign-language newspapers and magazines, as well as selling stamps and what seem to be the only postcards available anywhere in the city. A radical makeover has meanwhile turned the station bistro – once a fairly dismal place to hang out pending departure – into a pleasant, cheery venue with its own outdoor terrace; it's conveniently open for drinks, snacks and more substantial meals from 05.00 to 23.00. Public toilets (3kn) and shower facilities (45kn including towel, shampoo and hair dryer) are available at the west end of the main platform, beyond the bistro.

MAIN BUS STATION

Zagreb's main bus station – Autobusni Kolodvor – is the largest and busiest in the country, as you'd expect, with around 200 arrivals a day, from destinations both domestic and international. Like bus stations everywhere, it's a bit shabby, but has good facilities, including a small supermarket, several cafés, various fast-food outlets and newsagents. Up on the second floor there's also a post office and a bank, while down on the ground floor (at platforms 1 and 6) you'll find 24-hour left-luggage facilities – though at 1.20kn per hour for small bags and 2.30kn per hour for large ones, it's quite a bit more expensive than those at the train station (see above).

If you're planning on leaving by bus (not counting the airport transfer; see above), you should try and buy your ticket as early as possible – from the main ticket office on the first floor – as long-distance buses tend to be booked out ahead of time, especially in summer.

The bus station is 1.5km east of the main train station, which makes for a dull 15-minute walk (cross the railway lines, then walk west along Branimirova) or a four-stop ride on the #2 or #6 tram. Tram #6 also continues on past the station two stops to Trg Jelačića, Zagreb's central square.

Like the train station, the bus station also has a spanking new website in English (*www.akz.hr*), which makes getting timetable information a breeze (see page 48 for more details).

LOCAL TRAMS AND BUSES

Zagreb has excellent public transport, based around trams (and a tiny funicular) in the city centre, and a wide-ranging network of buses running to the inner and outer suburbs, all managed by ZET, Zagrebački Električni Tramvaj (*www.zet.hr* – in Croatian only) and all running from 05.00–midnight – with a selection of night trams and buses as well. Maps of the network are published at most tram stops, making the system easy to navigate.

There's a flat-fare ticket which costs 6.50kn from news stands or 8kn on board (you'll be expected to have the right money) and which is valid for 90 minutes from the time you punch it on board. Trips far into the suburbs cost two, three or even four tickets apiece, but everything in the city itself (and in this guide) is within the central zone, though all night trams and buses cost two tickets each. The on-the-spot fine for travelling without a ticket is 150kn.

A great-value day pass is available at 18kn, which is valid until 04.00 the following morning. And if you're here for three days or more, consider the 90kn Zagreb Card (see page 69), which covers not just all the public transport for 72 hours but also the cable car ride up to Sljeme on Mount Medvednica – and gives numerous discounts to boot.

TRAMS Trams have been part of the very fabric of Zagreb since the first horse-drawn variety was introduced in 1892, and particularly since the electric tram started up in 1910. Today there are 15 day routes, and another four night routes, which run from midnight–04.00. It's a good gag to get people to meet you at a #10 or #16 tram stop, as these routes don't exist.

The network is extremely efficient, though trams can get pretty crowded, particularly around the rush hour. All day routes run at least six times an hour, though as routes run in parallel you'll rarely find yourself waiting even five minutes for a ride. Night routes (#31, #32, #33, #34) go from the same stops as the day routes and are serviced about every 45 minutes, but take routes that even locals consider abstruse. When the tracks are being repaired, night trams are substituted by buses.

For quick reference, these are the stops you're most likely to use, and the trams which service them:

Jelačić Square	#1, #6, #11, #12, #13, #14
Glavni Kolodvor (train station)	#2, #3, #4, #6, #13
Autobusni Kolodvor (bus station)	#2, #5, #6, #7, #8

Westin	#12, #13, #14, #17
Sheraton	#4, #8, #9, #13
Bukovačka (Maksimir Park, zoo)	#4, #7, #11, #12

LOCAL BUSES Anywhere there isn't a tram you'll find a bus, with ZET operating some 120 routes in total (70 within the city and 50 to the outer suburbs); almost all of them connect neatly into the tram network. Frequency varies enormously, with some routes running up to eight times an hour and others operating every half-hour or hour; a few routes run only during the rush hour. Where specific buses will be useful to you we've provided details in the text.

FUNICULAR There's a charming little funicular which runs from the main shopping street, Ilica, up to Gradec, the old town. Originally opened in 1891, as a steam-powered affair, the funicular was electrified in the 1930s. It's said to be the shortest in Europe, and at just 66m in length it's certainly a plausible claim; it's also one of the steepest funiculars in the world, with a vertical gain of 30m. (Which makes you wonder, though, at what degree of steepness a railway becomes a funicular, and a funicular becomes a plain old-fashioned lift.) Anyway, it's a bit of fun, and well worth the 3.50kn fare, and it takes the legwork out of schlepping up to the Lotrščak Tower.

CABLE CAR If the funicular isn't enough of a thrill for you, then try the cable car which climbs up towards the highest peak on Mount Medvednica, Sljeme (1,030m).

Built in the early 1960s, it's due for a revamp, but still does a pretty effective job of getting you up the mountain – covering a horizontal distance of 4km and a vertical one of nearly 700m. The cable car costs 11kn one-way/17kn return, runs every hour on the hour (but not at all if it's windy), and the journey takes about 25 minutes. For more details on both the cable car and Medvednica, see page 221.

TAXIS

By local standards, taxis are a very expensive way indeed of getting around, though if you don't get stuck in traffic (which is, however, a real risk), it's a reasonable option, especially if there are three or four of you. Fares for radio taxis start at 25kn, and they charge 7kn per km on top of that, 80kn per hour for waiting time, and 5kn per bag, with a 20% surcharge at night and on holidays. You can pick up a taxi fairly easily in a number of public locations, including Trg Maršala Tita, by the theatre, or near the cathedral at Kaptol, as well as at any of the bigger hotels. If you're calling a taxi yourself, the central number to ring is ☏ 970; you can also try ☏ 668 2505, ☏ 660 0671 or ☏ 660 1235.

CARS

If you can find a way of avoiding driving in town, then do so. Zagreb is compact enough to manage easily on foot or using public transport, and having your own car with you is, frankly, a bit of a liability – we speak as those who know. A government credit on new cars, while good for the economy, has helped to further clog up Zagreb's arteries, while negotiating your way around the busy centre or the old town is made even harder by a tricky one-way system. Many streets are also car-free, designated for pedestrians or trams only.

If driving is a nightmare, parking is worse. Legitimate street parking spaces are a good deal scarcer than hens' teeth, but if you park illegally it's likely that the infamous 'spider' (*pauk*) will take your car away. If your car does disappear, try calling the spider on ☏ 631 1888, ☏ 631 1884 or ☏ 631 1881 before you panic and report its disappearance to the police – it might save you a lot of time and hassle. The pound – where you can pay the hefty fine and recover your car – is at Strojarska 14, just west of the bus station (it's the first right on Branimira heading east from the train station, after about 1km).

Street parking (it's hardly worth telling you this – but it's just possible you might find a space) is divided into three zones, red, yellow and green, corresponding to one-, two- and three-hour maximum stay respectively. You pay 12kn per hour in the red zone, 6n per hour in the yellow zone and 3kn per hour in the green zone. Payment is easy as pie: by getting vouchers (*Parkirna Karta*) at kiosks, paying in cash at automatic ticket dispensers, or – best by far – sending an SMS with your registration number (no spaces) from your mobile phone. Send it to 101 for the red zone, 102 for the yellow zone and 103 for the green zone. One SMS equals an hour's worth of parking, and you get a return SMS to confirm you've paid, and another SMS 5–10 minutes before your parking time expires.

There is also a growing number of underground car parks, which are safe and secure, though even here, at 5kn per hour, you can end up with a hefty bill if you're in the city for any length of time. The best located are at the Sheraton Hotel, the Branimir Centar, the Kaptol Centar (at Nova Ves) [4 E1], a block-and-a-half east of Jelačić Square (on the corner of Vlaška), and at the Importanne Centar [6 E8] near the train station – though the entrances can be hard to find and easy to miss, what with the one-way system and heavy traffic. More detailed information on parking can be found – but in Croatian only – at www.zagrebparking.hr.

You could also consider leaving your car in the suburbs, where there's ample daytime parking, and catching a tram or bus into town – but with car theft a real possibility, this may not be a great decision if you plan on leaving your vehicle unattended for days at a time.

A safer option – though not a cheaper one; prices vary from 60–120kn per day – is to choose a hotel with its own parking, where you'll have the peace of mind of knowing your car will be secure for the duration of your stay. It's also worth considering staying somewhere out of town for the Zagreb part of your trip if you have a car with you (Samobor, for example) and making the short journey into the city on the regular bus service – another advantage being that out-of-town hotels can offer excellent value for money.

CAR HIRE You shouldn't need a car in Zagreb itself, but you may well be going on somewhere else, or even just considering a day or two in the vicinity (see *Chapter*

12 for details) – and there's no doubt that having your own wheels out of town can save you a lot of time and hassle.

Car hire is easy to organise direct through any of the main agencies, which can all be found at the airport. If you're booking a holiday through any of the larger travel agencies, they should also be able to arrange this for you.

Avis Pleso Airport; ✎ 626 5190; www.avis.com. *Open Mon–Fri 07.00–23.00, Sat 08.00–23.00, Sun 08.00–23.00.* Also an office at the Sheraton Hotel, Kneza Borne 2; ✎ 467 6111. *Open Mon–Sat 08.00–20.00, Sun 08.00–12.00.*
Budget Pleso Airport; ✎ 626 5854; www.budget.hr/Rent-a-Car. *Open Mon–Sat 07.00–20.00, Sun 08.00–12.00.*
Dollar & Thrifty Pleso Airport; ✎ 626 5333; f 626 5444. *Open daily 07.00–21.00.* Also downtown at Sub Rosa, Radićeva 13; ✎ 483 6466; www.subrosa.hr.
Hertz Pleso Airport; ✎ 456 2635; www.hertz.hr. *Open daily 08.00–21.00.* Also at Vukotinovićeva 4; ✎ 484 6777. *Open Mon–Sat 08.00–20.00, Sun 08.00–12.00.*
National Pleso Airport; ✎ 621 5924; f 456 2550; www.nationalcar.hr. *Open daily 07.30–21.00.* Also at the Westin Hotel, Kršnjavoga 1; ✎ 481 1764. *Open daily 07.00–21.00.*
Sixt Pleso Airport; ✎ 665 1599; www.e-sixt.com. *Open daily 06.00–22.00.* Sheraton Four Points Hotel, Sportova Trg 9; ✎ 301 5303. *Open Mon–Fri 08.00–19.00, Sat 08.00–18.00, Sun 08.00–12.00.* Regent Esplanade Hotel, Mihanovićeva 1; ✎ 456 3789. *Open Mon–Sat 08.00–11.00 & 17.00–19.00.*

PETROL STATIONS With petrol stations dotted around the city, you shouldn't have any trouble finding fuel, but if you need to fill up late at night or very early before heading out of town, the following are open 24 hours:

Gradna south Autoroute south; ☎ 650 1900
Gradna north Autoroute north; ☎ 650 1908
Dubrava Dankovečka bb; ☎ 291 2602
Jagićeva Jagićeva bb; ☎ 377 4423
Ksaver Ksaverska c bb; ☎ 467 3954
Ljubljanska Avenija Ljubljanska south; ☎ 302 0054
Miramarska Miramarska bb; ☎ 611 0125
Spansko Avenija Ljubljanska bb; ☎ 389 8599
Stupnik west Jadranska bb; ☎ 652 5716

For more information in English – and indeed the details of every filling station in the country, as well as today's fuel prices – see www.ina.hr.

BICYCLES

As keen cyclists, we'd love to rave about what a fabulously cycle-friendly city Zagreb is, but the truth is that even though it ought to be perfect (mostly flat terrain, wide streets, large leafy squares, and 135km of cycle paths), it just isn't. City drivers aren't used to sharing their roads with cyclists, and can be somewhat aggressive, if not downright dangerous, so you're pretty much forced to use the pavements – which you then have to share, not just with pedestrian traffic but also illegally parked cars.

That said, continuous efforts are being made to make Zagreb a better place for cyclists, and, ironically, cycling on some the city's biggest thoroughfares, especially south of the railway line, is great, as the dedicated cycle paths there are kept well away from the traffic – notably along Vukovarska and Slavonska/Ljubljanska, and across both the central and eastern bridges over the Sava to Bundek and Novi Zagreb.

For the more athletic, there's fantastic cycling up on Mount Medvednica, and good cycle maps available which cover the trails through the woods, while a more leisurely spin can be had down on Lake Jarun or at Bundek – though both can get very busy on a summer Sunday afternoon. There's also excellent cycling available in Zagreb County, and you can pick up a whole raft of first-rate maps from the county tourist office (see page 69) which detail not just the routes along with profiles etc, but also places to stay and eat, and useful stuff like the locations of the nearest bike repair shops. Be warned, though, that you'll need a sturdy bike as quite a few trails take advantage of traffic-free gravel roads.

There aren't that many places you can rent bikes, but we can wholeheartedly recommend Vladimir Fumić, former pro and Croatian champion, who has a shop in town as well as a bigger rental place on Lake Jarun, which is open mainly at weekends and in summer. All bike rentals come with a lock and a helmet included, and prices (as of 2006) were one hour 20kn, two hours 30kn, half day 50kn, one day 80kn, one week 480kn. If you're renting for more than a couple of days, bike delivery to your hotel can be arranged. The shop is at Vlaška 81a (go into the courtyard) (☏ 466 4233; f 466 4247; www.fumic-bicikli.hr).

There's also a busy cycling association, which sponsors activities across Croatia, and is working notably on the major Danube cycle path project, as well as the popular 'Bike and Bed' initiative, which promotes cycle-tourism. Their website (Croatian only) is at www.bicikl.hr – though there is an English section for the 'Bike and Bed' programme, at www.bicikl.hr/bike-bed.

HITCHHIKING

Even out of town, where public transport can be patchy, hitchhiking isn't recommended. It's unlikely to be dangerous, but the chances are that tourists won't pick you up, and locals tend to be travelling only short distances.

5 Accommodation

Note: Prices in this chapter are given in euro, as this is the currency used for reservations and official accommodation quotations – your final bill, however, will still be in kuna. Prices were correct as of autumn 2006.

As a bustling, business-oriented capital city, Zagreb presents a problem if you're looking for true budget accommodation. Private rooms are in short supply (and twice the price of anywhere else in the country, with the exception of Dubrovnik), hostels fill up quickly, and there isn't a campsite we can honestly recommend.

Zagreb does have plenty of hotels, but they don't come especially cheap; there's nowhere within easy reach where you'll find a room for under €60 a night, and the most luxurious establishments charge a fairly breathtaking €250+ per night for a double, year round.

Of course the nicest places fill up fast at any time of year, so it's recommended that you reserve well ahead of time, and confirm by fax (email reservations have a habit of going astray).

HOTELS

While Zagreb hotels are classified by the standard international star system, it's a little bit hit and miss, so we've done our best to let you know what places are really like.

Breakfast is usually included in the room rate (though not always at the luxury end of the scale), and ranges from rolls, butter and jam to a full buffet, with a strong correlation between the quality of the food and the price of the room. You can save money by opting for half or full board – the supplement is usually under €20 per person per day – but bear in mind that you'll then also be condemning yourself to eating all your meals in the hotel, rather than enjoying the city's burgeoning restaurant scene.

In terms of location, since there aren't any hotels in the old town, the best place to be is amongst the Habsburg squares north of the railway line, which puts you within walking distance of the main attractions. Zagreb's excellent public transport system does mean, however, that even if your hotel is a bit out of the way, you can usually quickly get to where the action is – see the listings below, and the maps at the back of this guide for more details of hotel locations.

Hotels are detailed below in three categories – luxury, mid range/upmarket, and affordable – and are listed within each section in alphabetical order.

LUXURY Zagreb has three five-star hotels, which are almost exclusively used by business people on expenses, the jet set, or celebrities; most travellers lack the wherewithal to fork out upwards of €250 a night on accommodation.

🏠 **Regent Esplanade** (209 rooms) Mihanovićeva 1; 📞 456 6666; 📠 456 6020; www.regenthotels.com [6 D/E7]
Built in 1925 as a swanky stopover for *Orient Express* passengers *en route* to Istanbul, the Esplanade has now been restored to its former glory. The public areas reek of 1920s European opulence, the rooms are ultra-stylish & spacious, & the staff combine 5-star professionalism with unfailing friendliness. Check-in is a sit-down affair with complimentary fizz while the formalities are completed. The hotel offers discounts on weekends, & rooms include free internet access. Check out the fabulous Emerald Ballroom & the set of clocks inside the main entrance which tell the time in New York, Buenos Aires, London, Zagreb, Moscow, Tokyo & Sydney. B/fast is simply wonderful – but then so it should be, at 200kn a head. *Rooms from €220.*

🏠 **Sheraton Zagreb** (300 rooms) Kneza Borne 2; 📞 455 3535; 📠 455 3035; www.sheraton.com/zagreb [7 G7]
Located 2 blocks up & 3 blocks east of the station, the Sheraton is a glass-fronted city block with rooms (discounts available at weekends) offering as much luxury & all the facilities anyone's going to need, including a gym & an indoor pool – though you have to ask yourself which humourist was responsible for putting the fitness centre on the smokers' floor. *Dbls from €265.*

🏠 **Westin Zagreb** (378 rooms) Krsnjavoga 1; 📞 489 2000; 📠 489 2001; www.westin.com [6 B7]
Formerly known as the Opera (the National Theatre is just up the road), the hotel might be a bit of an architectural monstrosity, but inside it's all tasteful opulence & impeccable service. Rooms are spacious & comfortable, with a special emphasis on luxurious bed & bath facilities (though one could still argue that the bathrooms at the Esplanade are nicer). For fitness fans there's a gym & an indoor pool, & the b/fast (an additional 140kn pp) is terrific – unlimited *pršut, paški sir*, smoked salmon & the like, & dishes cooked to order. Secure parking is an extra 60kn a day; but the hotel does offer 20% discount on room rates at weekends. *Standard dbls €260.*

MID-RANGE/UPMARKET

🏠 **Arcotel Allegra** (150 rooms) Branimirova 29, Branimir Centar; ☎ 469 6000; 📠 469 6096; www.arcotel.at/allegra [7 G7]
Very modern, very chic, with spacious, minimalist rooms. Part of an Austrian chain, the Arcotel has earned a reputation for gay-friendliness in a town that's still a bit uneasy about same-sex couples.Count on substantial discounts at weekends. Internet access is free in the lobby, or you can sign up for WiFi in the room. If you plan to partake of the copious breakfast buffet, count an extra €15 per person – you can amuse yourself while you eat by trying to put names to the personalities pictured on the curtains, from Albert Einstein to Camille Claudel. *Sgls & dbls €120–160 per room, while suites range from €190–400.*

🏠 **Astoria (Best Western)** (102 rooms) Petrinjska 71; ☎ 480 8900; 📠 480 8908; www.bestwestern.com [7 F7]
With a very handy location in the town centre, this 4-star hotel has recently benefited from a major makeover from the American chain.Very comfortable rooms with internet access, complimentary HBO & satellite TV.The hotel also boasts a fairly upmarket Croatian restaurant, the Ragusa. *Sgls €115, dbls €150; executive rooms & suites go for €200 upwards.*

🏠 **Dubrovnik** (269 rooms) Gajeva 1; ☎ 487 3555; 📠 481 3506; www.hotel-dubrovnik.hr [4 E4]
If the exterior is a tribute to 1970s socialist architecture, the refurbished interior is starting to look a bit tired, & the staff can be a bit surly – but the Dubrovnik's location overlooking Jelačić Square is unbeatable if you want to be right in the thick of things. Rooms are comfortable & have AC, with those overlooking the square also noise-proofed against the coming & going of Zagreb's trams. Internet access is free at the minuscule business centre, or surprisingly expensive via dial-up in the room. *Small sgls from €105, dbls €140, & twins €160.*

🏠 **Four Points by Sheraton** (280 rooms) Trg Sportova 9; ☎ 365 8333; 📠 309 2657; www.starwoodhotels.com [1 B3]
A smart, business-oriented hotel about 3km southwest of the city centre.The very comfortable doubles have all the facilities you'd expect, with special offers usually available at weekends. *Rooms from €165.*

🏠 **International** (207 rooms) Miramarska 24; 📞 610 8800; 📠 610 8700; www.hup-zagreb.hr [1 C4]
Completely restored & refitted in 2006, this modern 4-star business hotel is a 10min walk south of the railway. It features elegantly appointed rooms (all with broadband internet access) & vast new underground parking for 400 cars. *Standard sgls/dbls €110–140, with larger superior rooms available for just a few euro more (20% discount at weekends).*

🏠 **Palace Hotel** (125 rooms) Strossmayerov 10; 📞 489 9600; 📠 481 1358; www.palace.hr [6 E6]
A Zagreb institution, the Palace was built in 1891 & has been a hotel since 1907. While it retains much of its old-fashioned secession-era charm, its rooms have all been thoroughly modernised, with AC & unlimited broadband internet access included in the room rate. If the mood takes you, treat yourself to an upmarket dinner in the hotel's swanky restaurant, or a less formal meal in the Belle Époque café. *Dbls €135–165, suites €220–315.*

🏠 **Villa Tina** (24 rooms) Bukovačka Cesta 213; 📞 244 5138; 📠 244 5204; www.vilatina.com [1 C3]
A modern Italianate villa set in the pleasant hills near Maksimir Park, Villa Tina is a stylish option. A small outdoor swimming pool is complemented by a jacuzzi, solarium & sauna, & there's also a nice restaurant. Given that the website wasn't working at the time of writing, don't count on internet access. To get there on public transport, take tram #1, #9 or #17 to Svetice (the stop before Borongaj, the terminus), & then bus #203, & look for the small stone lions flanking the hotel's gate on the left-hand side of Bukovačka, heading up the hill. *Rooms from €80–90, 2 trpls at €110.*

AFFORDABLE

🏠 **Central** (79 rooms) Branimirova 3; 📞 484 1122; 📠 484 1304; www.hotel-central.hr [7 F7]
An affordable 3-star hotel, the recently renovated Central is extremely well located just across from the railway station, & has straightforward AC dbls. If the building's façade is rather characterless, the friendly, helpful staff will do their best to make you feel at home – & most rooms have internet access. *Dbl €100–110.*

🏠 **Dora** (24 rooms) Trnjanska 11e; ☎ 631 1900; f 631 1909; www.zug.hr [1 C3]
A 10min walk south of the station, just off Vukovarska, & 20mins south of Jelačić Square. A simple, good-value hotel with pleasant rooms. While a bit out of the way, it's very handy for the main bus & train stations, & has its own private parking as well as affordable shared internet access. *Dbls €90.*

🏠 **Fala** (13 rooms) Trnjanske Ledine 18; ☎ 611 1062; f 619 4498; www.hotel-fala-zg.hr [1 C4]
Another pleasant affordable choice, with spotless, newly furnished – if a bit spartan – rooms. They even have cheap internet access from a shared computer. Convenient for public transport, the hotel also has a helpful multi-lingual website that includes maps & directions. To get there, simply take bus #219, #220, #221 or #268 from the main train or bus stations & head a couple of stops south towards Novi Zagreb. *Sgls €50, dbls €70.*

🏠 **Gaj** (29 rooms) Jezerska 24a; ☎ 381 7222; f 381 7225; www.hotelgaj.hr [1 B4]
A quiet, modern 3-star hotel offering AC rooms, as well as shared internet facilities, & free access to the solarium & fitness centre. An excellent option if you're arriving by car, as it's easy to drive to & has plenty of secure parking. While it looks to be well to the west of town, it's only a 3min walk from the terminus of the #118 bus, which sets off every 10mins from Trg Mažuranić. If you're arriving by bus from town, walk back to the first street on the right, & cross the stream over the footbridge at the end, & you'll see the hotel on your left. *Dbls €80, trpls €90, suites €95.*

🏠 **Ilica** (23 rooms, 1 suite) Ilica 102; ☎ 377 7622; f 377 7722; www.hotel-ilica.hr [4 A4]
Set in a courtyard just 2 tram stops (or 10–15mins' walk) west of Jelačić Square (& 100m west of Britanski Square), this cosy hotel is run by a rather mercurial owner. Rooms are individually furnished, & a few have balconies; all have wireless internet access, though it's not free. With some private parking & the convenience of a Konzum supermarket & DM store round the corner, rooms are still a bargain. They get booked up very fast indeed. *Sgls €60, dbls €70, twins €75, trpls €85, suite €125.*

🏠 **Jadran** (48 rooms) Vlaška 50; ☎ 455 3777; 📠 461 2151; www.hup-zagreb.hr [5 G4]
Although extremely well located on Vlaška, just a few minutes east of Trg Jelačića & round the corner from the cathedral, the Jadran has definitely seen better days – but the staff are friendly & the prices are very reasonable for a place this central. Most of the rooms have been recently (if modestly) refurbished. If you mind the smell of smoke, definitely ask for a non-smoking room. No internet access, but the Importanne Centar, which has, is just round the corner. *Dbls* €100.

🏠 **Jaegerhorn** (12 rooms) Ilica 14; ☎ 483 3877; 📠 483 3573; www.hotel-pansion-jaegerhorn.hr [4 D4]
Perfectly located, but tucked away from the hustle & bustle of Ilica itself, at the end of a narrow shopping arcade, this family-run hotel has simple, pleasant rooms. There's also a decent restaurant & leafy, tranquil garden terrace with a waterfall, backing onto the steep park which leads up to the old town. *Sgls, dbls & trpls from* €80–130.

🏠 **Meridijan 16** (25 rooms) Vukovarska 241; ☎ 606 5200; 📠 606 5201; www.meridijan16.com [1 C3]
Located bang on the 16th meridian, just 500m south of the main bus station, this new hotel's rooms are all tastefully furnished, with AC & equipped with dial-up internet access (be warned this is at premium rates). Private parking is available at €10 per day, & the situation, on most of Zagreb's main tram routes, makes getting in & out of town a breeze (#2 & #6 run direct to the bus & train stations, #6 & #13 direct to Jelačić Square). *Sgls* €65, *dbls* €85, *trpls* €105. There's also a very comfortable suite with a kitchen & small balcony for €85.

🏠 **Movie Hotel** (20 rooms) Savska 141; ☎ 605 5045; 📠 606 1911; www.the-movie-pub.com [1 B4]
Newly opened above the Movie Pub (see page 137), guests can choose themed rooms named after stars like Sharon Stone, Harrison Ford, Catherine Zeta-Jones & Al Pacino. With private car parking & a tram stop (#13, #14) just outside, the place is easy to get to – but you can't help feeling that most of the guests might be patrons from downstairs who've either been 'over-served' or struck it lucky. *Sgls* €40, *dbls* €75.

🏠 **Sliško** (18 rooms) Supilova 13; ☎ 619 4210; 🖷 619 4223; www.slisko.hr [1 C3]
A clean, well-run establishment located just 300m southeast of the main bus station in a quiet street with a couple of useful grocery stores nearby. Bright, airy rooms in pastel tones, an internet terminal on the first floor, & its own bar & café/restaurant. Very good value. *Sgls €55, dbls €75, trpls €90, quads €105.*

🏠 **Zagreb** (13 rooms) Bundek; ☎ 663 7333; 🖷 663 7229; www.hup-zagreb.hr [1 C4]
While the lake & park directly opposite have been newly restored, the same can't be said for this 2-star hotel, which manages to retain all its 1970s socialist-era functional feel – though you do get access to the internet at just 10kn per hour. The rooms are pretty basic, but clean & there is ample free parking. It's a great choice if you're on a tight budget, & don't mind a bit of a schlep into town (bus #219, #220 or #221 will take you straight to the train station, however). *Sgls €42, dbls €50.*

PRIVATE ROOMS/APARTMENTS

For a big city, Zagreb has a surprisingly limited supply of private rooms (*privatne sobe*), Croatia's rough equivalent to Britain's bed and breakfasts (though you may pay extra for breakfast). Generally clean, comfortable and friendly, their big advantage is the price, with most private doubles going for under €60 a night. Conversely, with real estate prices in downtown Zagreb skyrocketing, count yourself lucky if you manage to secure one of the few rooms in the city centre – more likely you'll find yourself out in the suburbs, using public transport to get into town.

Private rooms are officially classified into categories I, II and III. Category I rooms will be clean and functional, but you'll almost certainly be sharing a bathroom; in category II you'll be bathing en suite and may even have a television; while in category III you'll find yourself very well looked after.

In terms of cost, Zagreb's cheapest single private rooms (shared bathroom) start at about €30 per night, with doubles for around €45 (but bear in mind that unlike hotels, prices are usually quoted per person, not per room). If you're looking for a double room with its own bathroom, expect to pay anything from €50–80. A studio sleeping up to six people goes for €70–100 or so, depending on the size and location.

For short stays, the only agency currently handling private room bookings that's located in the city centre is **Evistas** (☎ 483 9546; f 483 9554; *open Mon–Fri 09.00–20.00, Sat 09.30–17.00*) at Šenoina 28, a block north of Branimirova (the main road running east–west in front of the train station). Rooms go quickly, so try to arrive early. Private room rates are always quoted per night for a minimum of two nights; add 20% to the standard per-night rate if you're planning only an overnight stay.

Zagreb also has a number of private apartments for let, usually on a longer-stay basis. If you're going to be in town for while, these can be great value, but try to arrange a visit before you commit to a lengthy rental contract. If you're in the market for a long-term rental, a good place to start is **Nest**, at Boškovićeva 7A (☎ 487 3225; f 481 8748; *www.nest.hr*). The agency says it specialises in pleasant, centrally located apartments and offers discounted rates for stays of more than 15 days – but it still hasn't bothered to answer our email.

The Zagreb Tourist Office also maintains a list of private accommodation options on its website (*www.zagreb-touristinfo.hr*) – you can find them by clicking on the 'Accommodation' option on the home page.

Finally, with both private rooms and apartments, don't be afraid to say 'no' if you don't like the look of the place – staying somewhere which doesn't suit you can really spoil your visit.

YOUTH HOSTELS AND STUDENT ACCOMMODATION

Zagreb has two official hostels which are part of the Croatian Youth Hostel Association (HFHS), one in the centre of town, and the other in the suburb of Remetinec, southwest of the city, across the river from the Jarun Lake. There's also an excellent private hostel in the suburb of Ravnice, east of the city centre and easily reachable on the tram. If you want to make advance bookings for other HFHS youth hostels in Croatia (there's just a handful) or get hold of an ISIC student card, you can do so at the HFHS office at Dežmanova 9 – see page 70 for details.

In summer it's also sometimes possible to get a bed in the university student dorms (ask at the Tourist Office on Jelačić Square), though prices aren't always as low as you might expect. A handful of other budget possibilities is posted on the Zagreb Tourist Office website (*www.zagreb-touristinfo.hr*); click on the 'Accommodation' section and follow the link 'For students and youth'.

🏠 **Ravnice Youth Hostel** (30 beds in 2-/4-/12-bed rooms) Ravnice 38d; ✆ 233 2325; f 234 5607; e ravnice-youth-hostel@zg.hinet.hr; www.ravnice-youth-hostel.hr [1 D3]

Located past the Dinamo Stadium & Maksimir Park, on the right-hand side, by the tennis courts (follow the wonderful smell emanating from the Kraš chocolate factory). From town, take tram #4, #7, #11 or #12 (direction Dubrava or Dubec) to the Ravnice stop, walk south for about 3mins, & look for the large hostel sign on the building itself. Opened in 2000, this bright, friendly family-run place sleeps 30 guests in spotless rooms that accommodate from 2–12 beds each. The price gets you clean bed linen & use of the large communal kitchen, pleasant sitting areas & a high-speed internet connection (16kn per hour); bring your own towel & food. The hostel is open 24hrs (reception is staffed from 09.00–22.00), & there are no curfew or age restrictions. Book directly over the internet, or by phone – owner Vera speaks excellent English, thanks to a stint in Australia. *€15 pp per night.*

🏠 **Remetinec Hostel** (37 rooms) Remetinečki Gaj 28; ✆ 614 0042; f 614 0039; e hostelremetinec@nazor.hr [1 B4]

A clean & friendly hostel, situated about 6km southwest of the city centre; bus #222 from the back of the main train station will get you there in about 20mins or so. *10 sgls at €28, 17 dbls at €50, & 10 trpls at €60, all with private bathroom.*

🏠 **Youth Hostel** (210 beds) Petrinjska 77; ✆ 484 1261; f 484 1269; e zagreb@hfhs.hr; www.hfhs.hr [7 F7]

Centrally located near the train station, but despite having a large number of beds, it's almost invariably full. While the staff do their best to keep it clean & friendly, it's also rather run down & can be a bit rough, especially if you're travelling alone. Plans are afoot to renovate the entire establishment in 2007 – a project that's sure to involve closing the facilities for some time, so be sure to check ahead before you visit. *Prices are €12 for a bed in a 6-bed room & €15 for a place in a 3-bed room, both pp. There are also some sgl rooms available at €25 (shared bathroom) or €33 (private bathroom), & a few dbls at €35 (shared bathroom) or €45 (private bathroom).*

CAMPING

At the time of writing, Zagreb really wasn't set up for campers at all, though a new campsite near the Jarun Lake, with some 1,500 places, is supposed to be ready for 2007 – check with the tourist office for the latest details if you're seriously intending to camp.

Pending the opening of the Jarun site, your only option is the campsite at the **Motel Plitvice** (↘ 653 0444; f 653 0445; e *motel@motel-plitvice.hr; www.motel-plitvice.hr* [1 A4]), which is rather dismally situated on the Plitvice road, southwest of the city, near the motorway junction. A bridge over the highway brings you to the service station, where you can at least take advantage of the shops and self-service restaurants there.

Finally, do remember that freelance camping in Croatia is illegal – and if you're caught you'll be subject to an immediate and fairly hefty fine.

6 Eating and Drinking

Food and drink are easy to find in Zagreb, with restaurants, bars and cafés for all tastes – and budgets – and a wonderful seven-days-a-week open market in Dolac, just north of Jelačić Square (see below).

As you'd expect in a fast-moving city, there are plenty of places where you can get a bite on the hoof, fast food coming in traditional (sausages etc) or contemporary (burgers and the like) formats, and the city having quite a few sandwich bars, both local- and US-style, as well as plentiful ice cream shops.

Before delving into the listings, it's worth taking a moment to look at what you might be eating and drinking while you're here.

FOOD AND DRINK

FOOD The day starts for most of us with breakfast, though it practically doesn't exist as a proper meal per se in Zagreb. If you're in a hotel though, then breakfast of some sort will usually be included in the price (not at the very top end, however) – usually in the form of a self-service buffet, with the quality and variety of fare on offer closely matching the price.

If you're not in a hotel, then you can rely on cafés, bakeries (*pekarnica*) and cake/ice cream shops (*slastičarnica*) to furnish the makings of breakfast. You can also still find *burek*, a traditional pastry filled with cheese (*sa sirom*), meat (*sa mesom*) and just occasionally spinach (*špinat*). It's cheap, filling and usually delicious – if occasionally too greasy for comfort – but a good deal harder to get hold of than it was a decade or so ago.

Cheaper restaurants and snack bars – sometimes billed as *bife* (bar) or *roštilj* (grill bar) – serve up *čevapi or čevapčiči* (spiced meatballs or small sausages, usually served with spring onions and spicy green peppers), *pljeskavica* (a wad of minced meat often served in pitta bread – the Croatian hamburger), *ražnjiči* (kebab), or plain old-fashioned sausages. Try any of these dishes with spicy *ajvar*, a sauce made from tomatoes, peppers and aubergines, with a dash of chilli.

At lunchtime, you'll also often notice cheaper places offering *gableci* – not, as you might expect, some exotic local speciality, but rather the generic name for home-cooked lunchtime *plats du jour*. Fare will be basic but hearty, and represents a tasty choice if you're wanting to fill up on a budget.

Pizzerias are the next step up the food chain, and are generally great value for money. Pizza here is fairly close to what you'd get in Italy, with a thinnish crust and a variety of toppings – including excellent chilli peppers. Pizzerias also tend to do good (and keenly priced) pasta dishes – though it's very rare to eat pasta anywhere in Croatia that isn't (by Italian standards, anyway) slightly overcooked.

Restaurants (*restoran, konoba or gostiona*) tend to focus on meat and/or fish dishes.

Meat isn't all that exciting, leaning towards pork and lamb chops and cutlets, pan-fried veal, or steak, but it's generally tasty enough. Fish for its part is delicious, but can turn out to be surprisingly pricey. For most white fish you'll pay by the raw weight, and a decent-size fish for two can come in at as much as 400kn. Whitebait, blue fish (sardines, mackerel, etc) and the ubiquitous calamari are, on the other hand, great value.

You'll also see lots of *pršut*, Croatia's answer to Italy's *prosciutto*, and pronounced (and produced) in almost exactly the same way. The air-dried ham is a Dalmatian and Istrian speciality and practically melts in the mouth when sliced thinly enough (which sadly it often isn't).

Of course if you're vegetarian, *pršut*, like much else on Croatian menus, is a non-starter – indeed it's a non-main and a non-dessert, too. Vegetarianism is no longer off the menu altogether, however, as even in restaurants that don't offer specific vegetarian options, you can usually get a cheese omelette (*omlet sa sirom*), a meat-free pasta dish, or a pizza, along with a range of salads.

You can also go for Zagreb's big speciality (and it is big), *štrukli*, which is something of a death by cream, doughy-pasta and cottage-cheese experience. It's somewhere between a giant cream-soaked ravioli and a cheese-stuffed dumpling. The dish technically comes from outside Zagreb, but the locals consume it here by the plate-load (boiled or baked; sweet or savoury; as a starter, main or dessert), and argue fiercely over where the best *štrukli* can be found (at the Regent Esplanade, in our opinion).

SOMETHING CHEESY

Croatia has some very palatable local cheeses, many of which are still made in the traditional fashion on small family-run farms. With country cheeses commanding better prices in Zagreb than at home, you'll find several varieties on sale in Dolac market (see page 139), and most sellers are happy to let you taste before you buy.

The prince of Croatian cheeses is indisputably *paški sir*, a firm cheese from the island of Pag. Made from the milk of sheep that graze on the island's salty sage-filled pastures, it's a local delicacy that's produced in tiny quantities – and priced accordingly. Sadly, in recent times a lack of stringent controls has seen the market flooded with inferior versions; once a rare treat, even in restaurants, it's now available pretty much on demand, and seems much the poorer for it.

Another popular local cheese comes from the Lika region, near Plitvice, where you often still see scarf-clad older women camped by the roadside selling their wares. Lika sellers also make the trek into town to sell their wares at Dolac.

Zagreb also has its very own chocolate factory, Kraš, beyond Maksimir Park, which smells absolutely mouth-watering from anywhere in the vicinity (notably the Ravnice Youth Hostel), and churns out a good wide range of tasty sweetmeats.

Eating times – unlike much of the rest of continental Europe – are pretty flexible, and you can get a bite to eat at most times of day, though it's worth checking the opening hours at the most upmarket places. That said, it doesn't seem to be exceptional for the moneyed classes to turn up for Sunday lunch at around three or four in the afternoon.

DRINK The most important thing to know is that you *can* drink the water – all publicly supplied water in Zagreb is safe unless it explicitly says otherwise. The next piece of good news for drinkers is that alcohol is reasonably priced, and certainly when compared with northern Europe.

A half litre of draught **beer** (*pivo*) costs anything from 10–20kn, depending on the waterhole. Premium and foreign brands go for a little more, but Croatian beers are just fine. *Točeno* will get you draught, which is best ordered by brand name – Ožujsko is Zagreb's major brewery, and the beer is wildly popular, though personally (we won't make any friends saying this) we prefer Karlovačko (from Karlovac) or Laško (from Slovenia). Zagreb also has a great micro-brewery called Zlatno, though its beer is not all that widely available (see page 129).

Croatia makes lots of **wine** (*vino*), and the quality – drinkable at worst – continues to improve. Almost the entire production is guzzled down domestically, however, so you're very unlikely to see it on the supermarket shelves at home. Equally, you won't see much in the way of non-local wine on menus or in the shops in Zagreb, so you're pretty much obliged to go the Croatian way.

In shops you can pay anything from 20–100kn for a bottle of wine, while in low- to mid-range pizzerias and restaurants a litre of the house red or white goes for

50–100kn and bottled wines start at around 80kn. Swankier establishments don't always sell house wine (it's always worth asking, however, even if it's not on the menu), and you can easily find yourself spending upwards of 200kn a bottle.

Increasingly, Graševina (a white grape variety) is coming to dominate local restaurant tables – a disappointing development given the country's many better wines. The reason, as usual, is economic – the Graševina grape is easy to grow and make into cheap but acceptable wine that offers restaurants a better sales margin. While that's not to say there aren't some good (and even excellent) Graševina wines, if given a choice it's worth making the effort to try some of the local Rieslings or Chardonnays too.

The nearest wine-growing region to Zagreb is the Plešivica vineyards, about 30km southwest of the city, which produce some great wines; a particular personal favourite is the white Rajnski Rizling, though you'll find local growers also pushing the local specialist red, Portugizać.

In bars and cafés, wine is less popular than it used to be, and more often than not you'll be offered a no-choice choice of whatever quarter-bottle of red or white happens to be on hand. If you want white wine and soda, then order a *špricer* for a small one or a *gemišt* for a larger version.

Spirits (*rakija*) are common, dangerous, and fairly cheap. In supermarkets you'll find Croatian brandies and other spirits at around 70–100kn a bottle, but you can also buy fiery and frequently excellent home-distilled spirits in the market for anything from 50–100kn a litre. The quality of spirits varies enormously and can't usually be determined from the label; price is a reasonable (but far from infallible) indicator.

Personal favourites are Velebitska travarica, which is made by monks up in the mountains and comes in an especially attractive bottle, and biska, an Istrian speciality with added mistletoe. On the other hand, do anything you can to avoid a drink called Pelinkovac. Piers once had three in a row in Zagreb, convinced that at some point the apparently re-bottled wood-stain would become palatable – but it never did. It brings a bad taste to the mouth, just writing about it.

Friendships, business deals and meetings are all cemented with *rakija*, and it's remarkable how often you can find yourself expected to down lethal drinks. If you don't drink at all, then it's not a bad idea to come up with a plausible reason why this is so (health is always a reliable standby), as Croatians, like most people, tend to be suspicious of those who won't join in.

If you're in a bar or café you'll notice a price difference between local (*domaće*) and imported (*uvozna*) spirits; for all but absolute sticklers, the local varieties are fine, especially if you're ordering drinks with mixers, such as G&T.

In marked contrast to the relative abundance of alcoholic choice, there are surprisingly few **soft drinks** available. You're basically limited to the usual mind-numbingly popular cola (but rarely the sugar-free variety), bottles of sweet fizzy orange, and mineral water. Those in search of local flavour might also like to try Cockta, a Slovenian-produced caffeine-free alternative to cola made from dog-rose berries, oranges, lemons and herbs.

Coffee is as popular here as everywhere, and in cafés tends to be excellent – though what you'll be served with breakfast in the lower-end hotels can be frankly disgusting. **Tea** is most often of the fruit variety or comes in dodgy-looking bags which tend to work better with lemon than milk. If you want ordinary 'English' tea, be sure to insist on black tea (*crni čaj*) – but don't expect to find anything you'll be able to stand a spoon in unless you bring your own. Tea and coffee will cost anything from 5–15kn in a café, depending on the classiness (or otherwise) of the establishment.

✖ RESTAURANTS

At places marked as inexpensive in the (alphabetical) listings below, expect to pay around 200kn for two, including wine; mid-range places will set you back 250–500kn for a couple; while at expensive restaurants two can easily pay 600kn and up – though there's nothing to stop you having a soup, a salad and a glass of wine at a ritzy place and coming away with change from 300kn for two.

Most restaurants catering to tourists stay open from around 11.00–23.00, though some (especially top-end establishments) will close for a period during the afternoon. Reservations are not normally expected (or accepted) except at the very upper end; where they *are* recommended, we've included the phone number with the listing.

We've listed restaurants here in four groupings for convenience: the upper town (everything from Gradec to Kaptol and along Tkalčićeva); Jelačić Square and the area west, south and east of it; the rest of the lower town (as far as the railway station); and restaurants a bit further afield (not including Mount Medvednica, which is covered separately in *Chapter 11*).

UPPER TOWN

✗ Agava Tkalčićeva 39 [4 E3]

The situation & setting – spread over several small terraces cascading down onto bustling Tkalčićeva – is just about unbeatable, & the food isn't bad either. Informal atmosphere, large range of salads, & an extensive choice of well-cooked pasta dishes (though they curiously had only one sort of pasta, fusilli, in stock, on the day we ate there). *Mid-range.*

✗ Atlanta Tkalčićeva 65; ☏ 481 3848 [4 E2]

Upscale place offering a wide choice of pasta, fish & seafood, steak & traditional Croatian dishes in a cosy, romantic atmosphere. Reservations recommended. *Mid-range to expensive.*

✗ Baltazar Nova Ves 4; ☏ 466 6999; www.restoran-baltazar.com [4 E1]

A traditional, upper-end restaurant just up from the cathedral, popular with business people & large groups, with an extensive menu featuring mainly meat dishes (for fish from the same kitchen, see Gašpar, below). Chef Tomislav Špiček carried off Croatia's coveted Chef of the Year award in 2003 & 2004. Reservations recommended. *Mid-range.*

✗ Gašpar Nova Ves 4; ☏ 466 6999; www.restoran-baltazar.com [4 E1]

Shares a kitchen with its neighbour Baltazar (see above), but specialises in seafood. A good choice of freshly prepared dishes, served in a polished-wood setting styled to resemble the interior of an ocean cruiser. Reservations recommended. *Mid-range to expensive. Closed Sun.*

✕ Ivica i Marica Tkalčićeva 70; ☎ 481 7321 [4 E2]
Taking its name from the Croatian for 'Hansel & Gretel' – look out for the gingerbread motifs – this upmarket option takes its food seriously. The emphasis is on organic, locally grown fresh produce, there's a good wine list, & manageable portion sizes mean you might even find room to indulge in one of their sumptuous desserts. If you're in the mood for something local, try the top-notch baked *štrukli* – one of the finest in town, & certainly the only serious rival in Zagreb (in our humble opinions) to Le Bistro at the Regent Esplanade (see below). Reservations recommended. *Mid-range to expensive. Closed Sun.*

✕ Kaptolska Klet Kaptol 5 [4 E3]
Right opposite the cathedral, with a large, rustic internal courtyard, this large restaurant is popular with tour groups & invariably busy. Service can be slow & rather offhand, but the food – traditional country-style Croatian cooking – is good for the price. *Inexpensive to mid-range.*

✕ Kapuciner Kaptol 6 [4 E3]
Next door to Kaptolska Klet, this place is popular with independent travellers in spite of (or perhaps because of) its simple, unpretentious décor. Efficient service, cheap prices & great pizza & pasta dishes with a view of the cathedral from the side terrace. *Inexpensive.*

✕ Katedralis Tome Bakača 9 [4 E3]
A conveniently located place in a pleasant setting facing the cathedral, you'll find most of the local staples at good prices, along with a tourist menu offering 4 courses for 90kn. 10% discount for cash. *Inexpensive.*

✕ Kerempuh Kaptol 3; ☎ 481 9000 [4 E3]
Right on the corner of the Dolac market square is our favourite restaurant in all of Zagreb. Run by the ever-cheerful

Nikica Vuksan, it's open only at lunchtime & at least half the tables seem to be permanently reserved by a varied bunch of retired university professors, former footballers & journalists. The menu is made fresh daily, & varies according to whatever head chef Anna Ugarković finds best in the market that morning. Chic, stylish interior, brisk, friendly service, & the view out over the market square from the newly extended terrace is wonderful. Reservations recommended. *Mid-range.*

✕ Lopud Kaptol 10; ☎ 481 8775 [4 E3]

A short stroll north from the cathedral. The menu here is limited to whatever fish has come in that day, & the wine list is positively spartan, but the Lopud's reputation as one of the best seafood places in town means reservations are highly advisable. *Expensive.*

✕ Maharadža Opatovina 19 [4 E3]

If you're in the mood for a curry, this welcoming place on the pedestrian street running north out of the Dolac market serves up a good range of classic favourites, authentically prepared – though don't expect it to compete with what you'd find in the UK. *Inexpensive to mid-range.*

✕ Mangiare Tkalčićeva 29 [4 E3]

A tiny, cosy place serving pizzas like they make them in Italy – wood-fired oven, thin crust & a good range of toppings. Large, appetising salads are also a speciality. *Inexpensive.*

✕ Mikina Klet Tkalčićeva 59 [4 E3]

With its vine-covered terrace & folksy, homespun interior (a *klet* is a small wooden house amongst the vineyards), this is a good place to enjoy traditional Croatian meat dishes like *čevapi* & *ražnjiči*, along with pizza & *štrukli*. *Inexpensive.*

Eating and Drinking RESTAURANTS

6

✕ Nažigač Kaptol 6 (in the alley, opposite Kapuciner's terrace) [4 E3]
Named after the informal word for 'lamplighter', this tiny place specialises in earthy local dishes served in hearty portions at great prices. One caveat – while the *grah* (heavy bean stew) is particularly good, traditional fare like horseburgers may not be to everyone's taste. Confusingly, the restaurant also seems to trade under the name 'National Fast Food'. *Inexpensive.*

✕ Nokturno Skalinska 4 [4 E3]
The ever-popular Nokturno, on the steep street running down from Kaptol to Tkalčićeva, serves up good pizzas & a wide range of pasta dishes in a simple, cheerful setting. There's a minuscule terrace, & their crisp Đakovo Riesling is among the most keenly priced in town. *Inexpensive.*

✕ Peperoncino Kamenita 5 [4 D3]
Fashionable, modern & informal Italian-style bistro just up from the Stone Gate, where grazers can choose from a range of bruschette or a keenly priced full brunch menu. Pasta dishes, including Istrian fuži, are also a speciality, & they do a good b/fast for 30kn. *Mid-range.*

✕ Pod Gričkim Topom, Zakmardijeve Stube 5 [4 D4]
Tucked away from the crowds just under Strossmayerovo Šetalište, with a fine view out over the lower town from the garden terrace, this friendly, professional place serves up well-cooked Croatian favourites in a homey setting. It's located at the top of the steps leading down to Ilica, or easily reachable on the path up from the bottom of Radićeva, or from the Lotršćak Tower. *Mid-range.*

✕ Takenoko Nova Ves 17 (in the Kaptol Centar); ✆ 486 8530; www.takenoko.hr [4 E1]
On the Tkalčićeva side of the Kaptol Centar, this very chic Japanese restaurant is a welcome addition to Zagreb's

rather Eurocentric restaurant scene, serving traditional sushi & sashimi along with more adventurous Japanese fusion cooking. Reservations recommended. *Expensive*.

✕ Tkalčina Vura Tkalčićeva 57 [4 E2]

A simple, friendly place right in the heart of bustling Tkalčićeva, with a pretty terrace & a good choice of well-priced standard fare – grilled meats, risotto, calamari & the like. *Inexpensive*.

ON AND OFF JELAČIĆ SQUARE

✕ Boban Gajeva 3 [6 E5]

This enduringly popular & well-located establishment (just down from Jelačić Square) is owned by former Croatian national team & AC Milan football superstar Zvonimir Boban. Underneath the café you'll find a busy Italian-themed restaurant in a brick-vaulted cellar, with excellent pasta dishes. *Mid-range*.

✕ Jaegerhorn Ilica 14 [4 D4]

Part of the Jaegerhorn Pansion, the restaurant is located at the end of a narrow arcade off Ilica, with a lovely summer terrace (though the fountain really is noisy) & a large indoor seating area for colder weather. Traditional Croatian fare. *Mid-range*.

✕ Lady Šram Mesnička 12; ☏ 485 1122 [4 C4]

A 5min walk west along Ilica from Jelačić Square, & up the hill a few steps, this place is named after a famous Croatian actress & beauty of the 1920s. The stylish Edwardian interior, soft lighting & upmarket ambience make this a great venue for a romantic evening out. With a chef who's passionate about keeping traditional recipes alive, expect a menu heavily slanted towards game, homemade patés & meat stews; & the homemade *štrukli* is also highly rated. Reservations recommended. *Mid-range*.

✖ **Piccolo Mondo** Gajeva 1 (in the Hotel Dubrovnik) [4 E4]
Don't be fooled by the rather middle-of-the-road décor; this place does some of the best *al dente* pasta in Croatia, along with pizzas & good international-style fish & meat dishes. Service is efficient & friendly, & the location (right on Jelačić Square) couldn't be more central. *Mid-range.*

✖ **Pizzeria Lav** Vlaška 23 [5 F4]
A basic place (the name means 'lion') just east of Jelačić Square with vaulted interior & a wee terrace tucked into an alleyway, serving decent pizzas from a wood-fired oven. Can get oppressively smoky inside. *Inexpensive.*

✖ **Pizzicato** Gundulićeva 4 [4 C4]
Another very simple pizzeria with a tiny courtyard terrace, but this time a block west of the flower market. Its location under a music academy means you'll munch your margarita to the background strains of aspiring local musicians – talented or otherwise. *Inexpensive.*

✖ **Purger** Petrinjska 33 [7 F5]
A wholesome Croatian place on the street running southeast out of Jelačić Square, named after the local word for 'citizen' (a variant on burgher). It's modestly priced, popular with local politicians, & has a terrace at the back in summer. *Inexpensive.*

✖ **Rossini** Vlaška 55; ☎ 455 1060; www.korum.hr [5 G4]
Very upscale Italian opposite the Jadran Hotel, complete with chic interior & an extensive menu of timeless favourites covering everything from antipasti to risotto, pasta & classic Italian meat & fish dishes. Reservations recommended. *Expensive.*

✘ Stari Fijakre Mesnička 6 [4 C4]

Just down from Lady Šram (see above). The name means 'old coach', & the emphasis is very much on old-fashioned country cooking from the Zagorje region north of Zagreb. The menu can be a little earthy for some – specialities include blood sausage, offal, turkey & *grah* (hearty bean stew), accompanied by an extensive selection of local & international beers. *Mid-range.*

✘ Vallis Aurea Tomićeva 4 [4 D4]

A rustic, down-to-earth place on the short pedestrian street off Ilica which leads up to the funicular, specialising in Slavonian & traditional Croatian dishes, served simply & in generous portions. Has a miniature terrace in summer on the street. *Inexpensive.*

LOWER TOWN

✘ Asia Šenoina 1 [7 F7]

With a new location overlooking Tomislav Square (it used to be at the Astoria Hotel), Asia is one of the very few places serving upmarket Asian food. Good range of traditional Chinese dishes, though if you're used to takeaway prices back home, you'll find it on the expensive side. *Mid-range.*

✘ Le Bistro Mihanovićeva 1 (in the Regent Esplanade); ↘ 456 6666 [6 D7/8]

Lovely French-style glass-roofed balcony & outdoor terrace, with pretty good value lunch options, excellent homemade pastries, & the very best *štrukli* in town. Reservations recommended. *Mid-range to expensive.*

✘ Fontana Kneza Borne 2 (at the Sheraton) [7 G7]

With swanky surroundings, a renowned buffet, & a fairly traditional à-la-carte menu, this restaurant is mainly favoured by the hotel's own business travellers & upmarket package tour groups.

✖ **Gallo** Hebrangova 34; ☏ 481 4014; www.gallo.hr [6 D6]
Located one block west of Preradovićeva in the atrium of the Castellum Centre, Gallo is one of Zagreb's most upmarket eateries. The décor & menu have a Mediterranean flavour, with lots of terracotta, wrought iron, Tuscan tones & a pleasant garden terrace complementing the seafood specialities. We have heard that it may be resting on its laurels a little – so let us know if that's untrue. Reservations recommended. *Expensive.*

✖ **Hrvatski Kulturni Klub** Trg Maršala Tita 10; ☏ 482 8084 [6 B6]
Tucked away in the basement of the Arts & Crafts Museum with a lovely terrace at the back, this traditional restaurant is popular with intellectuals & arty types, & serves up solid Croatian fare. Reservations recommended. *Mid-range.*

✖ **Huatian** Kneza Mislava 1 [7 G6]
Located opposite the Sheraton, a Chinese restaurant (signed *Kineski Restoran*) serving up unpretentious dishes at a reasonable price. Don't on any account be tempted by a shot of Pelinkovac as your after-dinner treat. *Inexpensive.*

✖ **Kaptol** Krsnjavoga 1 [6 B7]
The Westin Zagreb's large, airy restaurant is surprisingly good value (steady on the extensive & expensive wine list, however), mixing international dishes with good Croatian staples. *Mid-range to expensive.*

✖ **Mašklin i Lata** Hebrangova 11a [6 D6]
Located in the basement underneath the Old Pharmacy Pub (see below), this small family-run restaurant serves up Šibenik-style food with an emphasis – as you'd expect – on fish dishes. *Mid-range.*

✖ **Opium** Branimirova 29 (Branimir Centar); ☏ 461 5679 [7 G7]
A stylish new place serving upmarket southeast Asian & Japanese cuisine. Reservations recommended. *Expensive.*

✕ Palace Strossmayerov Trg 10; ☎ 481 4611 [6 E6]
A favourite venue for the city's better-heeled residents during the socialist era, the Palace's dining room retains a good deal of its old-world charm, even if the food lacks sparkle for a place of this calibre. Reservations recommended. *Mid-range to expensive.*

✕ Paviljon Trg Kralja Tomislava 22; ☎ 481 3066 [6 E7]
In an old glass & wrought-iron exhibition pavilion set in pleasant parkland opposite the station, the Paviljon is one of Zagreb's oldest upper-end restaurants. The spacious dining room & outdoor terrace attract diners with a decent expense account – which you'll certainly need if you're going for the vintage champagnes. Happily, those with more modest tastes can still get a first-rate plate of pasta here or a dish of *štrukli* without breaking the bank. Reservations recommended. *Mid-range to expensive.*

✕ Pivnica Tomislav Trg Kralja Tomsilava 18 (almost opposite the Paviljon) [6 E7]
Excellent hearty fixed-price lunch menus comprising soup plus main plus salad for 25–35kn, as well as an à-la-carte range of simple, home-cooked dishes. Very popular with locals, there's a small street-side café, with the main restaurant halfway underground indoors. *Inexpensive.*

✕ Radicchio Branimirova 29 (Branimir Centar) [7 G7]
Part of the Arcotel Allegra Hotel complex, this is modern, Mediterranean-inspired cuisine at its Croatian best. Good value for lunch, when they do a fixed-price menu including wine. *Mid-range to expensive.*

✕ Sorriso Boškovićeva 11; ☎ 487 6393 [7 F6]
A very stylish Mediterranean-inspired place, half a floor below street level in an old brick cellar, midway between Jelačić Square & the Sheraton Hotel. Modern Italian & French cuisines, beautifully presented, make this a popular choice for a special night out. Reservations recommended. *Expensive.*

✕ Zinfandel's Mihanovićeva 1 (in the Regent Esplanade); 📞 456 6666 [6 D7/8]
Belgian chef Marc Fontenelle heads up the Regent Esplanade's flagship restaurant, offering Mediterranean-inspired fare with an Asian twist. Named after the celebrated wine grape believed to have originated on the Adriatic coast, the restaurant's emphasis on using the very best Croatian produce means prices reflect quality. Modern, sumptuous interior, or eat out on the lovely Oleander Terrace in warm weather. Reservations recommended. *Expensive*.

FURTHER AFIELD

✕ Dubravkin Put Dubravkin Put 2; 📞 483 4970 [4 D2]
Northwest of the old town, tucked into the woods, this very fashionable restaurant serves up excellent fish, shellfish & meat dishes – all specialities of the Dubrovnik area. Reservations are essential, & with prices on the steep side, a flexible friend comes in very handy. *Expensive*.

✕ Kod Pavela Gračanska Cesta 46; 📞 467 5036 [1 C2]
Out of the way, but sumptuous Istrian cuisine in a charming garden setting, accompanied by a great selection of the region's best wines & liqueurs makes the journey worthwhile (take tram #8 or #14 to the terminus, then walk up the hill, signed Sljeme, for 10mins; the restaurant is on the right). Black & white truffles, homemade pasta & gnocchi, fresh sea fish, & gorgeous Italian-inspired desserts make this a great choice for a special lunch or evening out. It's much frequented by Zagreb's well-heeled set, so be sure to book ahead. *Expensive*.

✕ Mex Cantina Savska Cesta 154; 📞 619 2156; www.asker.com/mex-cantina [1 B4]
As Zagreb's most authentic Mexican diner, the slightly out-of-town location is worth the journey if you're in the mood for spicy home-cooked Tex-Mex treats in a cosy cantina-style atmosphere – take tram #13, #14 or #17 down Savska Cesta. Its popularity with students makes it worth booking ahead on busy nights. *Inexpensive*.

✘ Zlatni Medo Savska Cesta 56 (formerly Pivnica Medvedgrad) [1 B4]
On Savska Cesta about 10mins south of the Westin Zagreb (on the corner of Vukovarska; take tram #13, #14 or #17), this cavernous, noisy boutique brewery serves up its own range of beers & vast, wholesome platefuls of local food. In additional to the fabulous *weiss* beer, try the *zlatno* (lager), *trenk* (brown) or *ban* (dark) varieties, along with homemade dishes including various types of sausage & *čvarkuša*, a flavoursome cross between a Yorkshire pudding & a scone. While individual dishes aren't especially cheap, serving sizes are huge, making it exceptionally good value for money. *Inexpensive to mid-range.*

CAFÉS, BARS AND PUBS

With great summer weather and lots of visitors, there's no shortage of places to drink in Zagreb. Most restaurants with terraces will also be happy to serve you drinks between meals. Cafés and bars tend to open early – some from 06.00 – and close sometime between 23.00–01.00.

Café society is firmly centred in the area around Jelačić Square – the pedestrianised streets and squares to the southwest become one vast terrace in summer, and the ambience is wonderful, with frequent more or less impromptu live music in the area.

North of the main square, Tkalčićeva, a long, winding, pedestrianised street, is very much the humming heart of Zagreb nightlife. The charming old-style houses along here are now almost all cafés, bars and cheap restaurants – there's a great relaxed vibe just about any time of the day or night, and it's absolutely *the* place to kick off an evening out.

On Sunday mornings, Jelačić Square plays host to one of the most unusual spectacles in the world, when the Croatian political elite – from the president down – come out to sit at the café terraces and chew the fat. Blasé locals have been known to criticise this overt populism, but it's a refreshing change from the aloof remoteness of most of the world's leaders.

Saturdays are even busier, with the weekly *špica*, a Zagreb tradition which is a bit like a sit-down version of Italy's *passeggiata*. It basically involves dolling yourself up to the nines and meeting friends for a leisurely coffee/brunch at a favourite watering hole – for preference, one of the high-profile ones off to the southwest of Jelačić Square. The aim is to see and be seen, while catching up on the week's news and gossip in a relaxed, unhurried atmosphere. Again, don't be surprised if you see President Mesić at one of his favourite cafés; he used Charlie's, opposite the Hotel Dubrovnik, as the stump from which he launched his election – and subsequent re-election – campaign.

We've grouped cafés, bars and pubs – like restaurants, above – into four sections for convenience: the upper town (everything from Gradec to Kaptol and along Tkalčićeva); Jelačić Square and the area nearby to the west, south and east; the rest of the lower town (as far as the railway station); and places further afield (not including Mount Medvednica, which is covered separately in *Chapter 11*).

UPPER TOWN

Art Caffé Tkalčićeva 18 [4 E3]
Groovy place with a fashionably grungy interior.

🍺 Caffé Palainovka Ilirski Trg [4 D1]

In a picturesque part of the old town, right next to the Priest's Tower, this old-fashioned café boasts a lovely garden terrace & a 19th-century-inspired interior decorated with old photographs & even a penny-farthing bicycle. If you're planning to take part in the lamplighting tour of old Zagreb (see page 173), this is where you'll meet up with your friendly lamplighters.

🍺 Cica Tkalčićeva 8 [4 E3]

Groovy place decorated with bohemian bric-a-brac & specialising in exotically flavoured artisan *rakijas*. Honey & rose, blueberry, fig & pear took our fancy; a little research to find your own favourites will set you back 10kn a pop. If the bar staff are to be believed (we had had a few), the bar's name just means 'tits'.

🍺 Crenk Radićeva 23 [4 D3]

Popular with locals for its long opening hours, keen bar prices & appealing brick-vaulted interior. Has a leaning towards grungy rock music.

🍺 Fantasy Tolkein Pub Katarina Trg 3 [4 D3]

Hobbits will feel right at home in this homage to Dungeons & Dragons & all things Middle Earth up in a nice quiet part of the old town. Nice terrace. Open till late.

🍺 Giardino Tkalčićeva 37 [4 E3]

Comfy wicker sofas on the pavement for summer, & a post-modern interior for winter, marred only slightly by the presence of a large-screen TV. The terrace is one of the best places on the street for watching the world go by.

⌨ Gulliver Tržnica Dolac [4 E4]
One of several down-to-earth cafés along the mezzanine level on the steps leading up from Jelačić Square to Dolac market, & catering largely to traders & local customers. Large terrace, cheap beer.

⌨ Jackie Brown Nova Ves 17 (in the Kaptol Centar, but downstairs, actually on Tkalčićeva) [4 E1]
A trendy lounge bar with a retro-70s feel, attracting an affluent, older set. Large selection of upmarket whiskies & cognacs.

⌨ Khala Bar Nova Ves 11 [4 E1]
Also located in the Kaptol Centar at the very top of Tkalčićeva, another groovy lounge bar, but this time with a Persian/central Asian vibe. Serves up appetising nibbles & upmarket wines by the glass.

⌨ Oliver Twist Tkalčićeva 60 [4 E3]
Snuggled into a cutting about halfway along Tkalčićeva, the large green Tuborg umbrellas & vast terrace make it hard to miss. Or indeed pass up, with friendly service, a welcoming wood-&-brass interior for colder weather, & an extensive menu of foreign beers.

⌨ Strossmayer Bar Strossmayerovo Šetalište bb [4 D4]
Perched at the top of the steep climb up to the old town from Radićeva, serving keenly priced drinks on a quiet, shady terrace overlooking the Zagreb rooftops (also accessible by walking along from the bottom of the Lotrščak Tower, or down from the corner of St Catherine's Square). If you're game, you can venture indoors & shoot pool in a cavernous hall.

⌨ Žabica Opatička 5 [4 D2]
A traditional, refined, genuinely old haunt up in the old town, with lots of authentic detail & fabulous hot chocolate. Also doubles as a sometime internet café.

ON AND OFF JELAČIĆ SQUARE

Apartman Preradovićeva 7/1 [6 D5]
Retro bean bags, old school desks, tatty green felt, dark smoky ambience & live DJs, all combining to create a shabby, trendy atmosphere that attracts a hip young crowd. Like so many such places, it's rather soulless in the daytime.

Ban Caffé Jelačić Square [4 E4]
Like Mala Kavana next door, what you're paying for here is the location right on the main square. It's a great place to unwind after a tough morning's shopping in nearby Dolac market. Gradska Kavana, at the end of the square, is marginally less expensive, & if anything, swankier.

Charlie's Gajeva 4 [6 E5]
A popular Zagreb institution & one of the president's favourite watering holes. Founded by former Zagreb Dinamo player Mirko 'Charlie' Braun (who died in 2004), & easy to recognise by the black wicker chairs.

Dubrovnik Hotel Café Gajeva 1 (next to Charlie's) [4 E4]
With an ample terrace & an excellent location bordering on Jelačić Square, this place is a little pricey, but wonderfully convenient if you've been trawling around the city's shops.

Europa 92 Varšavska 3 [6 D5]
Part of the cinema complex. A nice enough terrace on a pedestrianised street, but be warned that it's probably named after the last year when the toilets were properly cleaned.

Gradska Kavana Jelačić Square [5 F4]
With an outdoor terrace & huge Art Deco-inspired interior on 3 levels, it's reputedly the favourite Sunday-morning coffee spot for the president & the political elite. The usual selection of cakes, coffee, soft drinks, wine & beer, at

133

prices marginally more modest than at the Ban Caffé & Mala Kavana along the square. There's an adjoining restaurant serving traditional dishes at moderate prices.

💻 Hole in One Vlaška 42 [5 F4]
Polished dark wood & brass railings make for a homely pub-like atmosphere, though prices are also scarily reminiscent of London. The smoky little pizzeria next door is part of the same establishment; for reasons unexplained, the day we were there it claimed to have no house wine, & wanted 180kn for a very ordinary-looking bottle of white – which we were easily able to resist.

💻 K&K (Knjiga & Kava) Jurišićeva 5 [5 F4]
Cosy café on 2 levels just east of Jelačić Square, with an old-world, bookish feel & walls crammed with vintage photos of Zagreb (the name just means 'books & coffee'). Ensconce yourself at one of the marble tables, or on the small outdoor terrace if the smoky atmosphere gets too much, & settle into a traditional sachertorte accompanied by coffee, beer or a glass of wine, all without blowing the budget. Owner Miličić is a popular local writer & a close friend of the great & the good.

💻 Kraljevac Caffé Britanski Trg 9 [4 A4]
This café 2 tram stops west of Jelačić Square comes into its own on Sundays, when the lively flea market at Britanski Trg gets into full swing. Take time out from perusing the bric-a-brac & haggling with the stall owners to enjoy a coffee, beer or a špricer on the green love seats.

💻 Mala Kavana [4 E4]
On the north side of Jelačić Square, next door to the Ban Caffé, the central location has made the Mala Kavana a long-standing favourite. Serves light snacks, cakes, ice cream sundaes & a selection of drinks, with prices at the upper end.

Maraschino Margaretska 1 [4 D4]

Just off Ilica, a very popular hang-out that takes its name from Zadar's world-famous cherry liqueur, known to locals as *maraska*. Good hot chocolate – their own version, infused with the aforementioned liqueur, is a special treat – & a selection of cocktails & Croatian wines. Particularly trendy at the time of writing in the summer of 2006.

Škola Bogovićeva 7 (third floor); www.skolaloungebar.com [6 D5]

A renovated school that's now one of the city's trendiest bars, with prices & snooty staff to match. A slick pure-white interior houses chic drinking & eating areas ranged over 2 levels; it's also one of the first places to offer a snack menu featuring a selection of Italian-inspired goodies. Very busy on Fri/Sat after 21.00, but otherwise a quiet haven for an afternoon drink. Email & blog addicts will revel in Škola's T-Mobile WiFi hotspot, safe in the knowledge that their MacBooks will blend perfectly with the all-white décor.

Tantra Gajeva 2 (second floor) [4 E4]

Very groovy lounge bar with wooden floors, indoor plants, & capacious armchairs & sofas which are particularly popular with snogging youth. Great views out over Jelačić Square, young, friendly staff, & reasonable prices. Their salsa nights on Thu & Sat are all the rage – for details ☎ 539 9551.

Uvijec Café Teslina 3 [6 E5]

One of Zagreb's last remaining socialist-era style cafés, featuring an old zinc counter & utilitarian floor-to-ceiling tiling designed for easy hosing-down rather than comfort. Charmless, really, yet historically compelling.

LOWER TOWN

Boom Bar Branimirova 29 (Branimir Centar) [7 G7]

1970s retro-décor, groovy ambience, & surprisingly expensive. Popular as a pre- & post-cinema hangout.

Hemingway Trg Maršala Tita 1 (opposite the Croatian National Theatre) [6 C6]
Spacious terrace, large cushioned benches & trendy but uncomfortable oriental glass & wicker stools. The interior is a spartan all-white affair with large photos of Papa. Extensive (& expensive) selection of cocktails, foreign beers & wines. Young, affluent crowd, but service can be on the surly side – & heaven only knows what the old man himself would have made of it.

Hopdevil Branimirova 29 (Branimir Centar) [7 G7]
Due to open in late 2006, this pub was planning to offer 101 types of Belgian beer & seating for 300, & seemed certain to be a huge hit with the locals.

Jo's Bar Branimirova 29 (Branimir Centar, at the Arcotel Allegra) [7 G7]
Modern, minimalist & gay-friendly; they also do light food, & sometimes have live jazz.

Kazališka Kavana Trg Maršala Tita 1 [6 C6]
Next door to Hemingway (see above), but with an altogether less affected, friendlier atmosphere, cheaper prices, & the same great view of the National Theatre across the road; the location of choice for pre-theatre drinks.

Lenuci Zrinjevac 15 [6 E6]
Just up from the Palace Hotel, this stylish, unpretentious wine bar is named after the man who designed Zagreb's 'green horseshoe'. Bold design & a spacious, airy interior spread over 1.5 floors, with subdued lighting & music to match. Popular with smart professionals.

Old Pharmacy Pub Hebranova 11 [6 D6]
On the south side of the street just east of Preradovićeva, this charming venue is a firm favourite with locals, who like to relax on the banquettes & sofas & partake of a coffee, beer or glass of wine in an authentic, fin de siècle atmosphere.

Sedmica Kačićeva 7a [6 A6]
Look out for the Guinness sign that marks the entrance to this fashionable, unpretentious place which remains popular with Zagreb's boho crowd (it's not far from the National Theatre). Marble bar tables flanked by tall bar stools, a retro, grungy look & a back room that's practically a semi-terrace.

FURTHER AFIELD

Dublin Pub Maksimirska 75 [1 C3]
With walls clad in photos of old Dublin, décor featuring the humble potato, & comfy brown leather sofas, this is as Irish an atmosphere as you're going to find in the heart of Croatia. Get there on tram #4, #11 or #12 towards the zoo & the Dinamo Stadium.

Godot Savska 23 [6 B8]
Authentic pub feel & cheap *travarica* at 7kn a shot, just south of the railway line. The youngish crowd reflects the bar's location in the student district.

Hemingway Bar Tuškanec 21/23 (behind the Kino Tuškanec cinema) [4 C3]
Zagreb's original Hemingway, west of the old town, has evolved from a swanky cocktail bar to an upmarket eatery/nightclub, mainly used for hosting functions. Smart, with prices to match.

Movie Pub Savska Cesta 141 [1 B4]
Take tram #13, #14 or #17. Enormously popular place out of the city centre, with seating for 350 & an authentic pub feel – though a little too faux-British (& pricey) for our tastes. If the crowd inside gets noisy, there's also a small but pleasant outdoor terrace. And if you've really overdone it, then there's always the Movie Hotel upstairs (see page 105).

🖵 **SPUNK** Hrvatske Bratske Zajednice bb [1 C4]

On the main road south to the Sava & Novi Zagreb, on the right-hand side, between Vukovarska & Slavonska, & part of the giant University Library complex. This small, modern bar is a favourite with students, not least because of its cheap beer & regular live music. Also makes for a handy freshener on your way out to the Močvara Club (see page 150).

ICE CREAM

Zagreb's first ice cream is believed to have been served up on 2 May 1847 by local restaurateur Mato Pallain in the coffee shop he'd opened on the city's North Promenade a decade earlier. Since then, it has firmly entrenched itself as a national staple whose enormous popularity is attested to by the large numbers of ice cream parlours – *slastičarnica* – dotting the city.

Croatians favour Italian-style *gelati*, though the local version tends to be somewhat heavier. But as in Italy, the cost of your cone or cup depends on the number of flavours you choose – be warned, however, that unless you speak Croatian, you'll have to 'fly by sight' when ordering, as English translations of the wealth of flavours available are rare.

✗ **Centar** On Jurišićeva, on the right-hand side heading away from Jelačić Square towards Palmotićeva [7 F5]

Our absolute number-one favourite in Zagreb, &, by the look of the queues, plenty of other people's too.

✗ **Hotel Dubrovnik** Gajeva 1 (though the shop is actually on Jelačić Square) [4 E4]

Mountains of luridly presented flavours; very popular with the locals.

✗ Millennium Bogovićeva 7 [6 D5]

Heavier & creamier than Centar's more Italian-style fare. Zagreb's most extensive & exotic choice of flavours.

✗ Orient Maksimirska 34 (close to the tram stop) [1 C3]

Run by 2 sisters who serve up the usual classic favourites along with more imaginative options like 'Ginger & Fred'. The homemade cakes are also much prized by sweet-toothed locals. A bit hard to find – look for the yellow & red cake sign outside.

✗ Trakošćan Bogovićeva 7 [6 D5]

Next door to Millennium, & longer-established & less flashy than its newer rival. Has a very loyal old-school following.

✗ Vincek Ilica 18 (& various other locations around the city) [4 D4]

A Zagreb institution offering excellent quality & a wide variety of flavours. Also makes an outrageous all-cream *torta* which goes for a very reasonable 10kn.

✗ Zagreb Masarykova (at the corner of Preradovićeva) [6 D5]

Another excellent choice, also selling a wicked range of popular cakes.

MARKETS, SUPERMARKETS AND BAKERIES

Seven mornings a week, **Dolac** market does its wonderful, bustling thing, with all kinds of fresh produce available, from seasonal fruit and vegetables on the upper level to meat, cheese and dairy goods, fresh pasta and delicatessen items in the basement, and the catch of the day in a separate fish section upstairs.

Locals still come here daily to sell their own vegetables and other produce, and most people in Zagreb are loyal to their preferred *kumica* (literally 'godmother') – usually an older woman who serves as their trusted source of the best home-grown produce. A bronze statue of a *kumica* has been placed in honour of the tradition at the top of the stairs up from Jelačić Square.

The action generally kicks off at about 07.00 – earlier for the fish market, where you'll be jostling for the choicest items with buyers from Zagreb's best restaurants – and winds up before 14.00, when the big clean-up begins, ready for the next day's trading. At the foot of the steps leading up to the market there's also a daily flower market, dominated, again, by local women selling their own cuttings.

If you're near the bus station, it's worth knowing that there's also a smaller daily market at the eastern end of Branimira, just north of the railway line. And if you're

STRAWBERRY FIELDS

If you're lucky enough to be in Zagreb from mid May to the end of June, you'll find the plaza around the main train station lined with local strawberry sellers offering half-kilo punnets of their own freshly picked fruit. Part of a highly successful initiative to encourage local production, prices start at around 12kn a punnet, dropping to just 8kn at the height of the season. The initiative is now being extended to blueberries, which go on sale – albeit in smaller quantities – around September-time.

west of the city centre, there's also a daily market on Britanski Trg, two tram stops along Ilica from Jelačić Square; on Sundays, bric-a-brac replaces the fruit and veg – see page 160 for details.

There are also plenty of **supermarkets** large and small in Zagreb, where you can stock up on essentials. The local Konzum chain is the most widespread, with branches throughout the city, but there are also quite a few independent shops. Prices are generally competitive, and there's usually a good selection of local produce as well as wholesale food. You can ask for sandwiches to be made up to order at the deli-counter in most supermarkets – just point at the type of bread you want filled, say '*sendvič*' and indicate your choice of filling(s); you're charged for just the ingredients by weight.

Bakeries (*pekarnica*) are also widespread and sell a good variety of breads and sometimes also offer ready-made sandwiches (*sendviči*) with cheese (*sir*), ham (*šunka*), tuna (*tuna*), egg (*jaja*) and occasionally more exotic fillings, as well as various pies, sausage rolls and the like.

Finally, if you find yourself craving American-style snacks, there's a doughnut shop two blocks east of Jelačić Square opposite the main post office, and a Subway sandwich outlet on Gajeva, right by the Hotel Dubrovnik, where you can sate your appetite with a foot-long sandwich or US-style muffins and cookies.

7 Entertainment and Nightlife

Zagreb boasts a sparkling cultural scene, with world-class opera, ballet, concerts, dance and theatre, and an action-packed programme of festivals and cultural events year round. In summer, you'll often find free street concerts taking place in and around the city, in addition to more organised happenings, and the capital is also endowed with a good number of clubs and venues large enough to attract big-name stars. Cinephiles are likewise spoilt for choice, with two large multiplexes and several smaller city cinemas screening mostly English-language films.

The festival season generally kicks off with the traditional February carnival marking the end of winter – if you get the chance, it's worth making the short trip out to Samobor to enjoy their version of the festivities (see page 254).

May marks the beginning of the summer concert and theatre programme, which, thanks to the city's warm, sunny weather, runs virtually uninterrupted until the end of September – though expect different kinds of festivities on Statehood Day (25 June), a national holiday sometimes accompanied by a military parade at Jarun Lake. Special events are also organised around Zagreb's City Day (16 November), and the year wraps up with a traditional German-style Christmas market centred around Bogovićeva.

FESTIVALS AND FAIRS

The most popular of Zagreb's many regular festivals and fairs are listed below, but it's also worth checking the Zagreb Tourist Information Centre website (*www.zagreb-touristinfo.hr*), the monthly *Events and Performances* guide, and street hoardings for details of other events as they come up.

FEBRUARY
Carnival See previous page.

MARCH
The Zagreb Auto Show One of central Europe's largest new car shows.
Springtime Jazz Fever Held at the popular BP Club (see below), featuring local and international acts.

APRIL
St Mark's Music Festival www.festivalsvmarka.hr. Focusing on classical and sacred music.
Music Biennial An internationally recognised festival of contemporary popular music, held in odd-numbered years.

MAY
Modern Dance Week www.danceweekfestival.com. Featuring the latest in contemporary performance.
European Short Story Festival Attracting young writers from across the continent.

JUNE

Cest is d'Best www.kraljeviulice.com. A colourful festival of street performance and busking, featuring 'kings of the street' from around the world.

Florart An international flower festival held around Bundek Lake.

Animafest www.animafest.hr. An annual festival of animated films held in conjunction with Zagreb's School of Animated Film, with a programme alternating between short films one year and features the next.

JULY

Amadeo A theatre and music festival featuring evening performances in the Natural History Museum's courtyard.

International Folk Festival www.msf.hr. One of Europe's largest folk gatherings, showcasing the music, dancing and costume traditions of Croatia alongside those of special guest nations. A real treat for lovers of local colour and culture.

Zagreb Baroque Festival www.zabaf.hr. Presenting top international and Croatian baroque musicians performing in historical locations around the old town.

INmusic www inmusicfestival.com. A festival of international music featuring some of Europe's most popular rock groups.

AUGUST

International Puppet Festival http://public.carnet.hr/pif-festival. Held since the 1960s, this event now welcomes some 350 puppet theatres from all continents.

SEPTEMBER

Zagreb International Autumn Fair www.zv.hr. The largest trade fair in south central Europe, showcasing a huge range of Croatian goods and services.

OCTOBER

Zagrebfest Zagreb's oldest popular music festival.
International Jazz Days www.jazz.hr. Featuring leading European bands and performers.
Zagreb Film Festival www.zagrebfilmfestival.com. A week-long event held at the city's Student Centre. Golden Pram awards are presented to the best feature, short and documentary.

NOVEMBER

The Zagreb Golden Pirouette An international ice-skating festival.
Nebo World Music Festival www.nebofestzagreb.com. Two days of the best music from around the world, held at the city's Student Centre.

DECEMBER

Zagreb Christmas Fair www.zv.hr. Centred around the Zagreb Fair exhibition grounds, Boćarski Dom, and Bogovićeva.

MUSIC, OPERA, BALLET AND THEATRE

Outside of festivals and fairs, there are plenty of excellent opportunities to listen to world-class classical music, thanks to a regular programme of concerts at the

Lisinski Concert Hall (*just south of the railway station, on Vukovarska*) by the Zagreb Philharmonic Orchestra, visiting artists, and the city's many other classical ensembles. The venue also offers a rich and varied programme featuring classical, jazz, contemporary world music and even popular rock acts, and you can choose, book and pay for your seats online in English (*www.lisinski.hr*). Collect your tickets from the box office 60 minutes before the performance begins.

For opera, ballet and theatre, the **Croatian National Theatre** (*Trg Maršala Tita 15, box office;* ℡ *482 8532; www.hnk.hr*) dominates, with an impressive year-round programme of new productions and revivals, featuring plenty of popular favourites mixed with more eclectic pieces. Unless you're fluent in Croatian, the theatre programme is hard work. Instead, head along to the opera or ballet, where you'll see and hear top local and visiting performers for just a fraction of the price you'd pay in the larger European capitals, while seated in *fin de siècle* Habsburg splendour. A few stray tickets are usually available at short notice (prices generally range from 75–145kn), but book in advance if possible to avoid disappointment. The theatre has a useful online facility (though for the moment only in Croatian) which shows seat availability and pricing; once you've made your choice, just ring the box office to reserve.

Croatian National Theatre

If it's **live gigs** you're interested in, keep your eyes peeled for posters around town advertising upcoming events, which mostly take place at one of the venues listed below (or, for the biggest names, at sports stadiums and open-air festivals). After a long period out in the cold during the socialist era, Zagreb simply can't get enough of popular bands, old and new. In just two weeks we saw Franz Ferdinand, the Buzzcocks, Morrissey, Motorhead, the Sisters of Mercy, the Pixies, and a host of other bands blaze their way through town. The Rolling Stones would have been amongst their number, if Keith Richards hadn't fallen out of a palm tree in Fiji (yes, quite ...).

Big names aside, Croatia has a thriving local music scene, of which Zagreb is the natural hub. There's plenty of talent about, and if you're relaxed about the fact that you won't usually understand the lyrics (though some artists do perform in English), it won't be long before you find yourself carried away by local bands' energy and enthusiasm.

NIGHTLIFE

Zagreb has plenty of late-evening lounge bars and cafés, and in summer popular haunts like Tkalčićeva stay humming until the wee hours. There's also a fair sprinkling of dance clubs, though the current fad for 'turbofolk' – an electronic take on the traditional Balkan theme – is unlikely to strike a chord with most visitors. In summer, the mainstream dance music scene – like much of the city's population – moves out to the Adriatic coast, and things stay pretty quiet in the capital until September. The reverse is true of live music, which consistently draws crowds large enough to ensure Zagreb remains a fixture on major European tours. The summer months welcome plenty of visiting bands, who play open-air festivals as well as the various live venues around town.

Nightclubs tend to open at around 22.00 and close any time between 02.00–06.00.

☆ **Aquarius** Aleja Matije Ljubeka; ☎ 364 0231; www.aquarius.hr; tram #17 to Horvati [1 B4]
Situated lakeside at Jarun, Zagreb's longest-established dance club is still the most popular, with dance floors thumping to commercial hip-hop, R&B & some of Europe's best celebrity DJs. The club has a massively popular offshoot in summer on the island of Pag, at Zrče Beach.

☆ **Best** Jarunski Cesta 5; ☎ 301 1943; www.thebest.hr; tram #14 or #17 to Savski Most [1 B4]
Huge, glitzy venue specialising in commercial techno, disco, house & hip-hop, along with special theme nights featuring soul, trance & the like.

☆ **Boogaloo** Vukovarska 68; ☎ 631 3021; www.boogaloo.hr; tram #13 to Miramarska [1 C4]
A vast place accommodating 1,000+, located in the OTV Dom building, a venue with a long history of breaking new ground in the Zagreb music scene. Features DJs & live bands.

☆ **BP Club** Teslina 7; ☎ 481 4444; www.bpclub.hr [6 D5]
Local jazz celebrity Boško Petrović manages this prestigious basement jazz venue, with graffiti on the walls attesting to the presence of big names like Ronnie Scott & Joe Pass. Cosy & intimate, there's also a good selection of international wines, beers & spirits.

☆ **Brazil** Veslačka; ⌂ 091 200 2481; tram #14 or #17 to Veslačka, then head to the riverbank [1 C4]
This dilapidated barge on the Sava stays open very late, making it a popular end-of-evening stopover for those on their way back from other venues like Močvara (see below). Reggae & world music, mostly.

☆ **Gallery** Aleja Matije Ljubeka; ⌂ 091 113 3221; tram #17 to Horvati [1 B4]
Another of Lake Jarun's popular nightspots, Gallery is the capital's most exclusive dance venue, with a very strict dress code (yep, no trainers) & a wealthy young crowd. The focus in the chic interior is on the latest celebrity DJs. At the time of writing, the only club to accept credit cards – & you'll quickly see why, if they deign to let you in.

☆ **KSET** Unska 3; ☎ 612 9999; www.kset.org [1 C4]
A small venue that's actually part of the University of Electrotechnical Science, KSET has a long tradition of pioneering new bands & hosting stylistically diverse genres, from punk & underground to avant jazz. Friendly atmosphere, & prices way cheaper than at the glitzier clubs.

☆ **Močvara** ('swamp') Trnjanski nasip; ☎ 605 5599; www.mochvara.hr; tram #13 to Lisinski, then walk south towards the river. [1 C4]
Set up in an old factory, this legendary venue down behind the Sava dyke is popular with an alternative crowd interested in punk, thrash, grunge & indie sounds, & puts on all manner of gigs & special events. Occasional DJ nights, & cheap drinks. If you're aiming to get home by taxi, you need to head across to the restaurant nearby, just 100m north of the venue.

☆ **Papillon** Veslačka, near Brazil (see above); ⌂ 091 250 3196; www.papillon-zg.hr; tram #14 or #17 to Veslačka [1 C4]
Another run down-looking place which attracts a young crowd, & which seems to get frequently closed down by the police.

☆ **Route 66** Paromlinska 47; ☎ 611 8737 [1 C4]
Behind the University Library complex (see SPUNK, below), on a parallel road heading down to the river. Classic rock & blues dive with a grungy feel & cheap beer, & popular with musicians. Also features country & western cover bands & demos from local new contenders.

☆ **Saloon** Tuškanac 1; ☎ 483 4903; www.saloon.hr [4 C2]
Smart, minimalist venue playing a mainstream disco sound; popular with the young & affluent.

☆ **Sax!** Palmotićeva 22; ☎ 487 2836; www.sax-zg.hr [7 F5]
A block or so east of Jelačić Square, & owned by the Croatian Musicians' Union. Informal venue hosting jazz sessions & album promotions from Tue–Sat.

☆ **SPUNK** Hrvatske bratske zajednice; ☎ 615 1528; tram #13 to Lisinski & then walk south towards the river; the bar's on the right [1 C4]
Part of the University Library complex, while technically a bar, this exceedingly popular student venue is also one of Zagreb's top spots for garage & underground music – & has the cheapest beer in town.

☆ **Tvornica** Šubićeva 2; ☎ 465 5007; www.tvornica-kulture.hr; tram #1 or #17 to Šubićeva station [7 K5]
A large (1,500+) live venue hosting names like David Byrne, Faithless, Madradeus & John Cale; also does big club nights.

CINEMA

Zagreb's two new multiplexes, at the Branimir Centar (13 screens) and the Kaptol Centar (five screens) show mostly mainstream Hollywood fare, but fortunately for

English-speakers, films are generally subtitled rather than dubbed. Tickets are cheap by UK standards, which makes a trip to the cinema a good-value night out at the end of a long day's sightseeing.

If art-house films are more your cup of tea, try the Kino Tuškanac, at Tuškanac 21–23 in front of Hemingway (the club, not the bar near the National Theatre), which is home to the Croatian Film Society (*www.hfs.hr*). For cinema listings, buy a copy of the local daily *Večernji List* from any news stand.

CASINOS

If you fancy a flutter on a turn of the wheel or a throw of the dice, Zagreb has two international-standard casinos open from early evening till late. Dress is smart.

☆ **Casino City** Hotel Regent Esplanade, Mihanovićeva 1; ☎ 450 1000 [6 D7] *Open daily 20.00–04.00.*
☆ **Vega Casino** Hotel Sheraton, Draškovićeva 43; ☎ 461 1886 [7 G7] *Open daily 20.00–06.00.*

There are also any number of 'Automat Klub' franchises around the city, if it's just the slots you're after.

GAY AND LESBIAN

After decades of being very firmly in the closet, Zagreb's burgeoning gay scene is beginning to come out with confidence, with a couple of good venues, its own annual Gay Pride march, and the Queer Zagreb festival. All too predictably, old Croatia's Catholic/macho culture means male gays are still better served than lesbians both for venues and cultural acceptance.

The city's Gay Pride march (*www.zagreb-pride.net*) takes place in June. While the event still seems to need vigorous policing, it's gradually gaining acceptance as part of the city's mainstream festival calendar. Queer Zagreb (*www.queerzagreb.org*), a cultural festival focusing on art, theory and activism, takes place in April, and is the largest event of its kind in eastern and central Europe.

At the time of writing, the Kino Tuškanac was also running a 'Queer Weekends' film programme, held on the third weekend of every month throughout 2006; check at www.queerzagreb.org to see whether screenings will be continued in 2007 and beyond.

♀ **David** Marulićev Trg 13; ✆ 091 533 7757; www.gay.hr/david [6 C7]
A friendly sauna and bar located down near the Botanic Gardens. *Open daily 15.00–23.00.*

☆ **Global** Pavla Hatza 14; ✆ 481 4878; www.globalclubzg.hr [7 F6/7]
Two blocks north of the train station, on a street running east from the 'green horseshoe'. Zagreb's only dedicated gay club, with 3 bars, a VIP lounge, a dance floor, a darkroom and a weekly programme of strippers and gay films. A happening spot at night; doubles as a sex shop and café by day.

8 Shopping

Zagreb's growing prosperity is reflected in the city's burgeoning retail scene. While hardly a shopper's paradise compared with other European capitals – the city's small size makes for limited choice, while prices are pretty much in line with its EU neighbours – Zagreb is beginning to develop its own style, particularly in the area of fashion.

Per capita, the city must surely boast more shoe shops than anywhere else on the planet. While there are still a few socialist-era stores selling the kind of sensible footwear your mother used to try and make you wear, today's accent is more on the latest Italian designs and status-symbol trainers – you'll have no trouble tracking down all the major sports brands, and may even pick up some sleek Italian sandals, boots or bags at attractive prices.

Zagreb's main shopping street is Ilica, a gently winding boulevard running west from Jelačić Square that's home to a wide range of shops – and the shopping crowds that go with them. Meanwhile, with brands like Diesel, Galliano, Gaultier, Lacoste and Moschino, Frankopanska, which runs south off Ilica about five minutes west of Jelačić Square, is taking over as the main centre for upmarket designer goods, and there is talk of pedestrianising it to make it more shopper-friendly. There is also a growing number of shopping centres, ranging from the more functional, like the Importanne

BARGAINING

While bargaining is *de rigueur* at the bric-a-brac market at Britanski Trg, or the car sales at Mladosti Most (see *Secondhand goods*, below), prices on shop goods are normally non-negotiable, and attempts to persuade staff to drop the ticket price will generally be met with an icy stare. That said, you can usually count on a small discount if you're buying in quantity – several pairs of shoes, or items of clothing, for example. The same goes for produce at Dolac and the daily flower market, where vendors will often lower prices if you're prepared to buy in volume. Play it by ear, though, and be sensitive too. Successfully knocking a couple of euro off the price of a wheel of cheese is nothing to crow about if it's being sold by a peasant woman who needs the money much more than you do.

Centar next to the train station, to swankier addresses like the Kaptol Centar, which is home to a number of upmarket bars and restaurants as well as chic clothing stores – and a newly opened Marks & Spencer.

DEPARTMENT STORES

Zagreb has only two shops that could broadly be called department stores, both of which are located a stone's throw from one another in the heart of the city centre.

Varteks, on Jelačić Square, is more upscale but much smaller than its rival **Nama**, at Ilica 4. Ranged over several floors, both sell the usual selection of goods, from cosmetics and clothing to home wares, bed and bath linen, and so forth.

SHOPPING CENTRES

Branimir Centar Branimirova 29, just east of the railway station [7 G7] A recent addition to Zagreb's shopping scene, offering a good mix of fashion, beauty, bars, restaurants, the 13-screen Cinestar cinema multiplex (films often shown in English), the Wettpunkt 24hr casino, & the Arcotel Allegra Hotel.

Kaptol Centar Nova Ves 17, just up from Kaptol, and connecting the top of Tkalčićeva with Nova Ves [4 E1] At the time of writing, Zagreb's newest & most glamorous shopping temple, housing big-name brands like Hugo Boss, Joop, Lacoste, Mandarina Duck, Max & Co, Paul & Shark & Tommy Hilfiger, along with Marks & Spencer (clothing only). The centre also boasts the Broadway 5 cinema multiplex & a few plush bars and restaurants – & is already busily expanding itself next door.

Importanne Centar Starčevićev Trg, located underground between the railway station and the Regent Esplanade [6 E8] Considerably more downmarket, but has a good selection of shops including fashion & jewellery, photo processing, shoes, stationery, etc. There's also a good number of takeaway sandwich & hot fast-food stalls, a biggish supermarket, a couple of newsagents & a branch of DM (for toiletries etc).

Importanne Galleria Iblerov Trg, on Vlaška, between Draškovićeva and Smičiklasova [5 H4] Just east of the Jadran Hotel, this modern complex covers everything from electronics, music, photo processing, jewellery, clothes & the inevitable shoe emporia, to pets, eyeglasses, perfume, toys & children's wear. There's a fast-food hall downstairs, along with a good supermarket & a large DM outlet. The centre also has a clothes alterations & repair service in the basement, for unexpected emergencies. The VIP Internet Café on the upper level offers fast & easy coin-operated internet access – & a lifetime's supply of secondhand smoke.

FASHION AND ACCESSORIES

Zagreb is fashion-conscious, so you'll see the usual global designer labels all over the city, both on people and in the shops. A few younger Croatian designers are also beginning to strike out on their own, with a growing number making a name for themselves abroad.

Croata In the Octagon at Ilica 5; also at Kaptol 13 [4 D4] You'll see men's ties for sale all over the place (they were invented here – see page 17), but Croatia's the place to go if you're in the market for quality neckwear of any kind – from silk ties to luxury scarves, shawls & wraps. Upmarket but reasonably priced, it specialises in everything from the latest looks & colours to modern takes on traditional Croatian designs.

Branka Donassy A designer with a host of international prizes to her name, she has based herself in Germany, but you'll find her sensual, Gothic-chic creations in several of the city's more upscale boutiques.

Gharani Štrok Dežmanova 5, on a narrow street running north of Ilica [4 C4] Another highly successful local name, & their shop is filled with the diaphanous, ultra-feminine creations that have seen the brand go global, successfully launch a more accessible line called 'GS', & begin to expand into jewellery & accessories.

I-GLE Radićeva 25 [4 D3] Cult label whose name is a pun on the words for 'sewing needle' & 'look', & which specialises in groovy, idiosyncratic street wear for both men & women.

Leonarda L Gajeva 9 [6 E5] Run by football star Zvonimir Boban's better half (his restaurant, Boban, is next door, natch), Leonarda L specialises in boho & occasionally outrageous numbers, but always worth a look.

Robert Sever Nova Ves 7 [4 E1] Another young rising star, with his own boutique, featuring bold creations reminiscent of younger Italian brands like Moschino & Prada.

Sinha-Stanić Quickly signed by prestigious Italian fashion group AEFFE having made a big splash at London Fashion Week 2005, doesn't have its own boutique in town – but is stocked at places like Victor (see below), as well as 'Harvey Nicks' in London.

Victor Kralja Držislava 10 – just west of the white marble Croatian Artists Centre [7 G6] This was Zagreb's first designer concept store, & features 3 trendy floors' worth of expensive clothing (including I-GLE & Sinha-Stanić), homewares & food.

SOUVENIRS, HANDICRAFTS AND GIFTS

If you're looking for souvenirs and gifts, there are several places specialising in Croatian handicrafts and local foods. Typical products from the Zagreb area include *licitarsko srce* (red-iced gingerbread hearts – although they're technically edible, make sure you have good dental insurance, since they're actually designed to be kept as decorations), locally produced wine, mustard, jams and honey, *paprenjak* (pepper) biscuits, various exotic kinds of *travarica* and *rakija*, Kraš chocolates, dried flowers and corn doilies, and traditional fabrics.

Extending the shopping list to other parts of Croatia means you can also include various white truffle sauces, *fuži* (homemade pasta), balsamic vinegar and *biska* (mistletoe brandy – surprisingly palatable) from Istria, hard cheese and lace products from the island of Pag, and brightly dyed fabrics and traditional clothing from Dalmatia.

Natura Croatia at Pod Zidom 5, just below Dolac market, has a good selection of all the above items, as does a slightly more downmarket shop right on the corner of Jelačić Square and Ilica. If you're based down near the Palace or Regent Esplanade hotels, **Babina Kuča** at Strossmayerov 7 – look for the poor old peasant woman chained up outside – has an extensive range of crafts and foodstuffs, while the best place to buy attractively packaged *paprenjak* biscuits (and the traditional wooden moulds for making them) is the small souvenir shop in the lobby at the **Regent Esplanade**. Many of the above items can also conveniently be picked up at the better-than-average **duty free shop** at the airport, if you're leaving by plane.

More durable items that might take your fancy include replicas of the iconic Vučedol partridge (available at the Archaeology Museum, and elsewhere around town), ceramic replicas of Dolac's bright-red umbrellas, Croatia scarves and ties (see above), glossy coffee-table books on Zagreb (Algoritam, see below, is a good place to look) and crystal and glassware. There's also a good shop selling antiques and local Croatian artists' work – from stylish ceramics to hand-designed glassware – next door to Charlie's, on Gajeva.

You'll also find a small but appealing range of different products for sale at the **Zagreb Tourist Information Office** on Jelačić Square, and at the office of the **Zagreb County Tourist Office** at Preradovićeva 42. Items are very reasonably priced, and profits go to local craftspeople and tourism development projects.

Finally, if you've cultivated a dangerous addiction to *štrukli* during your stay, the

Palace Hotel sells takeaway frozen packs which should survive the journey home and can be popped into your freezer when you get there.

SECONDHAND GOODS

For secondhand bargain hunters, there's an excellent Sunday crafts and bric-a-brac market at Britanski Trg, two tram stops west along Ilica from Jelačić Square. There's everything here from bayonets to wagon wheels, old china, music scores, clothing and wooden farming implements. If prices seem high at first, remember that bargaining is virtually obligatory, so expect to be able to knock off 20–40% – depending on your negotiating skills. Loads of fun, though you might have a job getting that 19th-century scythe through customs.

If it's a secondhand car or bike you're after, then head down to the last bridge across the Sava (Mladosti Most) on tram #6, #7 or #8, where you'll find a thriving regular Sunday market, with an astonishing variety of stuff – mostly junk – for sale. A smaller version is held on Wednesdays.

BOOKS, MAGAZINES AND MUSIC

Algoritam at Gajeva 1 has a good selection of foreign-language books, so when you run out of holiday reading you shouldn't have too much trouble finding something here – though expect to pay about 20% over the cover price for books in English. The shop also has a nice range of well-produced local books about Zagreb, which make good souvenirs or gifts.

Centrally based newsagents also sell a few foreign-language newspapers and magazines, though obviously not usually on the actual day of publication. The widest selection, not surprisingly, is available at the airport.

If you get hooked on the local music – and it happens – make sure you buy before you leave the country. There's a whole Croatian pop and rock music scene, as well as traditional folk music and the curiously popular 'turbofolk', but even in an online world, Croatian music is pretty hard to come by once you're out of the country. CDs are about the same price as in most of the EU.

OPENING HOURS AND PDV (VAT)

Opening hours vary, but you can expect supermarkets and the like to be open from 08.00 or 09.00 until 19.00 or 20.00 from Monday to Saturday. Department stores, fashion boutiques and shoe shops have shorter hours, and generally close early on a Saturday afternoon. Most shops are closed on Sundays and holidays.

Purchase tax (PDV, or VAT) is 22% on all goods except books and essentials. In theory visitors can get this reimbursed on single-ticket items costing over 500kn, but you have to really want the money. Fill in the PDV-P form at the point of sale and get it stamped, so that when you leave Croatia you can have the goods, receipts and forms certified by the Croatian Customs Service – not a process you should undertake if you're in any kind of a hurry. And that's just the easy part. You then post back the certified receipts and forms to the shop, along with your bank account details. Within a year or so, bingo, the money reappears. It's worth the hassle, of course, on really big-ticket items – but bear in mind when you're bringing goods back home that you may also be subject to import duties or asked to prove you've actually paid the VAT.

FCO TRAVEL ADVICE
know before you go
fco.gov.uk/travel

Bradt Travel Guides is a partner to the 'know before you go' campaign, masterminded by the UK Foreign and Commonwealth Office to promote the importance of finding out about a destination before you travel. By combining the up-to-date advice of the FCO with the in-depth knowledge of Bradt authors, you'll ensure that your trip will be as trouble-free as possible.

www.fco.gov.uk/travel

9 Walking Tours

Zagreb is a wonderful city for walking around – neither too big nor too small – and provides a wealth of historical detail, interesting places to visit, and plenty of bars, cafés and restaurants when you want to take a break.

We've suggested two walking tours, one of the upper town and one of the lower town, though of course these can be combined as, like everything else in Zagreb, they both start and end on Jelačić Square. Count on about two hours for each if you stop in at a few museums or churches, and allow time for a drink on the way. Finally, for something completely different, there's an excellent Lamplighters' tour you can join, helping light Zagreb's original gas lamps in the upper town (see page 173).

If you want to stretch your legs a little further, there are plenty of opportunities, either in Maksimir Park (where you'll also find the zoo) or on Mount Medvednica, behind the city. See *Chapter 11* for details of both, as well as other outdoor attractions.

WALK ONE: THE UPPER TOWN (GORNJI GRAD AND KAPTOL)

After admiring Ban Josip Jelačić on his horse, head west out of Jelačić Square on Ilica, Zagreb's longest street. After 250m you'll come to Tomislava, a short dead-end street which leads up to the diminutive **funicular** (see page 91), the easiest route up to the upper town (Gornji Grad, also known as Gradec).

The funicular leads straight up to **Strossmayerovo Šetalište**, a lovely west–east promenade giving magnificent views south out over the city, and the **Lotrščak Tower** (see page 183), one of the few vestiges of the original 13th-century city fortifications. The climb up to the tower's tiny rooftop terrace gives even finer panoramic views.

Once you've caught your breath, turn right along the promenade, and then up at the end, via the lovely café terrace here, onto **St Catherine's Square** (Katarina Trg). The northern side of the square is taken up with the Kulmer Palace, formerly the Museum of Contemporary Art (which is moving to Novi Zagreb), while on the southern side you'll find the Dverce Mansion and the Jesuit College, the 1607 Gymnasium, which is still a grammar school today. The Jesuits were also responsible for the square's main attraction, and Zagreb's finest Baroque church, **St Catherine's** (see page 188).

Before leaving the square, check out the small but dramatic sculpture opposite the **Klovićevi Dvori Gallery** (see page 216), of a fisherman wrestling with a vicious-looking snake, by Simeon Roksandić. Trivia fans will be pleased to know that there's a much larger version of the same statue in Belgrade's main park, up above the confluence of the Sava and Danube rivers.

TO ST MARK'S SQUARE The street running north from the corner of St Catherine's Square is Ćirilometodska, which leads along to St Mark's Square, Zagreb's political heart. On the way up the street notice the Greek Orthodox **Church of Sts Cyril**

and Methodius (see page 188), the chaps responsible for the Glagolitic alphabet. If you have time, you should also definitely pop in and see the **Croatian Museum of Naïve Art** (see page 214), next door.

At the corner of the street, as you come onto **St Mark's Square** (Markov Trg), is the **Zagreb City Hall**, which was originally built as a theatre in 1835 by a man called Stanković who had won a huge lottery the year before. It was used for various historic parliament meetings in the 19th century, and is today a place for ceremonial gatherings – and weddings, upstairs in the registry office. On the opposite corner you'll notice a sculpted stone head depicting the unfortunate Matija Gubec, leader of a 16th-century peasant uprising. Gubec was supposedly dramatically put to death right in front of the church here by the Austro-Hungarians, who held a mock coronation for him with a crown of red-hot iron.

Today the square is dominated by swanky German cars and lots of police – which is hardly surprising, as it's the seat of the Croatian government. On the left-hand side of the square is the original **Ban's Palace** (Jelačić himself lived and died here), which was the target of a Serb rocket attack on Zagreb in 1991 – Tuđman, Mesić and the Croatian prime minister were all inside when it happened, so it's lucky there were no casualties (see page 12 for more historical detail). On the other side of the square is the **Croatian Parliament**, the Sabor.

Between the two stands **St Mark's Church** (see page 187), its distinctive gaudily tiled roof bearing coats of arms of the Kingdom of Croatia, Slavonia and Dalmatia on the left, and Zagreb on the right.

FROM THE TOP OF GRADEC TO THE STONE GATE Head out of the far left corner of the square and up Mletačka, where you'll find the excellent **Meštrović Atelier** (see page 182) on the right-hand side, housed in the famous sculptor's house and studio. At the top of the street it's worth taking a detour down to the left, where you'll find the charmingly old-fashioned **Natural History Museum** (see page 203), and the elegant dead-end street of Visoka. Heading back up Demetrova, check out the classic façade of the Jelačić Mansion at number 7, home to the famous ban's brother, and the Balbi Mansion at number 11, with the old town's last original wooden well in the courtyard.

At the top of Demetrova turn left and then round the corner to the right, where you'll find the **Priest's Tower** (Popov Toranj), which was originally the only defence allowed to be used by neighbouring Kaptol, which had no defences of its own. It's now part of the tremendous **Museum of the City of Zagreb** (see page 190), which has its entrance on Opatička.

Continue down Opatička and then turn left into Kamenita, which leads to the Stone Gate. Before you get there, note two curiosities. On the left is a section of heavy black chain, which is supposed to have come from Nelson's ship, HMS *Victory*, though nobody seems to have the faintest idea how or why. On the other side of the street is a **pharmacy**, which has been in business since 1355, apparently, when it was opened by one of Dante's family – making it the second oldest in Europe, after Dubrovnik's.

The **Stone Gate** (see page 184) itself is the only one of the four original 13th-century city gates to have survived, although the present version is the 18th-century commemoration of the survival of an icon of the Virgin Mary, which miraculously escaped a fire, and is surrounded still by votive plaques and atmospheric candles illuminating the darkness.

Head through the Stone Gate and down the ramp, where you'll find a fine statue of St George and the (curiously catfish-faced, in this version) Dragon, with St George looking remarkably contrite. The road leads out onto Radićeva (originally called Duga Ulica, meaning 'long street' – and if you're heading uphill with a lot of shopping it certainly is), which continues downhill until it meets **Krvavi Most** (Blood Bridge), named for the bloody feuds between Gradec and Kaptol long ago (see page 5).

TO KAPTOL Krvavi Most connects the bottom of Radićeva with the bottom of Tkalčićeva, which is more or less one continuous café. It was originally a creek (hence the bridge), but it was diverted and the street paved over in 1899, as the stench from the tanneries upstream had become intolerable. Take a detour up the street – even if it's only for a coffee or a beer – and check out the statue on the left-hand side, of **Marija Zagorka**, Croatia's first female journalist and something of a proto-feminist (she died in 1957) as well as a popular novelist.

Returning to the bottom of Tkalčićeva, take the steps up past **St Mary's Church** (see page 189) to the market square, **Dolac** (see page 139), which was built in 1926 as a market hall with a big terrace roof, and still does regular business seven mornings a week.

Across the square are the unmistakable twin spires of the **cathedral** (see page 176), which is an absolute must. On the square in front of the cathedral stands a gilt Madonna, surrounded by four angels, by Fernkorn, the Austrian sculptor also responsible for the statue of Jelačić on his horse in the main square. The cathedral is flanked by the vast 18th-century Archbishop's Palace and the canons' distinctive houses, all that's now left of the great fortress which once dominated Kaptol.

After visiting the cathedral, head southeast down Stara Vlaška, which brings you onto Vlaška itself, and then turn right down Palmotićeva for a block — all of which is by way of getting you as far as **Centar**, which you'll see on the far side of Jurišićeva, halfway along the block to the left. It's our favourite ice cream shop in the whole of Zagreb, and after walking all that way, you deserve a break.

Gelati-fuelled, it's just a short walk west back to the starting point, Jelačić Square (and the start of the next walk, too).

WALK TWO: THE LOWER TOWN (DONJI GRAD)

After the winding streets and old houses of the upper town comes the planned munificence of the lower town (Donji Grad), which was made possible by the draining of the swamp below Kaptol and Gradec and the building of the railway embankment in the second half of the 19th century.

Head south out of Jelačić Square on Praška to the first of the three great, green leafy park-squares which eventually bring you down to the railway station. The squares – Zrinjevac, Strossmayerov and Tomislava – are lined with sober, imposing buildings, and closed off at the southern end with the formal elegance of the **railway station** (see page 86), which was completed in 1891.

ZRINJEVAC, STROSSMAYEROV AND TOMISLAVA The first attraction you come to on Zrinjevac, on the northern side of the square, is a rather charming 19th-century **meteorological station**, where you can check out the weather for your walk. Over on the right-hand side, if you're looking south, is the huge **Archaeological Museum** (see page 191), which is well worth a visit, if you have the time – and there's a very pleasant courtyard café behind it, if you're already in need of a break.

Further down towards the station, on the same side of the road as the Archaeological Museum, on the corner, is Zagreb's excellent and recently refurbished **Modern Gallery** (see page 209).

Centre stage in the square itself is the **Croatian Academy of Arts and Sciences** building, which you should pop into even if you don't want to visit the **Strossmayer Gallery of Old Masters** (see page 212), upstairs. The reason to check it out is that in the foyer are two particularly important bits of Croatian art/history: the first is the 11th-century Baška Tablet, which was found on the island of Krk, and records the gratitude of the local monastery to the king for his donation of a block of land. Originally part of a rood screen, the tablet was once coloured blue, yellow and green, and you can still see vestiges of paint in the upper left-hand corner. The Baška Tablet in Baška itself, since you're asking, is a good copy; this is the original.

Also in the atrium of the Academy is the magnificent *Sarcophagus of St Simeon*, supported by four angels. Although this time it's the one here that's the copy (the original is in Zadar), the benefit is that here you can see all the way round and admire the fabulous 15th-century gold-plated silverwork by Francesco da Milano. Check out the central panel on the front, which is directly inspired by one of Giotto's frescoes in the Scrovegni Chapel in Padua, and the panel to the left, which depicts the burial scene (even if it looks more like the poor chap's actually being chopped up). Round at the back, note the excellent medieval scene of a woman fainting melodramatically at the sight of the dead body.

Behind the Academy, looking pensively down towards the station, is Bishop Strossmayer himself, as portrayed by Ivan Meštrović ('What time *is* the last train to Đakovo, Ivan?' he muses, consulting an imaginary timetable).

At the top of the next square, Tomislava, is the charming **Art Pavilion**, which mainly does service these days as a good restaurant, Paviljon (see page 127). It's actually a prefabricated iron-framed structure, which was the brainchild of Vlaho Bukovac (see page 212), who had it built for the Millennium Exhibition in Budapest in 1896, and then shipped back to Zagreb afterwards (which, when you consider its size, is probably why it's not very far from the train station, even now). Indeed, the only thing

King Tomislav

separating it from the railway is enough of an expanse of lawn to set off the grand equestrian statue of **King Tomislav**, who was crowned in AD925 as medieval Croatia's first king.

From here, turn right, and head west from the station past the Esplanade Hotel (see page 101) to the **Botanical Gardens**, which have been providing an oasis of calm to generations of visitors since being opened to the public in 1894. It's a low-key affair, and the glasshouses are for botany enthusiasts only, but it's a pleasant place for a break.

MARULIĆA, MAŽURANIĆA AND MARŠALA TITA Running north from here are another three big squares, Marulića, Mažuranića and Maršala Tita. The first big building you'll see here is the **Croatian State Archives** (see page 200), which seems sober and formal enough until you notice the giant owls perched on the roof. In the square beyond, there's a statue of Marko Marulić, the father of Croatian literature, who was from Split.

On the west side of the next square north you'll find the undeservedly under-visited **Ethnographic Museum** (see page 197), where you can admire a comprehensive collection of Croatia's myriad national costumes. Round the corner, a block further west, and unmissable on Roosevelt Square, is the palatial neoclassical building (formerly a school) which houses the extraordinary **Mimara Museum** (see page 177), which is probably the one museum to visit in Zagreb even if you see no other.

171

Up from here, you come onto Maršala Tita, which is pretty much the last place in Zagreb to publicly acknowledge the man who created – and sowed the seeds of destruction of – modern Yugoslavia. On the left-hand side is the **Arts and Crafts Museum** (see page 202), in yet another huge, late 19th-century building (by Hermann Bollé). In the greenery, as you come out of the museum, look out for another Fernkorn sculpture, this time of St George slaying the dragon.

Across the square is the **Croatian National Theatre**, which was designed by the Viennese architects Ferdinand Fellner and Hermann Helmer, who made something of a career of theatre design, being responsible for over 40 across central Europe, from Switzerland to the Ukraine. An opportunity to see one of the frequent performances here (opera, ballet, theatre) shouldn't be missed (see page 147).

In front of the theatre is Meštrović's sculpture, the *Well of Life* (*Zdenac Života*), dating from 1905, and one of the clearest indicators that his early work was influenced by Rodin, whom he'd met and studied with – in this case the source of inspiration is clearly the *Burghers of Calais*, though the *Well of Life* itself couldn't be mistaken for a Rodin. Across the road, in front of the university's elegant Faculty of Law, is another Meštrović masterpiece, the *History of the Croats*, a simple composition of a single, seated woman, serene but stern, holding a stone tablet.

From the theatre, a few hundred metres up Masarykova will bring you to a shop called 'Zagreb' (see page 139), on the left-hand side, which will sort you out for an ice cream and a cake, and marks the beginning of the pedestrian zone heading up into Cvjetni Trg, the old flower market, and a wealth of places to sit and have a drink along Bogovićeva (where you'll also find more ice cream). At the end of Bogovićeva you'll see the 1970s plate-glass windows of the Hotel Dubrovnik, which brings you right back out onto Jelačić Square.

WALK THREE: LAMPLIGHTERS' TOUR

On the first and third Friday of every month, 'Bring light to the upper town' and join Zagreb's lamplighters as they wend their way through the maze of cobbled streets lighting the 270 original gas lanterns which still illuminate this part of the capital.

You'll be accompanied by young, enthusiastic tour organiser Helena Vajcner from Event Globtour and her colleagues (if you're lucky, dressed as some of Zagreb's most celebrated historical figures), and you'll get the chance to light some of the lamps yourself.

At the same time you can pick up all sorts of bits and pieces of history and trivia via a friendly game in which teams vie to light the most lamps and identify key sites of historical interest (assiduous study of this guide will guarantee you winning on the latter score, at least – including the fact that the local slang word for 'lamplighter' is *nažigač*). It's tremendous fun, with the tour starting at dusk, and lasting for about an hour.

For details, contact Helena (☏ *370 3092;* m *091 370 3553;* e *helena.vajcner@ event.hr – or her colleagues: event@event.hr; www.event.hr*). The place to meet for a drink before the tour is at Caffé Palainovka, on Ilirska Trg, next to the Priest's Tower, right at the top of the upper town.

10 What to See and Do

To see all of Zagreb's sights would take several intense weeks, with an astonishing 57 varieties of museum and gallery open to the public, not counting monuments, public sculptures or even churches. If you want to see the top-rated attractions, you'll need to allow three or four days – partly because opening hours don't always mesh as well as they might. For an idea of what's most interesting, and what you might expect or want to manage to see, depending on the length of your visit, see page 32.

There's a lot to see, but don't be too obsessive. Not everything needs a visit (or is open), and in the end the main sight is the city itself, along with the wealth of café terraces, bars and restaurants which make Zagreb such an agreeable place. A trip up to the top of Sljeme on the cable car followed by an alfresco dinner might turn out to be much more rewarding than religiously ticking off some of the more arcane subjects in the following pages.

Outdoor attractions such as the zoo or Mount Medvednica, and more out-of-the-way sights, such as the monastery church in Remete, are covered in the next chapter.

Museums are almost always closed at least one day a week and tend to have strange opening hours – see listings for more details – and some of Zagreb's more niche museums are open only by appointment. Churches are always open before, during and after services, but – with the exception of the cathedral and Stone Gate – many are closed outside these times.

In this chapter, within each section, the sights are listed very roughly speaking in order of merit.

UNMISSABLES

TRG JELAČIĆA [4 E4] Everything in Zagreb begins and ends on Trg Jelačića, the outsized central square. The main attraction here is the terrific equestrian statue of Ban Josip Jelačić himself. As the Viceroy of Croatia in the middle of the 19th century, Jelačić was a natural reformer, and did a great deal to advance the causes of Croatian statehood. After he died, the heroic statue (by the Austrian sculptor, Fernkorn) was erected in 1866, with Jelačić's drawn sword facing Budapest as a sign of defiance – by this time Croatia was already losing what little independence it had.

After World War II, the statue was torn down because it was considered unpatriotic within Tito's Yugoslavia, and the square was renamed Trg Republike. For more than 40 years, Jelačić languished in bits, in a cellar. When the statue was restored to its former glory, on Croatian independence, in 1991, however, it was put up facing the other way, towards Belgrade rather than Budapest – and today the drawn sword points uncompromisingly towards Knin, the short-lived capital of the erstwhile Republika Srpska Krajina (RSK). (For more Croatian history, see *Chapter 1*, pages

3–15.) Old photographs – such as those on the ground-floor corridor of the Hotel Dubrovnik, connecting the restaurant to reception – show the statue on the other side of the square, facing north.

THE CATHEDRAL [5 F3] The unmistakable twin spires of Zagreb's cathedral can be seen from all over town, which makes it a pity that they've been undergoing restoration for as long as anyone can remember, with no sign of the scaffolding ever coming down. Up close you can see just why the façade needs restoring: the sculpture is astonishingly worn and damaged after a mere century of existence; cheap sandstone is to blame.

The cathedral was built from the 13th to the 15th centuries on the site of an earlier Romanesque church, but what you see today is mostly the work of the Viennese architect Hermann Bollé, following the 1880 earthquake, including the neo-Gothic façade, and the 104m and 105m spires (don't ask). Inside, the cathedral's a light, spacious building, with an uncluttered feel to it. A touch of drama is added by the enormous 1941 Glagolitic Memorial, commemorating the 1,300th anniversary of the first contacts with the Holy See, during the reign of Pope John IV (AD640–642). It takes up most of the wall behind you as you come into the cathedral, and it really is a strange script, even to eyes used to Cyrillic.

(Just in case your Glagolitic's got a bit rusty, the inscription reads: 'Glory to God in the highest! In memory of the 1,300th anniversary of the conversion of the Croatian people, who promised an eternal allegiance to Peter the Rock, having received from him the promised protection in every trial. Placed by The Society of the Brotherhood of the Croatian Dragon – conserving the relics of our ancestors and commending the Croatian homeland to the Mother of God – 641–1941.')

There isn't a great deal in the cathedral which pre-dates the earthquake, though the inlaid choir stalls are early 16th century, and several of the altars and the pulpit are Baroque, from the beginning of the 18th century. There are also a few faded medieval fresco fragments in the sacristy, which date from the 13th century, along with an interesting triptych featuring the *Crucifixion of Golgotha* by Albrecht Dürer.

The biggest draws, however, are the monument and tomb of Alojzije Stepinac (see box); the monument is a great casket, with a life-size effigy of the cardinal, behind the altar, while his tomb is over on the north wall, with a touching Meštrović sculpture. Until 1991, and Croatia's independence, you'd have been unwise to spend much time near either; these days you'll be only one of many people paying your respects.

On your way out of the cathedral, check out the enormous organ, made by Walcker of Ludwigsburg, which was first installed in 1855, and expanded and renewed in 1912, 1939 and 1987. It's reckoned to be among the ten most valuable in the world.

MIMARA MUSEUM (MUZEJ MIMARA) *Roosevelt Square; open Tue, Wed, Fri & Sat 10.00–17.00, Thu 10.00–19.00, Sun 10.00–14.00; entry 20kn* [6 B6]

Without question, Zagreb's most interesting and intriguing museum is the Mimara.

CARDINAL STEPINAC

Nominated as Archbishop of Zagreb in 1937, Alojzije Stepinac courted controversy during World War II by not being quick enough to denounce the Ustaše fascists or the Independent State of Croatia (NDH) – though he subsequently not only criticised the regime but also helped Jews escape from it, and spoke out in favour of persecuted minorities, much to the ire of the NDH, and later the Germans.

He was no friend of Tito's communists, either, refusing to separate the Croatian Catholic Church from Rome, and after the war he was arrested. After a disgraceful show trial in 1948, he was condemned to 16 years' hard labour. He served five years of the sentence, in total isolation, and was then released, only to spend the rest of his life under house arrest in Krašić (see page 261).

In spite of being forbidden from pursuing his religious duties by the state, Stepinac was made a cardinal by the Pope in 1953, though he never went to Rome to receive the crimson, as he was certain he'd never be allowed home to his beloved Croatia. He died in 1960 (quite possibly of poisoning), and was beatified in 1998.

Housed in a palatial neoclassical building (formerly a school), it covers everything from Egyptian glassware to old masters, and medieval sculpture to French Impressionists. Altogether there are more than 1,500 items on display, so allow plenty of time, even if you're just intending to flit through.

The entire collection was given to the state in 1985 by Ante Topić Mimara and his wife Wiltrud. But how on earth did the ebullient, *bon vivant* Mimara manage to accumulate such a wealth of treasures? One answer may be his having lived in Berlin between the wars, a period of exceptionally ripe pickings for canny art collectors. Nonetheless, it's never been clear how Mimara came by either his money or the great majority of his artefacts, and many may well be … well, not quite the real thing. (Authenticity, of course, is especially troublesome to establish when the provenance is unknown.) Mimara himself was said not to be that bothered; he cared more about an object's beauty than its being 'genuine'.

The collection is broadly chronological in arrangement, but unless you have a particular speciality you want to start with, it's most easily handled from the top floor down, giving you time to appreciate the most famous and obvious works before succumbing to museum-fatigue.

Second floor – Western art At the top of the stairs on the second floor pop into the donor's room, where you'll find a bronze death mask of Mimara himself, looking positively beatific after a full and hedonistic existence.

Turn right out of here and head round the floor anticlockwise for a chronological tour through Western art, starting with icons in rooms 29 and 30 and sticking with solid religious themes through to room 35. The big draw here is Raphael's *St Luke the Evangelist*, which is almost certainly not by Raphael, though very much of the period/style.

Other attractions in the same room – which is the heart of the old masters' collection – include a disputed Rembrandt of a noble lady with a neck ruff the size of a wheel of brie, and van den Eekhout's *Ruth and Boaz*, which is very fine and almost certainly the real McCoy. Still staying in room 35, check out Rubens's vast *Virgin with the Innocents*, which brims over with more fleshy pink infant bottoms per square metre than was surely strictly necessary (or indeed tasteful), and an unusual Hoppner portrait of *Wellington and his Family*, all oddly disassociated from one another, as if they'd been PhotoShopped in later.

Moving on, there's a fleshy *Venus* in room 36 by Jordaens, notable mainly for the poor cupid doing his level best to hold up the goddess's extra chins, but it's the last room (number 40) which is most popular, with a disputed double-sided Renoir in the middle, and a couple of lovely Manet still lifes, with succulent oysters, and shiny, organic-looking apples.

First floor – archaeology, sculpture, arts and crafts Downstairs, on the first floor, start in room 13 (under the donor's room), which has some excellent and rare archaeological artefacts, including a fine lion's head which was probably the central boss of a shield and dates back to the 7th century BC, and a Persian pin and disc from the same period, with a lion/goddess in the centre, and pomegranates for fertility around the outside (picked up by Mimara in a market in Tehran in the 1930s, apparently).

Among Greek theatrical masks, Roman artefacts and Mesopotamian figures you'll also see a Hellenistic sculpture of an *ephebe* (young boy), claiming to be 3rd century BC, though the curator is pretty sure it's actually 16th-century German – not just because the hair and the base seem odd for the period, but because the statue has a distinctly slack Renaissance bum.

Rooms 14 to 28 cover a huge range of European sculpture and arts and crafts from the early Christian era right through to the beginning of the 20th century. There are hundreds of things to see, but look out for fishy lamps (room 14), an intricate English hunting horn carved from a walrus tusk (room 17), and a wooden monk carrying a cross and looking decidedly unsteady on his feet (room 19).

In room 20, there's an excellent wasp-waisted ballet dancer of a *St George* (Jacques de Baerze, 14th century) and a feisty 15th-century Flemish *Archangel Gabriel*, apparently in the act of saying 'Up yours!' Both the archangel and his attendant angels have been modelled on the likes of Felicity Kendal and Zoë Wanamaker.

Moving on, check out a 2ft wooden *Hercules* from 16th-century Florence (room 23), clearly inspired by the Farnese version of the same, and a stunning enamel jewellery box (room 24), dating from 1540 and possibly by Pierre Raymond. Finally, room 26 has some extraordinary ivory, including a Polish ivory-carved pyx (for consecrated communion bread) and a scabbard, both commemorating King Jan III Sobieski's 1683 defeat of the Turks in Vienna. When Poland approached Mimara to acquire them, he's said to have playfully agreed, but only in exchange for one of their better Rembrandts.

Ground floor – glass, carpets and Far Eastern art If your appetite's still unsated, head downstairs to the ground floor, where there's enough glass – ancient Egyptian, Roman, Islamic, Venetian, European – in rooms 1–5 to leave you utterly glassy-eyed, not to mention Oriental carpets in room 6, and an extensive collection of Far Eastern art in rooms 7–12. Amongst the bronze, ceramics, jade and porcelain, the most unusual artefact is an amazing pair of 19th-century 'goblets' in room 10, made from whole carved rhinoceros horns standing on intricately sculpted wooden bases depicting Taoist landscapes. You probably wouldn't want them at home.

MEŠTROVIĆ ATELIER (FONDACIJA IVANA MEŠTROVIĆA) *Mletačka 8; open Tue–Fri 09.00–14.00, Sat & Sun 10.00–14.00; entry 20kn* [4 D2]

Arguably the most interesting, and certainly the most accessible of Zagreb's galleries is the Meštrović Atelier. Ivan Meštrović was Croatia's most famous sculptor, and he lived at this house in the upper town between the two world wars, before emigrating to the USA.

Inside you'll find an excellent collection of the sculptor's work, in a much more intimate setting than the vast Meštrović Gallery in Split. The house itself is lovely, with the collection spread across three floors and the artist's studio, and demonstrating the diversity of his work. There's more than a nod to Rodin, who Meštrović befriended in Paris before World War I, but the sculpture goes a good deal deeper than that, and also owes a debt to Slavic culture, Christian iconography and the work of Michelangelo.

The collection is a fine introduction to some of the large Meštrović works dotted around Zagreb – *Bishop Strossmayer* behind the Strossmayer Gallery (see page 170), *Mažuranić* in front of the State Archives (see page 171), the *Well of Life* in front of the National Theatre (see page 172), the *History of the Croats* next to the Faculty of Law (see page 172), or the great *Crucifixion* in St Mark's Church (see page 188).

MONUMENTS, PUBLIC SPACES AND NOTEWORTHY BUILDINGS

TRG JELAČIĆA See page 175.

THE LOTRŠČAK TOWER *Open May–Oct, Tue–Sun 11.00–19.00* [4 D3]

At the top of Zagreb's tiny funicular (see page 91) stands the Lotrščak Tower, one of the very few vestiges of the old town's original 13th-century city fortifications. In summer it's well worth paying your 10kn and climbing up the spiral staircase to the tower's tiny rooftop terrace for excellent panoramic views over the city.

For centuries a bell was rung from the tower every evening to announce the closing of the city's four gates (only one survives – see below), but now it's the midday cannon which is the main attraction. The tradition started on New Year's Eve 1877, and has continued every day since. They're on the fourth cannon now (the other three are in the City Museum), with the current version being an American 76mm model from World War II; a gift from the Yugoslav army for the 1987 University Games in Zagreb.

If you climb the tower shortly before noon you can see the cannon being fired by Stjepan Možar, who's practically become a Zagreb institution since taking on the job more than 30 years ago (he started work on 12 April 1974). For the first 20 years, he didn't take a single day off, though now he has the occasional holiday, with the army ensuring the cannon still goes off at noon – but he has no plans to retire, and he'll continue for as long as he's able. Get close enough, and you can see that Stjepan has three separate watches to make sure he gets the timing right – though he's sure he could do it no problem using his finely tuned internal clock, and after a third of a century you have to believe him.

THE STONE GATE [4 D3] The Stone Gate (Porta Lapidea) is the only one of the four original 13th-century city gates, which were closed at nightfall and reopened at dawn the following day, to protect the old settlement of Gradec from outsiders, and notably from their neighbours in Kaptol.

The gate owes its present appearance to a fire which ravaged the town in 1731. Amongst the ashes in a first-floor flat a perfectly preserved icon of the Virgin Mary (provenance unknown) was found, so in 1760 a church was built into the fabric of the gate, and the icon given pride of place (the gold gem-studded crowns were added in 1931, to celebrate the bicentennial of the miracle).

The Stone Gate

A protective iron grille was added in 1778, presumably to keep grubby fingers away from the miraculous icon, and – in spite of curiously persistent calls for the gate's demolition over the centuries – it's still a major place of pilgrimage today. The walls are cluttered with votive plaques thanking the Virgin for her intercession in answering prayers, and a multitude of candles sends flickering shadows over the faces of the faithful in the semi-darkness. It's an atmospheric place, whatever your religious beliefs (or lack thereof).

LENUCI'S 'GREEN HORSESHOE' [6 C6–6 D8–6 E5] Milan Lenuci was an urban planner who did much to make Zagreb the city it is today, most notably by using the catastrophic 1880 earthquake as a good excuse for laying out the great, grand, leafy squares which dominate the lower town between the train station and Jelačić Square.

The idea was to create a 'green horseshoe', with the Botanical Gardens at the bottom, and two wings running from south to north. It doesn't quite come off – the western arm is less well defined than the eastern one. But it does create large green spaces in the middle of the city, where you'll also find some of the great national Croatian institutions – such as the State Archives, the National Theatre, the Academy of Sciences and Arts, and the Art Pavilion – as well as lots of public sculpture, large and small. See page 168 for more information.

There's a small plaque to Lenuci himself just to the right of the Palace Hotel's front door.

THE STOCK EXCHANGE [7 G5] Zagreb's most dramatic neoclassical building is the former stock exchange, now home to the Croatian National Bank. It was designed by the architect Viktor Kovačić (see page 206), though he didn't live to see its completion; it was finished off in 1927 by his associate Hugo Erlich.

The front of the building is a striking white marble porch, supported by Ionic columns, which dominates the square it's on. If you get a chance to peek inside, do (it's not all that likely, but there's no harm in trying). A tremendous staircase leads up from the entrance hall to the foyer of the original trading floor, a great circular room topped by a huge cupola with a round opening to let in the light.

THE CROATIAN ARTISTS CENTRE *Open Tue–Sun 14.00–18.00* [7 H6]
All roads in the eastern part of the lower town seem to home in on Zagreb's only large circular building, the white marble Croatian Artists Centre (*Dom Hrvatskih Likovnih Umjetnika*). Supported by a colonnade of fine white marble pillars, the building was designed by Ivan Meštrović (see page 182) to house temporary art exhibitions, a function it still performs to this day (though it's also seen service as a mosque and a socialist museum in the meantime). It's worth popping in, even if the current exhibition's not something you're mad about, just to see the great space, diffusely lit from above by its glass ceiling.

THE GOLDEN HALL *Opatička 10; open for private functions only* [4 D2]
In the old town, and easy to find because of the big wrought-iron gates, is the

mansion housing the Croatian History Institute. And inside that, there's an extraordinary Baroque room called the Golden Hall, which is used mainly for swanky functions. If you ever get the chance to see inside, it's well worth it, with the abundant gilding which gives it its name, and major paintings celebrating great Croatian moments in history. Best of the lot is the dramatic depiction by Vlaho Bukovac (see page 212) of Emperor Franz Josef arriving in Zagreb, with the back of what's now the Mimara Museum (it was then a school) clearly visible behind the assembled welcome reception.

✟ CHURCHES

CATHEDRAL See page 176.

ST MARK'S CHURCH [4 D3] Bang in the middle of the old town's main square, with the president's palace on one side and the Croatian parliament (Sabor) on the other, St Mark's Church sits right at the heart of the political capital.

St Mark's Church

The most dramatic thing about the church is its distinctive roof, gaudily tiled in the fashion of seaside resorts with clock flowerbeds. The left-hand coat of arms is that of the Kingdom of Croatia (the chequerboard you still see on the national team's football shirts today), Slavonia (a kuna running between two rivers, the Sava and the Drava) and Dalmatia (three lions); on the right-hand side is the city of Zagreb's.

The original church here was built in the 13th century, with 14th- and 15th-century additions. Most of the church of this era has long since disappeared, though the southern portal, with 15 beautifully carved statues by the Parler family, from Prague, dates from 1420; if they ever finish restoring it, it's well worth a look.

Most of the rest of the church is a late 19th-century Gothic reconstruction. Like so much of post-1880 earthquake Zagreb, it's by Hermann Bollé, though the bell tower is an 1841 original. The interior was refurbished in the late 1930s by the painter Kljaković and the sculptor Meštrović; the former's frescoes are closer to Socialist Realism than Gothic masterpieces, but the latter's crucifix is suitably imposing and dramatic.

ST CATHERINE'S CHURCH [4 D3] Zagreb's principal Jesuit and finest Baroque church is St Catherine's, also in the old town. Built between 1620 and 1632, it features some highly superior 18th-century stucco work and an amazing *trompe l'oeil* altarpiece (those aren't real pillars), an extraordinary work from 1762, by the Slovene painter Kristof Andrej Jelovšek. No prizes for guessing who was responsible for the renovation of the plain façade after the 1880 earthquake: yep, Hermann Bollé.

CHURCH OF STS CYRIL AND METHODIUS [4 D3] Halfway between St Catherine's and St Mark's, and boxed rather uncomfortably between two small town houses, is the

Church of Sts Cyril and Methodius. Cyril and Method were the men responsible for the Glagolitic script (the best example of which is in the cathedral, see above), and ultimately, the Cyrillic alphabet. The Greek Catholic church (see page 260) was built on the site of the former Church of St Basil following the 1880 earthquake by … well, we won't go on; we all know who was chief church architect around then. To see inside – typical Orthodox layout with an iconostasis separating the clergy from the congregation, and not much in the way of furniture – you normally need to ask at the Greek Catholic seminary next door.

ST MARY'S CHURCH [4 E3] The last remnant of the Cistercian abbey which was pulled down to make room for Dolac, the main market square, St Mary's Church is the one you see not just from the market but from most of the cafés and bars along Tkalčićeva. And get this: Bollé didn't even get a look in, as the church was one of the few buildings to be spared by the earthquake. Although the foundations of St Mary's are 13th century or so, the current model is mostly 18th century, including a fine fresco behind the altar by Jelovšek, the man also responsible for the great frescoes in St Catherine's (see above).

ORTHODOX CHURCH (CHURCH OF THE HOLY TRANSFIGURATION) [4 D4] Situated behind the old flower market, the rather drab exterior of the 19th-century Orthodox church hides quite an imposing iconostasis and a dramatic deep-blue fresco across the apse depicting an unusually benign-looking Jesus with outspread arms. It's a particularly atmospheric place when there's a service on, with lots of smoke and incense on the go.

ST BLAISE'S CHURCH [6 A5] Situated a few blocks west of the National Theatre, St Blaise's Church is mainly famous for its reinforced concrete dome. The church was the brainchild of local architect Viktor Kovačić (see page 206), and was built according to his designs between 1912 and 1915. Sceptics were certain that the 18m-wide dome would collapse the moment the supporting pillars were removed, so Kovačić sat out the night underneath it to confound his critics, and the dome still looks pretty solid today. The church is quite plain inside, and usually closed (except during services), but you can get into the porch and have a peek through the bars if you're keen.

 MUSEUMS

MIMARA See page 177.

MUSEUM OF THE CITY OF ZAGREB (MUZEJ GRADA ZAGREBA) *Opatička 20; open Tue–Fri 10.00–18.00, Sat & Sun 10.00–13.00; entry 20kn* [4 D2]
It might seem unlikely, but the City Museum is one of Zagreb's most appealing. The museum was founded in 1907 and originally housed – bizarrely – in the Stone Gate (see page 184), before being transferred in 1925 to the Art Pavilion (see page 170),

and finally finding a permanent home in 1947 in a former convent at the top of the old town, abutting onto the Priest's Tower (see page 166). It's a wonderful museum, with good English-language labelling (sadly still something of a rarity in Croatia) and imaginative displays, and well worth a visit; happily, only a small fraction of the total of 75,000 items in the collection are on display.

The visit starts with an excellent archaeological dig within the museum itself, and moves engagingly through Zagreb's history, giving you a real flavour of life at different periods from Neolithic times right up to the damaged furniture from the 1991 rocket attack on the Ban's Palace.

There are some fine bits of sculpture from the portal of the original pre-earthquake cathedral, as well as pennants, charters, Golden Bulls and coats of arms, as well as a genuinely unpleasant 17th-century cast-iron 'mask of shame', used to punish miscreant market traders.

Perhaps most interesting of all, however, are the reconstructions of various shops from the past and the working rooms of several Croatian notables, along with our personal favourite, a fabulous room with a coloured map of the city inlaid into the floor, with scale models of the main buildings on small pedestals.

ARCHAEOLOGICAL MUSEUM (ARHEOLOŠKI MUZEJ) *Zrinjevac; open Tue–Fri 10.00–17.00, Sat & Sun 10.00–13.00; entry 20kn* [6 E5]

The Archaeological Museum on the west side of Zrinjevac is a truly monumental collection ranging from prehistoric times through to the early medieval period.

Most of the four million or so objects here were collected in the 19th century, but thanks to major revamps since 1999, and the very best in modern display techniques, the museum is a light and airy place, and well worth a visit if you have even a glancing interest in archaeology, Egyptology, classical studies or numismatics. Clearly numbered explanations in Croatian and English go a long way to help.

Start at the top floor, where you'll find the recently renovated prehistoric and Egyptian displays. The prehistoric collection is excellent, with highlights including a headless Bronze Age figurine from Dalj (near Osijek) decorated with geometric patterns, and large collections of Bronze Age and Iron Age pots, axe-heads, jewellery and cloak pins, etc, all well displayed. Also noteworthy is the *Lapodium* collection; the Lapods were an ethnic group from the Plitvice Lakes area, and cultural finds on display here (mostly from gravesites) are characterised by unusual headdresses and the lavish use of chunky amber jewellery.

The star attraction, though, is the so-called *Vučedol Dove* (which should really be the Vučedol Partridge). The three-footed Copper Age vessel dates back to the 4th millennium BC, and is one of the best artefacts from the period ever found. It's decorated with the grooved geometrical patterns typical of objects from this era and area (along the Danube, near Vukovar), with the white paste filling the grooves being made from sea shells. The partridge became a major symbol for Croatian peace and unity, and a memorial for Vukovar, after the 1990s war, so you'll see it everywhere – including on the 20kn note.

The Egyptian collection is also outstanding, with several hundred artefacts including painted coffins and treasures from tombs, mainly from the Ptolemaic period (1070BC to AD30). In its own separate room is the real prize of the collection, the Zagreb Mummy, who was the wife of a tailor at the court of the Pharaoh, and still looks frighteningly deathlike today.

The mummy was acquired by Zagreb in 1859, and when unwrapped, it was discovered that the linen bandages were actually an Etruscan manuscript. At around 1,200 words, the *Linen Book of Zagreb* is the longest text ever found in that obscure, still undeciphered, language. It appears to be an Etruscan liturgical calendar; if you have any clearer notions, or indeed a translation, I'm sure the museum curators would be delighted to hear from you.

Head downstairs to the newly renovated Greek, Roman and medieval displays (which should be opening again to the public in 2007). Among an impressive collection of Greek vases and Roman artefacts of all kinds, check out one of the more unusual and tranquil works from antiquity, the 2nd-century *Head of a Girl from Solin*.

Hopefully, you'll also be able to admire the astonishing *Apoxyomenos* statue, which was found by a Belgian diver off the coast of Lošinj in 1998. The larger than life-size figure of a young Greek athlete is believed to be a Hellenic copy of a classical piece, and was painstakingly restored over many years before finally going on display in 2006. 'Hopefully', because it's not yet certain where the statue will eventually end up.

Finally, numismatists will hardly be able to contain themselves in their rush to see the museum's stunning coin collection; one of the world's most comprehensive, with over a quarter of a million pieces.

When you've had enough – or even if you just fancy a break during the visit – scope out the café in the courtyard behind the museum, where you can sit outside amongst ancient sculpture (fragments from the 1st to 4th centuries) and enjoy a pleasant drink (see page 169).

TECHNICAL MUSEUM (TEHNIČKI MUZEJ) *Savska 18; open Tue–Fri 09.00–17.00, Sat & Sun 09.00–13.00; entry 10kn* [6 A8]

Zagreb's Technical Museum is a bit out of the way, but well worth the detour – and trams #13, #14 and #17 take you straight there. If you're in town with kids of almost any age, then it's a must; as grown-up kids ourselves, it ranks amongst my favourite diversions in the city. The museum is housed in an industrial-looking barn on the right-hand side of Savska, not far past the railway bridge.

The collection starts with fire engines, including Zagreb's first, a horse-drawn number that was bought for the city by a public-spirited lottery winner. It goes on to cover various machines, ancient and modern, which are used to transform energy, from watermills to great steam engines to a whole collection of aircraft engines.

The main central hall houses a wide range of goodies, from a pint-size 1935 Fiat tank to an Italian submarine abandoned during World War II near the island of

Lošinj, to various old cars, including a 1926 Renault NN and a Mercedes sportster from the same period, with a frightening top speed of 170km/h. Even more terrifying is a motor sleigh from 1931, which was powered by a giant propeller on the back and has no visible means of stopping.

Also on display is Dubrovnik's last tram – after derailing and killing two people, it was permanently taken out of service (as anyone who's battled with Dubrovnik's traffic today will still lament); a replica of an old horse-drawn Zagreb tram; and the delightful *Samoborček*, the mini steam train that made the short run over to Samobor from 1930–60, so the locals could indulge in their weekend *kremšnite* (see page 255).

To one side there are scale models of ships (everything from a 5th-century BC Greek trireme to a 17th-century Venetian galley to modern warships), while hanging from the ceiling are various flying machines, from biplanes to a US Thunderbolt to the tatty-looking helicopter which was pressed back into service during the war of the 1990s.

Two other displays on the ground floor are of particular note. The first deals with early aviation, and in particular the pioneer Otto Lilienthal, who made 2,000 successful glider flights in planes of his own design, but died after falling 17m and breaking his spine on his 2,001st flight. His last words were *'Opfer müssen gebracht werden!'* ('Sacrifices must be made!'). The photos make you realise just how unsuited humans are for winged flight.

There's also a good display on the dirigibles pioneered by Croatian aviator David Schwarz – called Schwarzoplans, naturally. They were commissioned by the German army and tested in 1897 in Berlin, but although successful, one also crashed; Schwarz died of a heart attack soon after, reportedly brought on by the news that the invention had actually been accepted. Schwarz's widow sold the plans to a certain Count Ferdinand von Zeppelin, who of course went on to build his eponymous airships, including the extraordinary *Hindenburg*.

Upstairs there's a rather dry exhibition on the 'basics of agriculture', but the effort is amply rewarded by a fantastic bee exhibit at the far end, consisting of three working beehives with glass sides and tubes giving access to the great outdoors, allowing you to see what the bees are really getting up to. It's an excellent display.

Also upstairs is an optical planetarium, which gives you anatomically correct views of the star-filled night sky at any time of year and from the poles to the Equator. It costs an extra 10kn to get in, and is usually only open during the hour before the museum closes.

Back downstairs, there are two more major highlights, both only visitable by guided tour. The first, underneath the museum, is a mine, with some 300m of tunnels, showing what working conditions in mines at different periods were (and indeed are) like – tours usually go at 15.00 daily, 11.00 at weekends, or you can try and hitch onto the back of a group visit. It's a truly excellent experience.

And finally, there's an amazing reconstruction of some of Nikola Tesla's working experiments, including both 3MW and 12MW sparks around a Faraday Cage (lightning is around 20MW, for comparison), along with an interactive exhibition, which has been fully revamped in honour of the 150th anniversary of the inventor's birth in Croatia. Tours happen at 15.30 on weekdays, 11.30 at weekends.

Tesla was an extraordinary man, pretty much defining the way we use electricity even today, and also inventing the radio ahead of Marconi – though this wasn't recognised until after Tesla's death, impoverished and forgotten, in 1943. Tesla demonstrated a radio-controlled boat in Manhattan, almost 50 years earlier, in 1897, though such things didn't become commonplace until the 1960s, and at the time of his death, he was working on a teleforce weapon, or death-ray (intended of course as a peace-ray).

ETHNOGRAPHIC MUSEUM (ETNOGRAFSKI MUZEJ) *Mažuranićeva; open Tue–Thu 10.00–18.00, Fri–Sun 10.00–13.00; entry 10kn, free Thu* [6 B/C6]

The Ethnographic Museum is occasionally invaded by noisy school groups, but usually curiously deserted – which is unfair, as it's a tremendous insight into the way life was lived by most Croatian people until relatively recent times.

The collection is housed in a Jugendstil building which was originally designed at the turn of the century to be a museum of trade and commerce (check out the allegorical figures around the dome). After World War I, it took on its new function as the Ethnographic Museum, focusing on everyday village life, special festive items, and national costumes – and unless you're in Zagreb on the right dates in July (see page 145), this will be the absolute best chance you get to see the huge variety from across the country.

The current exhibition dates back to 1972, and is definitely showing its age – and certainly hasn't been helped by the wilful removal of all the English captions (which were a good deal too Yugoslav for comfort) after the 1990s war. Happily, full renovations are planned for 2008.

The permanent collection upstairs starts with a simple village house interior. Note the photograph of a large village clan of over 30 people; the abolition of the feudal system by Jelačić (see page 175) in 1848 saw most clans disintegrate, but some persisted through until the 1930s.

Opposite the house interior there's a display of decorative women's headwear from northern Croatia, which tells you a lot about hair-related superstition. Young girls' hair is allowed to be seen, but married women's woven bonnets cover it all up, and bridal bonnets are often highly reflective to ward off the evil eye. The superstition reigned that a woman's strength and goodness lay in her hair, and so this should be reserved for the family; as a result, any hair lost had to be burnt, to prevent witches from getting hold of it. In some of the more remote villages of Croatia, these beliefs still persist today. Even in Zagreb, you'll find people being superstitious about chimney sweeps (you see them in the streets) and nuns, with one for good luck, two for bad, three for good, etc. It can't be a coincidence that both nuns and sweeps usually work in pairs.

Looking at the fabrics and costumes, you'll see lots of red, black and white. Red was believed to ward off evil spirits, and was often used during childbirth to divide the room, to separate the women from the rest of the household. Red dresses also symbolise youth and vitality. Black, of course, is usually associated with death – to wrap the body for burial or cover the burial chest. But until around a century ago, white was the traditional colour for mourning across most of Europe, and still is in Croatia, Hungary, and even parts of Spain today. White was the simplest fabric, so the total absence of decoration and colour signifies a lack of interest in personal appearance in the wake of tragedy.

In the main display rooms you'll also see rustic furniture, communal ovens, baking implements and valuable bridal chests, usually made from wood from the island of Rab. The wood was sold off so enthusiastically to the Italians and French — it was a favourite for cognac casks — that the island eventually became denuded and entirely barren on the east side, and remains so today.

Also noteworthy are hand-operated corn mills, which were once the 'morning music' heard in every village; primitive wooden carnival masks used to chase away the evil winter spirits (local carnivals continue today, and there's a huge one in Rijeka); small wax votives (of limbs in need of repair, or sick animals); and the ubiquitous red-iced gingerbread hearts (*licitarsko srce*) decorated with mirrors, traditionally given by young men to their brides-to-be: 'Look who I have in my heart'.

Among the costumes themselves, look out for the grass capes used by shepherds to keep the rain off, and the shaggy (positively hippy) costumes and rugs from the Lika region, which come from vertical looms which can't be used to make linen.

Richer garments reflect wealthier parts of the country, and notably the Slavonian costumes, with silver and gold thread, complex embroidery, and an abundance of fabric, as well as necklaces with coins sewn into them for unmarried daughters, symbolically representing their dowry.

Downstairs, don't miss the unusual – and quite entertaining – foreign ethnographic collection, with artefacts and costumes from India, Bengal, the Pacific islands, Australia, Africa, Easter Island, Japan, Brazil and Latin America. Most of the material here came from the expeditions led at the turn of the 20th century by Mirko and Stjepan Seljan, an exotic pair of explorer brothers from Karlovac.

And last but not least, see what's happening on the rest of the ground floor; the temporary exhibitions here are generally first-rate.

CROATIAN STATE ARCHIVES (HRVATSKI DRŽAVNI ARHIV) *Marulićeva; open Mon–Fri 12.00, 13.00 & 14.00; at other times by special arrangement; ☏ 480 1981; entry 20kn* [6 C7]

The Croatian State Archives (Guided tours in English, German and Croatian) are housed in Zagreb's finest Jugendstil building, down near the Botanical Gardens. If you have the time, it's well worth taking a tour, as the inside is as grand as the exterior.

At first sight, the edifice seems as sober and formal as you'd expect from something which was originally built as a monumental university library in 1913, but wait until you see the four sets of giant green owls supporting globes on the roof – they're fabulous! Before you go inside, also check out the four sets of reliefs above the main entrance, which are allegories of the four collegiate sciences – from left to right as you're looking at them, *Medicine*, *Theology*, *Philosophy* (Socrates confronting the very naked truth indeed) and *Law*.

The magnificent building is the work of local boy Rudolf Lubynski, who used the knowledge he gained studying architecture in Karlsruhe to create Zagreb's first concrete building. He also took charge of the sumptuous interior decoration, which includes geometric marble inlay floors, Bohemian crystal glass panelling, Slavonian oak wainscoting, and light fittings from Murano, all set off by tasteful touches of gold leaf decoration.

Inside the main hall, notice the mosaic depictions of some of Croatia's most important sites, including Đakovo, Dubrovnik, Senj and of course Zagreb. There are plenty of other owls around too, symbolising illumination and knowledge.

The tour takes in the lovely Professors' Reading Room, which features comfortable reading desks and fine Art Nouveau lamps, as well as several large allegorical paintings by Ivan Tišov, depicting the natural sciences, the liberal arts and the scholastic arts. Above the entrance hangs Robert Auer's image of Athene Palladia holding a figure of Athene Nike, a pictorial embodiment of the maxim 'Through knowledge to victory'.

The other main attraction inside is the aptly named and genuinely enormous Large Reading Room, which is still in use today. Two vast chandeliers (imported from Prague and weighing in at over a tonne apiece) complement the elegant beaded reading lamps and the lovely stained glass in the ceiling.

On the north wall (above the entrance doors) are three imposing paintings by Mirko Rački, depicting *Science in Antiquity* to the left (note Homer), *Science in the Middle Ages* to the right (featuring Dante), and *Science in the Modern Age* in the middle. The huge canvas opposite is the *Evolution of Croatian Culture* by Vlaho

Bukovac (see page 212), and features 27 Croatian luminaries – with a little knowledge and a sharp eye you can spot the playwright Ivan Gundulić, Bishop Strossmayer and Ljudevit Gaj, while that person on the right-hand side peeking out from behind the figure in a green cape may well be Lubynski himself.

Back outside, dizzy from all the accumulated knowledge and wisdom – not to mention the owls – see if the small graffito telling you what it's really all about ('Sex and Money and Guns') has been cleaned off yet. It's on one of the small pillars holding up the chain fence, to the left as you leave – or it was in the summer of 2006, anyway.

ARTS AND CRAFTS MUSEUM (MUZEJ ZA UMJETNOST I OBRT) *Trg Maršala Tita; open Tue–Sat 10.00–19.00, Sun 10.00–14.00; entry 20kn* [6 B6]

Zagreb also has an outstanding Arts and Crafts Museum, housed in yet another huge, late 19th-century building (Bollé, again), just across the square from the National Theatre. The only real disappointment is the almost complete lack of English-language captions and legends.

The great pastel edifice was purpose-built for the museum, and was designed to house a 'collection of samples for masters, craftsmen and artists' – a remit it certainly manages to fulfil to this day, covering pretty much everything from the 14th to the 20th centuries, and displaying around 3,000 objects from its total collection of over 150,000 artefacts.

What you find most appealing will depend on your own specialist areas of interest: you can choose from furniture; textiles and clothing; ceramics; glass; Gothic and Baroque sculpture; European miniatures from the 17th to 19th centuries; ivory; silverware; musical instruments; religious art and liturgical objects; a magnificent collection of 400 clocks and some 200 pocket and wristwatches; and pretty much all the Secession and Biedermeier you can eat.

If that's not enough to knock the stuffing out of you, there are also sections on printing, graphic and industrial design, and photography – with both old photographic equipment and photographs on display, including early daguerreotypes, documentary photographs from World War I, and pictures from dashing mountaineering expeditions of the 1920s. Finally, there's an interesting collection of European art, with the focus primarily on the 17th century. Rembrandt's student Ferdinand Bol is represented here, along with Charles Le Brun, the painter who (with Poussin) pretty much determined the course of 17th-century French painting.

The museum has a nice, classy shop, where you can buy good reproductions as well as modern ceramics and textiles, and downstairs (with its own courtyard at the back) is the Hrvatski Kulturni Klub – nothing whatsoever to do with a Croatian Boy George, but instead a rather good café and restaurant (see page 126).

NATURAL HISTORY MUSEUM (HRVATSKI PRIRODOSLOVNI MUZEJ) Demetrova 1;
open Tue–Fri 10.00–17.00, Sat & Sun 10.00–13.00; entry 15kn [4 C2]
If you fancy a trip back in time, then Zagreb's Natural History Museum is just the ticket. Situated up in the old town in a palatial but rather run-down building, the

collection comprises around two million specimens, most of them in anachronistic wooden glass-fronted cabinets.

Get past the surly socialist-era ticket sellers, and you can lose yourself in room after room of rocks and fossils, moon dust and meteorites, and bones, skeletons and specimens you'd rather not think about in formaldehyde-filled glass jars.

The top floor is the main attraction, especially if you're travelling with kids. Here you'll find seriously old-fashioned displays of stuffed and preserved animals from throughout Europe, including a large shark in a suitably aquamarine environment, and a long corridor of specimen jars leading through to mammals, birds, insects and some very fine butterflies.

For serious naturalists, the museum also houses a library of some 40,000 volumes which you can consult; the oldest is a natural history encyclopaedia in Latin dating from 1638.

Before you leave, make sure you step into the museum's courtyard, where you can check out the excellent mineralogical map of Croatia, made from a bit of stone from each part of the country, and a geological column stretching from 350 million BC to about 10,000 years ago. One side shows rocks from Mediterranean Croatia; the other stone from the continental interior, including various fossils representative of different eras.

Finally, don't be surprised if you see anthropologists of world renown snooping around the museum, as it's also the repository of the extraordinary Krapina Man find, the world's largest collection of Neanderthal fossils from a single site. This isn't

KRAPINA MAN

Krapina Man was discovered in August 1899 by Dragutin Gorjanović-Kramberger – or to be more accurate, a fossilised human molar was found, pointing to the existence of a Neanderthal settlement in the area some 130,000 years ago. Thanks to Gorjanović-Kramberger's enormous diligence, scholarship and plain hard work, the collection grew in size to become the world's largest and most important set of Neanderthal fossils from a single site, comprising 900 pieces from 70 to 80 individuals.

The current curator, Jakov Radovčić, has dedicated a great part of his life to the collection, and is the author of a fascinating biography of the finder, see page 298). Radovčić is currently setting up a new database with the help of EU funding, which will allow for extensive data sharing, without the need for the priceless original specimens to be handled.

His great personal achievement – after decades of lobbying – is the new, state-of-the-art interactive museum being developed at Krapina (see page 247), which will display replicas of the collection, and recount what we know about Neanderthal man. Much of the museum will be underground, as it has been conceived as a labyrinth, a voyage of discovery into the development of European thought about ancient man, along with the history of the site itself and its discovery. The museum is expected to be open by 2008.

open to the public, but a wonderful dedicated museum on the subject will open in 2007 or 2008 near Krapina itself (see page 247); in the meantime see the box on page 205.

CROATIA HISTORICAL MUSEUM (HRVATSKI POVIJESNI MUZEJ) *Matoševa 9; open Tue–Fri 10.00–17.00, Sat & Sun 10.00–13.00; entry 10kn* [4 C3]

If you're kicking your heels or it's a rainy day, pop into the Croatia Historical Museum which has temporary exhibitions focusing on – yep – Croatia's history. The museum is one block west of St Mark's Square in the old town.

There's no permanent exhibition, which is a pity, as they have all sorts of important goodies in stock, from Jelačić's 1848 flag to armour, weapons, stone sculpture, painting, clocks, maps and photographs. The temporary exhibitions are usually good, but the amount of information you'll get in English varies.

VIKTOR KOVAČIĆ APARTMENT *Masarykova 21; open Thu 10.00–17.00; ☏ 485 5911 to arrange a visit* [6 C5]

The Viktor Kovačić Apartment is a touching tribute to the life of one of Croatia's greatest architects. Kovačić was given the attic apartment in lieu of payment for designing the building it's in and the one next door, and he lived here from 1906 until his death in 1924, aged just 51.

The flat has been preserved exactly as it was when Kovačić lived here, and gives a fascinating glimpse into early 20th-century urban life. It's also a testament to

Kovačić's eclectic tastes: an oriental wallpapered, black-and-white tiled entrance hall leads into an elegantly appointed dining room and sitting room, the latter papered with a striking gold geometric design. The sitting room features a small library as well – guides to Paris, Venice and Switzerland reflecting Kovačić's love of travel – and the room also contains folios showing some of Kovačić's designs and sketches, including a prize-winning plan for the redevelopment of the zone around the cathedral (ultimately never realised). The best examples of Kovačić's work you can see today in Zagreb are the stock exchange building (see page 186) and St Blaise's Church (see page 190).

BELA AND MIROSLAV KRLEŽA HOUSE *Krležin Gvozd 23; open Tue & Fri 11.00–17.00; ✆ 483 4922 to arrange a visit* [4 C2]

If you want to nose around in another famous person's residence, look no further than the Bela and Miroslav Krleža House. Bela was one of Croatia's most celebrated actresses, while Miroslav was one of Yugoslavia's most distinguished writers; they lived together at this address from 1954 until they died within a few months of each other in 1981.

In spite of the lack of any information in English, the place shows just how the famous couple lived, and gives a great snapshot of Zagreb life at the end of the Tito era. On entering you're greeted by a cheery Miroslav in the mirror, before coming into the small dining room – which was fine, as they apparently only ever entertained one couple at a time.

Bela's card room and bedroom come next, with a marvellous hotchpotch of furniture, furnishings and decoration. There's an amazing 18th-century Italian inlaid table, lots of pictures of the famous actress, and the original official 1973 radio for tuning in to Tito's regular broadcasts.

Miroslav's study and bedroom are full of books and papers as you'd expect, and very 1950s. Check out the last newspapers he ever read, which were *Le Monde* and *France Soir* on 16 November 1981, with Indira Gandhi on the front page, trying to do peace deals in New Delhi. The bedroom leads into the bathroom, which is now a museum of all the different editions of his books – including his homily to Tito which was forcibly pressed upon one of the authors in Belgrade over 20 years ago.

Finally, there's a collection of interesting personal effects, including pre-tied bow ties, battered hats, a gun, letters from Tito, Yugoslav awards, and some rather morbid pictures of the couple's funerals. Most interesting of all is a picture of Miroslav playing chess with Tito as a guest on the Brijuni Islands, near Pula, which Tito kept as a private playground. You can just picture Miroslav letting Tito win every time.

COLLECTION OF ANKA GVOZDANOVIĆ *Visoka 8* [4 C2]

One of Zagreb's most unlikely museums is the Collection of Anka Gvozdanović, in the old town. Although it's currently open only to arts and crafts professionals (it's actually an offshoot of the Arts and Crafts Museum; ℩ 488 2111 if you need to know more), there are plans to open it up to the public, perhaps in 2008.

The museum is the house of Dragutin Gvozdanović, a late 19th-century judge and landowner, and was bequeathed to Zagreb by his (much, much younger) wife Anka, on her death in 1968. So what you get is a good look at the life of the Zagreb upper crust around a century ago. Gvozdanović was an important member of Zagreb's *faux* masonic lodge, *kvak* (meaning 'frog'), which met here regularly for dinner from 1875 to 1945, along with their silly froggy nicknames.

Indeed, there's froggy imagery everywhere – but what you come to see is an extensive collection of period furniture and lavish furnishings, painted wall decorations, numberless portraits and photographs, porcelain stoves, display cases full of ornaments and china, a black room, a green room, a red room and a blue room, a smoking room, a massive dining room, and an even more massive ballroom.

The house backs onto Tuškanec Park, far below, and there are lovely sweeping staircases down to the road beneath – though they're badly in need of shoring up.

GALLERIES

MEŠTROVIĆ ATELIER See page 182.

THE MODERN GALLERY (MODERNA GALERIJA) *Strossmayerov; open Tue–Fri 10.00–18.00, Sat & Sun 10.00–13.00; entry 30kn* [6 E6]
The Modern Gallery houses 'Two centuries of Croatian Visual Arts'. In spite of one of the steepest entry fees in Zagreb, and the works being mainly by artists most of us haven't heard of, this is nonetheless one of the best galleries in Zagreb.

It's recently been expensively and beautifully restored, and the rooms are bright, light and airy, running chronologically from around 1800 onwards. For us personally, the show is stolen by Vlaho Bukovac (see box, page 212), and the gallery holds some great works by him – but don't let that stop you enjoying the rest of what's on show here.

The first room you come into sets you up a treat, with a symbolic feast from the 'School of Zagreb' painters, dominated by a vast *Bacchanalia* from Celestin Mato Medović. That leads you into something of a vacuum in the next couple of rooms, but it's worth sparing a moment for Fernkorn's models of the statues of *St George and the Dragon*, and *Ban Jelačić*, the full-scale versions of which you'll have seen in the city. There are also four very strange portraits by Vjekoslav Karas, which fall uncomfortably between the naïve and the expressive, and were painted before the young artist drowned himself in Karlovac in 1858 (see page 268).

The next room's more cheerful altogether, with some wonderful Bukovac works, and a couple of excellent hyper-realistic sculptures by Robert Frageš Mihanović; his *St Dominic* is particularly good.

In the next long room check out the transition from Jugendstil to Symbolism, and a fine picture of water lilies by Croatia's first important female painter, Slava Raškaj; a deaf mute, she died before the age of 30 in an institution. In the same room, there's a fine diptych in a Jugendstil frame by one of Croatia's most influential painters, Emanuel Vidović – it's entitled *Mali Svjet* (Small World); the house he was born in is on the left, and the graveyard where he will be buried on the right.

The main oval room which comes next showcases the arrival of German expressionism, and sees Vidović retreat into his dream-world of *The City of the Dead*. Also check out the photographically framed seascapes by Menci Clement Crnčić, and some dramatic portraits by the short-lived Josip Račić (he died when he was just 23), including the *Lady in White*.

Moving on, there are two excellent self-portraits by Miroslav Kraljević, who made it to the ripe old age of 28 before dying of consumption; a great painting of a woman with a gun by Croatia's second great female painter, Nasta Rojc; a fabulous 1923 self-portrait by Milivoj Uzelac – Schiele-influenced and expressionism at its cruellest; and a 1927 Picasso-feel self-portrait by Ivo Režek.

Head upstairs and check out the works by the socially committed architect Drago Ibler in the first room – distinguished by the brick wall backgrounds denoting lack of choice. There are also some fantastic photographs in the same room of 1930s workers by Tošo Dabac, and a couple of very late works by Vidović of Split and Trogir cathedrals.

After World War II you get everything from beauty to landscapes to social realism and – post 1951 – geometrical abstractionism. Look out for works by the husband-and-wife team Frano Šimunović and Ksenija Kantoci: abstract landscapes of fields and dry stone walls from the Dalmatian hinterland from the former, and abstract sculptures from the same landscapes, usually of peasant women, from the latter.

The exhibition ends with art which was banned during the Yugoslav era, including an excellent conceptual work featuring doctored hyper-inflation banknotes and worthless coins being scooped up by a ladle.

VLAHO BUKOVAC – VIRTUOSO PAINTER

Vlaho Bukovac was born in Cavtat (just south of Dubrovnik) in 1855, and showed prodigious talent from an early age. In 1877, he went to the Beaux-Arts in Paris to complete his studies and a year later became the first Croatian painter to be accepted into the prestigious Paris Salon. Travelling widely around Europe, Bukovac nonetheless played a vital part in the development of Croatian art – not just by being enormously prolific himself (he left over 2,000 works) but by supporting younger artists as well.

At their best, Bukovac's paintings are simply marvellous, combining an almost photographic realism with impressionistic touches, and some of his portraits are truly stunning. As a virtuoso painter, he seems to have had a penchant for technically difficult or daring compositions, adding inlaid furniture, tapestries or wild wallpaper designs to his pictures, just for the hell of it.

STROSSMAYER GALLERY OF OLD MASTERS (STROSSMAYEROVA GALERIJA)
Strossmayerov; open Tue 10.00–13.00 & 17.00–19.00, Wed–Sun 10.00–13.00; entry 20kn [6 E6]
In the square across the street from the Modern Gallery you'll find the Croatian Academy of Arts and Sciences (see page 169), the top floor of which is given over to the excellent Strossmayer Gallery of Old Masters. Josip Juraj Strossmayer was the

fervently pro-Croat bishop of Đakovo, in eastern Slavonia, and was the founder of the Academy. He was also a serious art collector, and what you get here is his private collection of 256 works from 1884, supplemented by various donations over the years from the likes of Augustinčić (see page 244) and Mimara (see page 177).

The gallery is at the top of the stairs, and spans religious works from the Renaissance right through to 19th-century France. The lack of English-language captions is a pity, but not the end of the world.

Heading clockwise, chronologically around the gallery, the first room is noteworthy for a fine 15th-century work by Frangelico depicting *St Francis and St Peter*, and a *Madonna and Child* by Roselli, featuring dreary-looking angels – even by the standards of the day.

The next room houses Strossmayer's own favourite works, and notably another *Madonna and Child*, this time by a follower of Raphael. Rooms 3 and 4 make the small stylistic leap from the Ferrara school to the Venetian school – a bit less detail in the works, but still camp as Christmas. Look out for a dramatic *Resurrection* from Carpaccio, with Jesus positively leaping out of his grave and stepping on the sleeping soldiers on his way out, an inspiringly simple *Ecco Homo* by Filippo Mazzolo, and a suggestive *San Sebastian* by Andrea del Sarto.

In the next three rooms, check out Ribera's dramatic *Jerome* (clearly inspired by Caravaggio), a wonderful *Mary Magdalene* by El Greco (centuries ahead of his time as usual), and a great treatment of *Salome*, by Elisabetta Sirani, who managed to churn out more than 170 oils by the time of her death, aged just 27, in 1665.

Rooms 8, 9 and 10 take you through Croatian, Flemish and French works for the most part, with the likes of Bruegel, Poussin, Delacroix and Courbet on show – and a fantastically stodgy portrait of famous beauty and salon-hostess *Juliette Récamier* by Antoine-Jean Gros.

As you leave, look out for Carpaux's bust of Eugène-Emmanuel-Ernest d'Halwyn, Marquis de Piennes, who was France's ambassador to Zagreb under Napoleon III – and known here as plain old Etienne. Piennes bequeathed his private art collection to the Strossmayer Gallery on his death in 1911.

CROATIAN MUSEUM OF NAÏVE ART (MUZEJ NAIVNE UMJETNOSTI) *Ćirilometodska 3; open Tue–Fri 10.00–17.00, Sat & Sun 10.00–13.00; entry 20kn* [4 D3]
One of Zagreb's most interesting galleries is the Croatian Museum of Naïve Art. The gallery was opened in 1952, as the Peasant Art Gallery, making it the oldest museum of naïve art in the world. From 1956 it was called the Gallery of Primitive Art, and in 1994 took its present name. There are around 80 works on show, from a total collection of over 1,600, covering naïve artists who had no professional training and little or no education – but all went on to make a living from their work.

Croatian naïve art developed from the 1930s in Hlebine, near the Hungarian border, with the first important artist being Ivan Generalić, who showed in Paris to great critical and commercial acclaim in 1953. Characteristic of Generalić and his followers was the technique of painting highly stylised rural scenes on glass, which was then reversed for framing. Apart from being valuable in its own right, the movement was particularly important for giving us a record of the terrible hardships of peasant life until quite recent times.

A common motif is the rooster, a symbol of rebirth (as it is in the work of Federico García Lorca); look out for the Godzilla-sized version on the barn roof in one of the paintings in the first room, which is dedicated to Generalić's work, or the particularly colourful cockerel in *The Death of Virius*, a homage to another painter from Hlebine who died during World War II – note the dead trees and concentration camp, with life going on far behind the barbed wire. Finally, check out the striking self-portrait from 1975, with its absolutely uniform background and Generalić looking down in contemplation.

In complete contrast is follower Ivan Večenaj's *Evangelists on Calvary*, with blood pouring down the Cross, the evangelists present in their metaphorical form (ox, lion, eagle, angel), people strung up in the trees, inscribed parchments everywhere, and a blood-red sky: the stuff of nightmares. If you don't like it, you probably won't much enjoy his portrait of an inbred peasant woman with her cat, either.

More palatable are the winter landscapes by Mijo Kovačić. Reminiscent somewhat of Bruegel, particularly good examples are 1962's *Singeing a Pig* (using burning straw to remove the pig's skin), 1967's *Swineherd,* and 1974's *Frozen in the Snow*, depicting dead Partisans in a super-realistic snowdrift.

Moving into the third room, check out the large, accomplished work by Genaralić's son Josip, *Guiana '78*, which deals with the mass suicide of Jim Jones and his 900 followers that year, and marks the start of a general trend towards the depiction of more modern life, rather than simply peasant culture.

Two other artists are particularly worth singling out: Emerik Feješ and Ivan Rabuzin. You can spot a Feješ a mile off, as the scenes are mostly geometric multi-coloured churches, including Vienna and Milan cathedrals, St Mark's in Venice and Sainte-Chapelle in Paris.

Rabuzin's work is also highly distinctive, and he's arguably the most accessible of all the naïve artists, as he leaves people out of the picture (literally; he believed that the presence of people was a 'blot' on the beauty of the world). His bright, optimistic pastel landscapes feature repetitive geometric forms in the trees and flowers – and I even once saw a reproduction in a French hotel.

Finally, check out the work of naïve sculptor Petar Smajić, and particularly his charming *Adam and Eve*, which is Henry Moore-like in its simplicity.

If you're really serious about naïve art, then it's well worth making the trip up to Hlebine, a couple of hours northeast of Zagreb, where you can visit both a state gallery and the private collection of Generalić father and son. The virgin landscape of the early paintings may no longer exist, but the old way of life persists.

KLOVIĆEVI DVORI *Jesuitski Trg 4; opening hours vary for each exhibition* [4 D3]
Next door to St Catherine's Church, the four wings of the former Jesuit monastery have been converted into a lovely space which is used for major temporary exhibitions. It's well worth checking out what's on there – though for reasons which

remain entirely opaque, even the best internationally mounted exhibitions seem to lack translations in English.

MUSEUM OF CONTEMPORARY ART (MUZEJ SUVREMENE UMJETNOSTI) *Under construction in Novi Zagreb*

For a long while the Museum of Contemporary Art was housed in the Kulmer Palace, on the other side of St Catherine's Church, but the space was much too small for comfort. As a result, a large new museum building is currently (at the time of writing) under construction in Novi Zagreb, which will be wholly dedicated to international art, mainly from the 1950s and 1960s. It should be open sometime in 2007 or 2008; check the tourist office for the latest details.

11 Outdoor Attractions

If you've just worked your way through everything in the previous chapter you'll clearly be after a breath of fresh air and some outdoor attractions. Happily, Zagreb has plenty to offer here too, from one of the best cemeteries anywhere, **Mirogoj**, to the huge city park, **Maksimir**, where you'll also find a great **zoo**, to a cable car ride up to the easily accessible Sljeme, the peak of **Mount Medvednica**. Zagreb even has its own beaches, at **Jarun Lake** and **Bundek** – and if that's still not enough, there's also the charming monastery church of **Remete** to visit in the northern suburbs.

MIROGOJ CEMETERY

You don't have to be in the least bit morbid to enjoy a trip up to Mirogoj Cemetery [1 C2], one of the best burial grounds we've ever visited. Just hop on bus #106, which runs up from Kaptol, above the cathedral, and get off ten minutes later when you see the semicircular entrance gate to the cemetery, dominated by the dome of the main chapel.

Mirogoj was opened in 1876 as the city's monumental municipal cemetery, and the main feature is a series of divine, greening cupola'd arcades running either way along the inside of the walls. They're the work of Hermann Bollé, and in their own way every bit as impressive as the cathedral.

The cemetery is not just non-denominational but a positive pantheon, housing Jews and Muslims, Orthodox Christians and Catholics, communist Partisans and the German dead from World War II. There are literally thousands of touching memorials to individuals, families, and different historical tragedies, with sculpture from pretty much every notable Croatian artist.

The largest and most impressive memorial of all is right at the top of the main avenue, where Croatia's first president, Franjo Tuđman, is honoured by a vast expanse of black marble. It's big, but it's not as poignant as the memorial to Stjepan Radić, who was shot in Belgrade's parliament in 1928 (see page 7), which you'll find to the right of the entrance as you come in, under the arcades. Just before Radić is the memorial to the poet Petar Preradović, which features a wonderfully sculpted mourner laying a single flower on the bier, while four cupolas beyond, check out the lovely monument to Emanuel Prister (whoever he was), with a tremendous depiction of a woman closed in upon herself with grief.

Once you've paid your respects, you can return to the city on the bus, or simply walk down the hill – it takes around half an hour,

Mirogoj Cemetery

heading down Mirogojska (head straight out of the cemetery, not left down Hermana Bolléa) until you reach the tram stop at the bottom of the hill, and then make your way across at the lights to the top end of Medvedgradska, which runs down the hill until it becomes Tkalčićeva (it's one street across from the top of Nova Ves, which then becomes Kaptol).

MAKSIMIR PARK AND THE ZOO

A few kilometres east of the city centre is the sprawling Maksimir Park [1 D3], easily reached on tram #4, #7, #11 or #12 (get off at the Bukovačka stop, heading towards Dubrava or Dubec), which also plays host to Zagreb's wonderful zoo. It's right across the street from the Dinamo Stadium, home to Zagreb's 'Bad Blue Boys', the local – and enormously popular – football team.

Maksimir itself is a real oasis of calm, feeling far, far away from the noisy city streets. Measuring around 2km by 1.5km, it was landscaped in the manner of a 19th-century English park, and features lakes, woods, hidden paths, meadows and even the occasional folly to divert you. It's a great place for a stroll, and an even better one for a picnic.

Zagreb's zoo (*www.zoo.hr; open daily 09.00–18.00; entry 20kn*) is spread along the southern edge of Maksimir Park, and is absolutely first-rate, putting far bigger cities like London and Paris to shame. From its founding in 1925, when it boasted just three young foxes and a pair of owls, it's grown – and indeed matured – to become one of the nicest zoos in Europe.

Many of the 2,000 or so animals here, from nearly 300 species, live in modern, airy, outdoor enclosures, rather than cages, and there are some real treats in store for visitors, from a fearsome pack of wolves, to the most charming red panda ever seen, to a pygmy hippo (called 'Hypo' after the local mortgage lender), to a comic pool of savvy seals and sea lions. There are excellently themed didactic exhibitions covering different regions of the world, with the emphasis on eco-systems rather than simply the fauna to be found there.

Two particular exhibits make the zoo stand out even further. The first is a house which shows off domestic fauna in its actual setting, from mice in the cupboards to cockroaches under the floorboards to birds nesting in the roof. The second is even more adventurous, comprising two cages marked 'Homo Sapiens', complete with full species data, such as height, weight, longevity and average number of young. You can go inside, of course, to see what it's like behind the bars, but the trick is: you get to choose whether you want the cage furnished with plastic and non-renewable materials, and junk food on the table, or the cage done out with wooden and cane furniture, and a bowl of fresh fruit.

MOUNT MEDVEDNICA

For a real breath of fresh air, look no further than Mount Medvednica, the mountain which provides Zagreb's permanent backdrop and an excellent local resource. As a well-managed Nature Park, there's lots to see and do up here, from pleasant not-too-strenuous walking to cycling, to just taking in the views and the cooler air above the city. The biodiversity here is wonderful, with 1,200 plant species on Medvednica, compared with 1,600 in the whole of Great Britain.

If that's not enough to tempt you up the mountain, there's also Medvedgrad (a splendid medieval castle), a bat cave to explore, and a small reconstructed mine to visit, as well as places you can stay and eat. In winter you can even ski down the back of the mountain and pretend you're local hero and four-time Olympic winner Janica Kostelić.

GETTING THERE (AND SKIING) Getting up the mountain isn't difficult at all, and can be comfortably managed in a half-day trip, using public transport. Take tram #8 or #14 to the Mihaljevac terminus, followed by tram #15 to the end of the line at Dolje. From here it's a pleasant ten-minute walk through a short tunnel and up a forest path to the cable-car station (*Žičara Sljeme*), and a 23-minute ride (hourly, on the hour) up to the 1,030m peak of **Sljeme** [1 B1], the highest point on Mount Medvednica. If it's windy, the cable car doesn't operate, and they usefully post a notice at the Mihaljevac terminus saying so (*Žičara ne vozi*). The price of the ride is currently 11kn one-way, 17kn return (free with the Zagreb Card).

By road (assuming you have your own wheels), head north from the city and follow signs to Sljeme, turning right at the Mihaljevac tram and bus terminus, and then left a couple of kilometres further on, at Bliznec. The road which winds up the mountain, along the top, and down again a few kilometres west, is a one-way system (after you've passed the Nature Park's office on the first left-hand hairpin), so when you come down the mountain it's actually into the suburb of Šestine – more or less due north of Britanski Square, on Ilica.

If you're planning on skiing, you can rent kit at the top of the mountain – but be warned that since the Kostelić phenomenon kicked in, Zagreb's gone skiing mad, and it can get pretty busy. Best fun of all is the Snow Queen, a twice-weekly night-slalom which takes place throughout the season (from the end of November to the beginning of April).

PRACTICALITIES You can get heaps of information from the cheerful, friendly and helpful staff at the **Nature Park** (*Park Prirode Medvednica;* ☏ 458 6317; f 458 6318; *www.pp-medvednica.hr*) [1 A2–C1], whose office is situated on the main road into the park, above Bliznec – you can hardly miss it, as there's a fabulous bear trimmed from a large bush on the corner. Just below the park office, criss-crossing the stream, is an excellent nature trail, which – in a world-first for the blind – has all the legends in Braille as well as access for the disabled.

There are several places to stay on Medvednica, most notably the **Tomislav Dom** (☏ 456 0400; f 456 0401) [1 B1], which is just a few minutes up from the top of the cable car. Chalet-like doubles go for €100–120 per night, which is a bit expensive for something this far out of town. Another option if you want to stay up here is the **Pansion Medvednica** (☏ 455 0737; f 455 5845; *www.pansion-medvednica.com*), which does four-bed rooms for a very reasonable €70 – but it is pretty basic, catering mainly to student groups, and it's a 15-minute walk west from the top of the cable car. Finally, there's also the **Pansion Zvonimir** (*formerly Hunjka;* \ 458 0397; f 455 2185), which has pleasant double rooms at €70 in a largish chalet overlooking the Hunjka meadow, about 4km east of Sljeme, on the old road heading down off the back of the mountain.

You're also unlikely to go hungry on top of Medvednica as there are several cafés and restaurants at the top of the mountain (as well as the two near Medvedgrad, see above). Our personal favourite is **Puntijarka** [1 C1], in the Ivan Pačkovski mountain lodge. It's out of the way a bit, about 3km east of Sljeme, but serves up lashings of mountain food at unbeatable prices. Fill up on a delicious bowl of *grah* (heavy, meaty bean soup) for just 15kn, or turkey with *mlinci* (thin homemade doughy pasta) for 40kn. Be warned: portion sizes are almost as big as the mountain itself.

MEDVEDGRAD FORTRESS [1 B2] From the top of the cable car, it's a little under an hour on foot to the 13th-century Medvedgrad Fortress. This was abandoned in the late 16th century and fell into ruin, but was expensively restored in the 1990s, as a patriotic gesture by Franjo Tuđman – it's become something of a nationalist symbol, and as such is mildly controversial: could the money have been better spent on something else, the locals ask. Whatever the politics, it's an atmospheric place in a great location, all the same, on a bluff with lovely views out over the city, and a fine restaurant in the vaults.

If you're coming by car, Medvedgrad is a bit non-intuitive to find, as it has its own access road. If you're coming down the mountain, pass the Šestinski Lagvić

Restaurant, then turn right at the attractive, gaudily roofed **Šestine Church** [1 B2], towards Talane, and then right again at the next junction, which is signed for Medvedgrad; the road takes you straight up to the castle.

The **Šestinski Lagvić Restaurant** [1 B2] itself is an excellent place to eat, but quite pricey. For something a little more reasonable, there's the **Kraljičin Zdenac Restaurant** [1 B1] further up the hill (ie: before you get to Šestinski Lagvić, if you're driving). If you fancy a stroll, it's a lovely shady walk up to Kraljičin Zdenac along the Kraljevic stream, avoiding the road.

If you're driving (or cycling) down the hill, look out for the huge, newly restored mansion to the right, after you come out of the woods and before you get to Šestine Church; it's called **Kulmerovi Dvori**, and now belongs to the Todorić family, the owners of the successful Konzum supermarket chain.

THE VETERNICA CAVE *Entry 25kn* [1 A2]
On the southwestern corner of Medvednica is the Veternica Cave complex (named after the eddies of wind at the entrance which led to its discovery), over 7km of which have been explored. On Sundays from May to August you can visit the first well-lit 400m of the cave as part of an excellent guided tour (call the Nature Park office for more detailed information; see below), which covers the cave's geological and natural history, as well as its former use as (probably) a Neanderthal shrine of some kind; over 100 bear skulls were found in the cave, but the original entrance is too small for bears.

You'll also see a date on one wall in an inner cave. This was daubed here by a daring young blood called Fabrici, who came all the way inside in the dark in 1934; unfortunately his mates didn't believe he'd actually done the deed, so he had to climb the cathedral tower instead to prove his worth – happily without unfortunate consequences.

Serious speleologists can go much deeper into the complex (by arrangement with the Nature Park authorities), and squirm their way on hands and knees up the Stairs of Calvary, past the Stinky Lake and through Ramses's Passage (ooh-err).

Outside the summer season, the cave is closed to the public, as it's the natural hibernation place for 14 of Croatia's species of bat, as well as all sorts of other unusual wildlife, including the peculiar *Chthonius jalzici*, a mock scorpion endemic to Veternica which was classified only in 1988.

The easiest route to Veternica is the 20-minute hike downhill from the **Glavica mountain hut** [1 B2], though that does rather raise the question of how you get to the hut first. The other route to the cave is by taking tram #2, #6 or #11 to the Črnomerec terminus, and then bus #124 to the end of the line, after which it's a kilometre or so uphill (walking trail #3 on the map) to the cave entrance – allow 45 minutes up and 30 minutes back.

THE ZRINSKI MINE *Open Sat & Sun & public holidays (when it's not snow-covered) 10.00–16.00, & also by arrangement (with the park office, see below) for groups; entry 20kn* [1 B1]

More historical nuggets (though no silver ones, these days) can be gleaned from the Zrinski Mine (also called Rudarski Vrt, especially on maps – meaning 'miners' garden'), which has been excellently and evocatively reconstructed to give you a feel for miners' life in the 16th century.

What that feel is, mostly, is of just how hard a miner's life was (and in many places still is). If mining was your chosen (or designated) career up here, you could expect to start work at age 12, and die of lead poisoning by the time you were 30. In the brief years between, you worked the mine, doing a 12-hour shift, six days a week, plus the 1.5-hour commute each way from the bottom of the mountain (ironically where you'll now find Zagreb's ritziest real estate). Each day, you would dig out, with the other 15 miners on your watch, around a tonne of rock, which might yield a little silver and a bit more lead.

The mine was abandoned for over 400 years, but has now been restored (by the Nature Park) to show something of its history and workings. Most important of all is the presence in mines everywhere of St Barbara, the patron saint of miners. Why St Barbara should be their protector is a bit of a mystery, as the unfortunate Barbara is best known for having her head cut off by her father, and her father then being killed by lightning by God (so why didn't He throw the lightning bolt before Barbara's untimely decapitation, you have to ask).

The tour is enlivened by talking wooden statues of Zagorje mining types (whose accents are apparently especially hard for Dalmatians to understand), the first of which is the mine manager – you can tell by the silver buttons on his coat. With low ceilings and narrow corridors, along with drippy-water sound effects, it's an atmospheric experience and especially worthwhile if you're here with kids.

The mine is located about 25 minutes' walk west of the top of the cable car, on the main road, just below the Grafičar hut. If you're walking up from Medvedgrad, allow around 40 minutes.

WALKING AND CYCLING Medvednica is ideal for both walking and cycling, and there are good maps available for both pursuits – available either direct from the park office or at the main tourist office on Jelačić Square. The walking is on the whole rather less demanding than the cycling (walkers can use the cable car to cut out a good deal of the legwork), which requires you to get up the mountain in the first place. The cycling map – available for the time being in Croatian only – details 15 different rides of varying difficulty, and helpfully gives not just distances and routes, but profiles too, as well as the total climb you're in for.

JARUN LAKE

About 5km southwest of the city centre, Jarun Lake is an artificial playground tucked into a bend of the River Sava. It was built for the 1987 World University Games, and comprises a great big lake, with a handful of islands, long pebbled swimming (and sunning) beaches, cycle paths, jogging tracks and places you can rent bikes, pedalos, deckchairs, canoes and even sculls.

As the lake warms up quickly and stays that way throughout the summer months, with average water temperatures of around 24°C, it can get pretty busy with swimmers and strollers on summer weekends. And as you'd expect, there are plenty of bars and cafés as well as snack and ice cream establishments to keep you going. Jarun is also home to a couple of Zagreb's most important nightspots, Aquarius (see page 149) and Gallery (see page 150).

You can get to Jarun Lake easily enough, either directly on the #113 bus from behind the main railway station (Jarun is the last stop), or almost all the way on tram #5 or #17 to the Jarun stop, which is just a few minutes' walk north from the lake.

BUNDEK

For years, Bundek, just across the River Sava on the way to Novi Zagreb, and opposite the racecourse and fairgrounds, was an edgy area where you were more likely to tread on a needle or find last night's forgotten undergarments. Happily, that's all changed now, with a major redevelopment of the lake and surrounding park, which reopened in 2006.

As a result, you'll now find lovely flowerbeds and a glistening lake spanned by an elegant bridge at its narrowest point, as well as numerous cycle paths, pebble beaches and lots of lawn space for sitting around on. It's all very pleasant, and very popular at weekends.

If you're looking for a bit of an excursion, then the monastery Church of St Mary in the northern suburb of Remete is a nice place to visit – but don't go unless you've really covered a lot of ground already, or are particularly passionate about Mary, as it's a little over 5km from the city centre and not that easy to get to without your own transport (take bus #203 or #226).

The church is famous primarily for the wooden sculpted Virgin Mary, which the faithful still come to admire, particularly on the Feast of the Assumption (15 August), though it's also a popular place to get married, or – if you're sufficiently famous – buried. Before you go inside, check out the excellent reliefs outside the front door, with the saint on the left apparently holding a dodo, and the one on the right standing on a wild boar.

Inside, apart from the Holy Virgin herself, the big deal is the wealth of amateurish but powerful frescoes depicting her intervention in a huge range of domestic dramas. On the right-hand side, on the upper wall near the door, there's an endearing gentleman who looks as if he's definitely had one *travarica* too many.

12 Beyond the City

There's a whole lot you can see and do on easy day trips out of Zagreb, and if you have the time, efforts to explore the surrounding region will be well rewarded. For a more in-depth view of the region, turn to the excellent *Croatia: The Bradt Travel Guide*.

HIGHLIGHTS

The attractions are listed here working very roughly anticlockwise from Varaždin to the north, round to Lonjsko Polje in the southeast. But first, a selection of our own personal favourites (in no particular order) would have to include the following, any of which can be handled in a single day, or combined with others to make for a longer excursion:

MOUNT MEDVEDNICA (page 221) So close to Zagreb, it's been included in the previous chapter. Take the cable car to the summit, and get a breath of fresh mountain air.

KEY
Motorway
Main road
Other road
International boundary
National park
Nature reserve

HUNGARY

Budapest

Drava

ČAKOVEC

KOPRIVNICA

Đurđevac

BJELOVAR

Kutina

N

Bradt

Lonjsko Polje

E70

VARAŽDIN

Zlatar

Križevci

E65/71

Ivanić Grad

Sava

SISAK

Petrinja

ZAGORJE

1030m

Mt Medvednica

ZAGREB

TUROPOLJE

Glina

Kupa

Krapina

Zabok

E59

Zaprešić

Samobor

Plešivica

Jastrebarsko

E65/71

KARLOVAC

Vojnić

Žumberak

Bosanci

Vrbovsko

1181m

Ogulin

Klek

Josipdol

Jezerane

Otočac

Vrelo

Plitvice National Park

Slunj

Jasenak

1534m

Bjelolasica

SLOVENIA

Velebit

BOSNIA & HERZEGOVINA

0   20km
0   10 miles

SAMOBOR AND THE ŽUMBERAK (page 254) A charming little town just half an hour from the capital, with a couple of excellent accommodation options and easy access to the low mountains, remote villages and fine vineyards of the Žumberak.

THE PLITVICE LAKES (page 271) Croatia's most-visited attraction, but nonetheless lovely for that, with a series of pristine lakes connected by waterfalls large and small.

VARAŽDIN (page 234) Croatia's northern provincial capital is a Baroque masterpiece, with easy access to the unspoilt Međimurje region up against the Hungarian border.

THE PLEŠIVICA WINE ROAD (page 263) Just an hour out of the city; the narrow roads, rounded hills and abundant vineyards are among the most beautiful in Croatia.

THE ZAGORJE (page 242) The area just north of Mount Medvednica has hundreds of churches and dozens of castles and country houses set amongst wooded hills, as well as the preserved museum-village of Kumrovec and an amazing new ethnographic museum in Krapina.

KARLOVAC (page 265) The purpose-built Renaissance fortress town of Karlovac has an appealing town centre set amongst abandoned 16th-century fortifications, a fine castle on a hilltop, and a lovely river to bathe in.

STORK COUNTRY, FROM THE TUROPOLJE TO LONJSKO POLJE (pages 276–280) With old wooden village houses and churches, and marshy wetlands, the region southeast of Zagreb is home to a large population of nesting storks.

CYCLING IN ZAGREB COUNTY Cyclists should jump at the opportunity of taking advantage of an excellent new series of maps entitled *Biking Routes of Zagreb County* which were published for the first time in 2004 by the Zagreb County Tourist Board (✆ 487 3665; f 487 3670; www.tzzz.hr). These describe a series of routes to the north and west of the capital following low-traffic-density roads across beautiful rolling countryside, and range from the easy to the moderately strenuous. Altitude and distance profiles let you know exactly what you're up for and full details are provided of everything you could possibly need along the way from restaurants and accommodation options to bike repair shops. It's a wonderful initiative – but go for knobbly tyres, as quite a few of the trails go off the tarmac and onto gravel to avoid the traffic. There's another good map of bicycle trails covering the Žumberak Nature Park (see page 258), which you can pick up in Samobor.

VARAŽDIN

Tucked into the northernmost corner of Croatia, about 80km north of Zagreb and just 45km from the Hungarian border, Varaždin is a provincial capital and a Baroque delight. It has great architecture, a fine castle, a wonderful pedestrianised city centre, and enough to see and do without being anything like hard work. The city is the most cycle-friendly in Croatia (over 20,000 bicycles for a population of just 50,000), and one of the most wealthy – the elegant buildings and spacious streets are the result of centuries of prosperous agriculture and trade, and very little damage from recent wars.

HISTORY Known as Garestin in Roman times, little of importance happened here until Varaždin was recognised by Hungary in AD1181, and then developed first as an administrative and later as a defensive centre – from the 15th century on, the city was on the front line against the Ottoman Empire.

With the Turkish threat under control by the early 17th century, Varaždin became an affluent and influential city, and in 1756 even became the capital of Croatia. It wasn't to last – after a catastrophic fire in 1776, the ban (the local governor) moved to Zagreb. Varaždin was still a prosperous city, however, and its wealthy merchants didn't miss the opportunity of rebuilding their houses and palaces according to the latest fashion of the day.

Today, the Baroque centre of town has been beautifully restored, and deserves to win its bid to be included on UNESCO's World Heritage list. With everything comfortably within walking distance in the centre, and plaques on many of the buildings in Croatian, English and German, it's also an easy place to visit.

GETTING THERE AND AROUND Varaždin is easy to reach, with buses running at least once an hour from Zagreb, and trains making the journey a dozen times a day. Buses take around 1.5 hours, while trains rarely achieve the distance in under 2.5, though the notoriously slow train ride is a much more picturesque way of making the journey. Varaždin is also a stop on the major international bus and train routes north to Austria and Hungary. By car, it's not much more than half an hour on the motorway from Zagreb, once you've cleared the city. Parking is metered in the city centre, and you can pay in cash or by sending an SMS from your mobile phone.

The bus station is five minutes southwest of the town centre, while the train station is ten minutes away to the east. Most of the old town is pedestrianised, with the curving shopping street Gundulića leading up to the main square Trg Kralja Tomislava. A block northwest, on Padovca, you'll find a friendly and helpful tourist information office. The expanded city map is well worth the 25kn, though if you're on a tight budget you can certainly get by with the free materials.

 WHERE TO STAY AND EAT Varaždin's short on accommodation, with just three plainish hotels: the smaller **Garestin** and **Maltar**, or the slightly bigger **Turist** (contact the tourist office for information). A better option is to head out of town to **Zlatne Gorice** (\f 042 666 054; dbls €50), 4km south, on the main road to Varaždinske Toplice (Varaždin's spa complex), in the locality called Turčin – it's on the left, at the top of the hill. It's actually an upmarket restaurant, with individually furnished dining rooms, but upstairs they have three brand-new, comfortable doubles – and they make their own excellent wine too.

As a prosperous town, Varaždin has no shortage of places to eat and drink, and some of the restaurants and bars have terraces in pleasant courtyards hidden away behind the Baroque façades, or overlooking the town park. The best of the bars is **Aquamarin**, just north of the main square, next to the town hall, which is trendy and popular for its cocktails, though **Mea Culpa**, a groovy lounge bar next door to the tourist office, is a serious contender.

The smartest place to eat is **Zlatna Guska** (☏ 042 213 393), the only place in town for which you'd really need to think about making reservations. It overlooks the park and has a medieval-style vaulted interior downstairs, complete with crests, maces, lances and colourful banners.

WHAT TO SEE The main sight in Varaždin is the harmonious old town, which you'll likely be approaching from the south, as this is where the hotels and bus station are. Across the bottom of town is a lovely park, with the **National Theatre** on the southwest corner – if you have the chance to look inside, or see a performance here, you'll find it a sumptuous red velvet and gilded treat.

In the **park** itself, look out for the statue of **Vatroslav Jagić**, the Slavic-languages expert who was born here in 1838. His statue's a bit of an embarrassment for local clothes manufacturer Varteks (Varaždinska Tekstilna), as his coat buttons are on the wrong side for a gentleman's garment. Worse, his legs are at a weird angle, the result of a botched repair job after the heavy statue was dropped when it was originally being installed.

Moving up into town, stop at the **Church of St Nicholas** on Trg Slobode (Freedom Square). Nicholas is usually the patron of seafaring cities, but got chosen here because of Varaždin's dependence on the Drava River for trade. The church is also dedicated to St Florian, with his red flag – he's the patron saint of firemen, as a reminder of the 1776 fire. Up on the tower, there's a stone bear; the legend is that the poor bear turned to stone on returning to the site of the church to find her cubs gone.

Turn up into Gundulića, which is known locally as Dučanska, as this is the place to shop (*dućan* = shop). Note the casement windows at the corner of Habdelića, which were designed so that wealthy ladies could snoop on what was going on below. At the top of the street, take a detour left to the 17th-century **Franciscan Church**, which was built on the foundations of something much earlier – its tower, at 54m, is the tallest thing in Varaždin.

Outside the church, anyone who's been to Split will recognise the pint-sized version of Ivan Meštrović's most distinctive statue, *Grgur Ninski* – strangely undramatic in its reduced form. As in Split, the erstwhile bishop's big toe has been worn golden by people hoping their wishes will come true.

Almost next door, and an absolute must for entomologists, is Varaždin's wonderful **World of Insects** museum, featuring 1,000 species of bugs and more than 4,000 exhibits. It was the work of Franjo Košćec, who spent decades collecting the specimens here, and was personally responsible for the museum's creation in 1954. It's one of the best collections of its kind, demonstrating not only Croatia's endemic species, but also the life cycle and habitats of various insects, in a modern, stylish setting – and there's even a charming re-creation of Košćec's study. If you're interested, or have kids, the interactive *Kukci* CD-Rom for sale here is simply excellent.

Heading back the way you came brings you to Varaždin's 17th-century **cathedral**, on the right, with a plain Baroque façade giving away few secrets about the riotous over-the-top altarpiece inside. Multi-coloured pillars frame dramatic saints in late medieval garb, overlooked by gesticulating angels and overflown by abundant *putti*. It's absolutely marvellous – but you wouldn't want one at home. The doors, dating from 2002, celebrate Varaždin's becoming a diocese, with its own bishop.

On the corner of the main square opposite the cathedral stands the Drašković Palace, which was the ban's residence during Varaždin's (very) brief stint as Croatia's capital in the 18th century. The main square itself – **Trg Kralja Tomislava** – is dominated by the town hall, dating from 1523, with an unlikely spire rising from its centre. Look out for the mermaid sign hanging outside the Bonbonniere Kraš sweet shop on one side of the square – the sign formerly denoted a shop selling exotic goods sourced from abroad (the original sign is in the town museum, if you want to see it). You'll also notice the Ritz and Jacomini buildings side by side in the main square; the family plots are also side by side in the cemetery (see below). Finally, while you're here, scope out the arcades which lead off the square and the surrounding streets, which shelter enticing boutiques, cafés and restaurants.

Heading north from the main square brings you round onto Trg Milijenka Stančića, which faces onto the drawbridge and gatehouse leading across to the castle and town museum. On the square itself, in a gaudily fronted palace, is the **Municipal Art Gallery**, which mostly comprises old works by artists you won't have heard of – but it's nonetheless interesting for that.

From here head through the gate into the park housing Varaždin's trademark whitewashed fortress, the **Stari Grad**. Set amongst defensive earthworks which have pleasantly metamorphosed into lovely gardens, the fortress was originally built in the 14th century, before becoming a major defence against the Turks in the 15th century, and evolving into its present shape during the 16th century.

The fortress now houses the **Town Museum**, which was established in 1925, and is one of the best municipal collections outside Zagreb. Even if you're not especially into the paintings, weaponry and furnishings on display here, the entry fee is amply repaid by the chance to wander round the rooms and the two three-tiered courtyards – and there are some old and droll hunting targets on display, including one which features the faces of the marksmen's wives. Of particular interest is a series of rooms each furnished in a different period style, from the 17th century through to Biedermeier, with original paintings, furniture and furnishings. Finally, don't miss the chapel and sacristy built into the tower on the first floor – and drop us a line if you have the faintest idea how they got that massive piece of furniture in there.

From the fortress it's a ten-minute stroll west to the town's wonderful **emetery**, which has much more in common with a well-tended garden than a traditional resting place, with plants and shrubs dominating the graves. It's the life's work of Herman Haller, who ran the cemetery from 1905 until 1946, with the intention of creating a 'park of the living' rather than a 'place of the dead'. You'll find all sorts of wonderful memorials here, amongst the avenues and promenades, including 376 red rose bushes commemorating the town's World War 1 fallen. One of the most interesting graves is that of the mountaineer Lucijan Zlatko, which features a piece of rock from every peak he climbed. It seems terribly ironic that as a climber he lived to the age of 93, while his wife Vera succumbed at only 48.

If all the sightseeing's left you hot and bothered, and you have your own transport, head a few kilometres east out of town to **Aqua City**, where you'll find a lake to swim in, a shingle beach to sun yourself on, and a restaurant. Without wheels you can still get the shore-side experience by walking 20 minutes northeast of the old town to the **Dravska Park Šuma**, where you'll find jogging paths along the banks of the great, still River Drava.

Varaždin festivals Varaždin is the perfect venue for any number of festivals during the year, with the two largest being the 'Špancirfest' at the end of August and the Festival of Baroque Music in late September. There are also weekly festivals every Saturday from April to October, which feature workshops around the old town highlighting traditional métiers and arts and crafts, along with music and theatre for children.

ČAKOVEC AND THE MEĐIMURJE Situated just 13km northeast of Varaždin, Čakovec is the northernmost town in Croatia, and though there's not a whole lot to do or see, it's worth a visit even if only to take in the **Museum of the Međimurje**, housed in the wonderfully shabby Zrinski Castle. The collection ranges from Neolithic finds to period furniture, arts and crafts, and silverware and glass. In town, also look out for the wacky secessionist **Trade Union Hall**, which was built in 1904 and still looks moderately bonkers today, with its frivolous decorative brickwork quite unsuited to the serious business of organised labour.

Across the street is the friendly **Tourist Office**, which will help you out with local information and give you details of the Međimurje Wine Road, as well as accommodation options in the region.

THE ZAGORJE

The northwestern corner of Croatia, known as the Zagorje, is one of the most beautiful parts of the country, with scores of castles, country houses and hilltop churches looking down across rolling wooded hills and vineyards. It's largely neglected by foreigners on their way to the beach, but it's no secret to locals, who come out here at weekends to relax.

Many of the old houses – and especially the little buildings adjoining the vineyards (*klets*) – have been converted into weekenders for people escaping Zagreb, but come here on the right Tuesday in February, and you'll find the local winemakers' wives getting plastered in *klets* on every vineyard; seems like a splendid tradition to me. Many of the castles (the French word *châteaux* is more appropriate, really) are in a state of disrepair, empty and abandoned, and could do with fixing up, and of those which have been restored, most are in private hands and can't be visited – though some are in the process of being transformed into upmarket hotels.

It is difficult to get the most out of the Zagorje without your own wheels: even though many of the sights can be reached on public transport, it may take you all day to see a place worth only an hour of your time. Consider renting a car for a couple of days – but be prepared for narrow and windy roads off the beaten track.

There aren't that many places to stay, with most of the area's hotels being attached to the various spas in the region, but there are a couple of excellent exceptions listed within this section. Zagorje eating is usually a treat, with lots of hearty local specialities, and notably *štrukli* (see page 113), which is often at its best here. The red-iced gingerbread hearts you see everywhere (*licitarsko srce*, see page 158) are intended for decoration rather than eating, however.

The following attractions are ordered in an itinerary heading very roughly clockwise from Zagreb towards Varaždin and back again, with those to the east of the main road to Hungary appearing at the end of the section. Covering the whole lot would make for a fairly hectic two- or more relaxed three-day tour.

ZABOK AND KLANJEC Heading northwest out of Zagreb, it's around 20km to Zabok, which is nothing special, but as you come off the motorway you'll see a newly restored mansion up on the hill which is now a nice hotel called **Dvorac Gjalski** (☏ *049 201 100;* f *049 201 135; www.dvorac-gjalski.hr*). It makes an agreeable stopover, even though the views to the back of Mount Medvednica are blighted somewhat by the light industrial landscape in between – fortunately there's a lovely terrace behind the hotel, and a fine restaurant within. The rooms are impeccable, too, and very good value indeed at €70 for doubles and €82 for a suite.

From here it's under 20km northwest to the small town of **Klanjec**, nestled right up against the Slovenian border. The main reason to stop here is to visit the **Antun Augustinčić Gallery**, which maintains a comprehensive collection of the sculptor's work from the 1920s right through to the 1970s. You may not think you've heard of Augustinčić, but if you've ever seen the monumental horse and rider outside the UN building in New York, or the pick-wielding miner outside the International Labour Office (ILO) in Geneva, then you'll recognise his work.

KUMROVEC Continuing north, another 10km up the road brings you to the ethnographic museum-village of Kumrovec. For half a century the name was synonymous with Josip Broz Tito, Yugoslavia's erstwhile leader, as he was born here, but these days that angle's very much downplayed.

Today the museum part of the village consists of more than 30 houses, each displaying a different feature of life as it would have been lived at the end of the 19th century, when Tito was a boy. Mannequins in period costume, the full range of authentic furnishings, tools and implements, and excellent labelling in English, make this easily the best of Croatia's many ethnographic museums.

In different houses you can imagine what it must have been like (hard work, mostly) to be a wheelwright, a baker, a blacksmith, a linen manufacturer, a toymaker, a potter or a gingerbread man. One house is given over to a wedding feast, with a shy bride-to-be in her bedroom, doubtless deafened by the jolly music-making going on at the banquet across the hall.

The Broz family house (obvious because of the heroic Augustinčić statue outside) is a low-key testament to Tito's fairly humble origins. The main room is given over to a small collection of Tito memorabilia – a few documents, one of his wartime uniforms, and a handful of photos of Tito with other heads of state from Churchill to Nixon. Without exception, the whole lot look as if they've been amusingly doctored to include Tito after the fact. In 1956, Nasser and Nehru shake hands, but Tito appears to have been pasted in behind; by 1963, it's John and Jackie Kennedy in the frame, with Tito scissored-in on the left-hand side.

The chickens wandering around and the hay drying on the attractive Slovenian-style lattice frames should alert you to the fact that not all the houses are part of the museum – before you wander unannounced into someone else's authentically rustic living room (as Piers once did), check for telltale trainers or gumboots outside.

Within the museum complex there's a nice place to eat, the **Zagorska Klet**, where you'll find a wholesome range of local food at reasonable prices. You can then pick up a *licitar* heart, in the gift shop.

Heading up the Slovenian border from Kumrovec, the countryside becomes ever more beautiful, with Austro-Hungarian spires crowning hilltop churches – stop briefly for the photo-op at Zagorskje Sela, where from **St Catherine's Church** you get lovely views across the valley into Slovenia. Not much further up the road from here, as you come into Miljana, is the turn-off to Desinić, which is the road for Veliki Tabor.

VELIKI TABOR, PREGRADA AND DVORAC BEŽANEC A few kilometres up the road, on a 333m hill, is **Veliki Tabor**, arguably the most picturesque authentic castle in Croatia. Originally dating from the 12th century, the distinctive defensive round towers were added in the 16th century. From the road there's a lovely view – as indeed there is from the excellent and authentically rustic **Grešna Gorica Restaurant**, clearly signed off the main road, a few hundred metres beyond the steep track leading up to the castle.

Unfortunately the castle itself doesn't really deliver on its promise. The lovely five-sided, three-tiered courtyard is undergoing much-needed restoration, and it looks as if it'll take years. The rooms leading off the galleries house a fairly mundane collection, and the art and pikes don't really warrant the 20kn entrance fee.

Like all good medieval castles, Veliki Tabor has its own romantic fable attached to it. In this case the local landowner's son wouldn't renounce the peasant girl of his desires, and was imprisoned in the castle until his death. The girl, for her part in the sorry story, was bricked up into the castle walls – they say the skull in the chapel here is hers. Count yourself lucky if you live in a time or country where you can choose whom you marry.

Eight kilometres east of Veliki Tabor is the village of **Pregrada**, where the local parish church is so big it's known locally as the Zagorje Cathedral. It's 38m long and 19m wide, and its two 45m towers dominate the village. Inside, check out the monumental organ (avoiding 'monumental organ' jokes of course), by Focht, which used to belong to Zagreb Cathedral, until they sold it to Pregrada for 600 forints in 1854. Frankly, it's much better value than the 600 forints the church spent eight years later on the vast altarpiece of *The Adoration*, which looks like it can only have been bought by the square metre, or indeed the rather drudgy modern stained glass in some of the church's windows.

Another 4km east leads to **Dvorac Bežanec** (☎ *049 376 800;* f *049 376 810; www.bezanec.hr*), which is in a great setting and has been converted into a swanky hotel and conference centre. Originally built in the 17th century, the château was remodelled in 1830 in the Classicist style, and it can be a wonderfully luxurious place to stay, with nice suites at €100–120 a night. Be fussy about your room, however – some of the standard doubles (at €82) could really use a lick of paint, and there's no excuse in a place this nice for thin towels or plastic shower curtains. The hotel's restaurant – which serves up meals in the courtyard or out on the terrace in fine weather – is absolutely first-rate.

KRAPINA A further 12km east brings you to Krapina, which is on the main road running north from Zagreb to Maribor (in Slovenia) and Graz (in Austria). It's a busy, commercial little town, but the main reason for visiting is that in 1899, on the

Hušnjakovo hill above town, the site of an important Neanderthal settlement dating back 130,000 years was found.

Krapina Man was discovered by Dragutin Gorjanović-Kramberger, who went on to collect the world's largest and most important set of Neanderthal fossils from a single site, comprising 900 pieces from 70 to 80 individuals. The original bones are safely under lock and key in the Natural History Museum in Zagreb (see page 203), but a new, state-of-the-art interactive museum is being developed at Krapina, which will display replicas of the collection, and recount what we know about Neanderthal man. Much of the museum will be underground, as it has been conceived as a labyrinth, a voyage of discovery into the development of European thought about ancient man, along with the history of the site itself and its discovery. The museum is expected to be open by 2008.

In the meantime, you can visit the old museum here, and then walk up the path to the actual site, where you'll find life-size (and quite lifelike) statues of the Neanderthals brandishing clubs. One of them looks alarmingly like the exchange student Piers had in his last year at school.

If you want to stay, look no further than **Vuglec Breg** (✆ 049 345 015; f 049 345 032; www.vuglec-breg.hr), in the locality known as Škarićevo, in a fabulous location up in the hills between Krapina and Krapinske Toplice. A handful of old village houses have been beautifully restored and converted into accommodation with all mod cons, and there's a restaurant and vineyard attached, with excellent local wines (especially the whites). A double room goes for €70, while for €130 you get a small thatched house that sleeps six.

TRAKOŠĆAN Northeast from Krapina is the Zagorje's most-visited attraction, Trakošćan. It's billed as a 13th-century castle, but you don't have to read much of the small print – or use much architectural intelligence – to work out that what you're seeing here isn't medieval at all but mid-19th-century neo-Romantic all over. That doesn't make it any less worth visiting – although it's all a bit shabby and run down, it's still extraordinary inside and out, with a complete collection of the original (19th-century) furniture and fittings.

The castle was given to the powerful Drašković family in 1584, probably as a belated thank you for its role in putting down the peasants' uprising a decade earlier (see *Gornja Stubica* below). After the first century or so, the family didn't do much with Trakošćan, preferring to live at the better-appointed Klenovik (see below). But with the Romantic revival in full swing, they then spent a fortune – and more than 20 years – building the castle you see today, and damming and flooding the valley below to give themselves a decent lake.

Access is up a lovely spiralling path and through mock-defensive gates, overlooked by imaginatively crenellated walls and ramparts. Inside it's all heavy neo-Gothic. On the ground floor you'll find the Knights' Room, with lots of clumsy-looking armour and the usual gruesome array of pikes and swords. There's also a curious fireplace, with wooden dragons supporting the mantelpiece. At the other end of the building there's a Hunting Hall which verges dangerously close to self-parody.

Upstairs there's room after room of heavy furniture and heavier furnishings, hideous to most modern sensibilities, but a real insight into the mid-19th-century mindset of the ruling classes. You'll also see ten generations of smug Drašković portraits, by the famous local painter Nepozanti Slikar, and presumably his eponymous descendants – since they date from 1680 to at least 1823. (No, we're kidding – *nepozanti slikar* just means 'anonymous painter'.)

Far from anonymous are the paintings by Julijana Drašković (née Erdödy, 1847–1901). Much of her surviving work is here in the castle and – although most of it doesn't stand up to extended 21st-century scrutiny – there are several excellent impressionistic portraits.

Other things to look out for, amongst the absurdly chunky Baroque furniture, are an unusual three-seater neo-Gothic sofa (inspired no doubt by church architecture), superb stoves in every room (usually fed from behind, to avoid the unpleasantness of intrusive servants), and what must have been a boy's room on the top floor, with wallpaper consisting of tapestries depicting massive armies of tin soldiers on parade.

You can clear your head outside by a promenade around the lake – the whole circuit takes a leisurely 1.5 hours.

LEPOGLAVA AND KLENOVIK From Trakošćan it's about 10km southeast to **Lepoglava**, (in)famous mainly for being the site of Croatia's largest prison. The main reason for coming here – the town's pleasant enough, but nothing special – is the fine whitewashed Austro-Hungarian church, with saints in niches on the outside. Inside, the church has a curious right-curving nave, colourful frescoes and a big

Baroque altar – which you can see even if the church is closed, as there's a grille inside the portico you can peek through.

Northeast 10km from Lepoglava is Croatia's biggest castle, **Klenovik**, which claims to have 90 rooms and 365 windows. Built in the 17th century, it was for a brief time the seat of the Croatian parliament and is now a sanatorium, dealing mainly with respiratory complaints. You only visit today can if you're (a) patient.

BELEC Barely 10km southeast of Lepoglava as the crow flies, but on the other side of the 1,100m Ivančićica Mountains (you have to skirt round through Zlatar, and then head 8km north), is the village of Belec, and more importantly the **Church of St Mary of the Snow**. Simple enough on the outside, it's profligate Baroque gone mad once you get inside.

There's hardly an unadorned surface in sight. *Putti* proliferate off every balcony, mantelpiece and archway, extravagantly gestured saints camp it up, and the accumulated wealth of gilt, carving and paintwork is completely overwhelming. Restrained simplicity it ain't – it has to be seen to be believed. Although it's usually open only on Sunday mornings, the woman who lives opposite the gate has a key, and will let you in. Expect to make a small donation to the restoration fund.

MARIJA BISTRICA Heading south 10km from Zlatar brings you into Marija Bistrica, a pleasant little town dedicated to looking after the more than 600,000 pilgrims who come here every year, making it Croatia's premier pilgrimage site.

The reason? A late 15th- or early 16th-century Black Madonna, which already had a huge following, even before a fire in 1880 destroyed almost everything except the statue itself.

With pilgrims on the increase for centuries, the congregation has frequently outgrown the church, and the church has equally frequently had to be expanded. The current incarnation was completed in 1883 by Hermann Bollé, the man behind lots of buildings in Zagreb, including the cathedral.

From the outside, the **Pilgrimage Church of St Mary** is halfway between a castle and a cathedral. An elegant piazza leads through a gate into a half-cloister, lined with thousands of marble plaques of gratitude from pilgrims whose wishes have been granted over the years, and topped with paintings of specific miracles attributable to the Black Madonna.

Inside, the church is a quiet, reverential place, with a continuously shifting congregation of the hopeful (mostly older women) saying their prayers, but also seizing the opportunity to photograph and film the famous Madonna behind the altar.

Behind the church, there's an enormous open-air auditorium, which was built for the Pope's visit in 1998 (when he came here to beatify Cardinal Stepinac), and a Way of the Cross, leading up Calvary Hill. The church and town look lovely from the top, even if you haven't climbed up here on your knees.

You may want to steer clear, however – unless of course you're a pilgrim yourself – on 15 August, when thousands of people come to celebrate the Assumption of the Virgin Mary.

GORNJA STUBICA From Marija Bistrica it's 11km west to Gornja Stubica, home to the radically named **Museum of Peasant Uprisings** (Muzej Seljačkih Buna), housed in the local Oršić Palace.

In the 16th century, peasants were treated appallingly, overloaded with dues to foreign overlords, expected to fight their battles for them, and driven to the brink of starvation by people who lived idle lives in opulent palaces. By 1573, in this area, it was all too much, and the peasants revolted. The uprising was quickly and ruthlessly put down by the Bishop of Zagreb, a Drašković, who spread word that the ringleader, Matija Gubec, had been made king of the peasants. Within weeks he was horribly executed in St Mark's Square, in Zagreb, by being 'crowned' peasant king with a band of red-hot iron.

There's a dramatic communist-era statue of Gubec on the hill above the town, framed by a huge bronze frieze by Augustinčić (see page 244), depicting revolting peasants. The museum, over the hill behind the monument, is actually a bit of a misnomer, telling you more about the luxurious lifestyle of the oppressors than the beaten-down existence of the oppressed – though maybe that's the point: this is what you're meant to revolt against.

A roomful of furniture and trinkets only confirms the distance between rich and poor, though you can't help admiring the pocket sundial dating from 1755. 'What time is it, your honour?' 'I'm afraid I can't tell you – it's raining.' From here there's a bridge through to the rest of the collection, with a group of ragged-looking peasants on one side, and a couple of well-shod militia on the other. You can see that the peasants wouldn't have stood a chance.

Less than 20km from downtown Zagreb, and just five minutes from the Slovenian border, Samobor is an attractive little town, with a compact heart set on an elegant, elongated square. A shallow, trout-filled stream is spanned by narrow bridges, and it's a lovely place to sit and soak up the atmosphere while you're tucking into Samobor's culinary specialities.

With buses from Zagreb every half-hour (hourly on Sundays), it's easy to reach, and even makes a realistic alternative to staying in the capital. The friendly tourist office, located right on the main square, will set you up with good local information, and maps of the surrounding area, including the lovely Žumberak region, to which Samobor is the natural gateway.

 WHERE TO STAY AND EAT Samobor has one of our favourite hotels anywhere, the **Hotel Livadić** (⤫ 01 336 5850; f 01 336 5851; www.hotel-livadic.hr; dbls €65, suites €100), with a lovely flower-bedecked central courtyard and utterly charming rooms, with old furniture and good-sized bathrooms. It's an absolute steal compared with anything in Zagreb, with the real treat being a handful of gorgeous, beautifully renovated suites at the top of the building. An alternative is the **Hotel Lavica** (⤫ 01 332 4946; f 01 336 6611; www.lavica-hotel.hr; dbl €45), just across the river, with simple rooms and a brick-vaulted restaurant.

As a long-standing day treat for Zagreb's workers, Samobor is big on edible treats, and notably its famous *Samoborska kremšnita*, a mountain of cream filling, sandwiched between two slices of flaky pastry. The 'recipe' published by the tourist board makes it sound all too simple: 'Dress lightly. Throw a sweater over your shoulder. Take a vehicle of some kind. Go to main square of Samobor. Take a seat. Order and enjoy.'

The two best places to buy *kremšnita* – we did several tests – are U Prolazu and Gradska Slastičarnica, both on the main square, the latter slightly sweeter, but with lighter pastry than the former. But personally, in the cake department, our money's on the *rudarska greblica*, which is big on walnuts and not quite so creamy. As its name implies, it comes from the village of Rude, just up the valley toward Plešivica.

Samobor is also big on sausages, with a **Salami Festival** in April, and produces excellent local *muštarda* to go with them. If you're going the whole hog (insert sausage joke here), also make sure you try the local aperitif, *bermet*, which is red wine flavoured with herbs and spices; it's not to all tastes, but the locals love it.

For sit-down eating and drinking, Samobor is particularly blessed, although – perhaps because it's still focused on visitors from Zagreb, rather than international tourism – there's nothing especially upmarket.

The nicest bars are along the river (try **Ara**, **Gradua** or **Labirint**), though the **Havana Kafé** on the main square is groovy and popular.

For eats, the **Samoborska Klet**, off the north side of the main square down a short alley, offers a regular selection of sensibly priced dishes, while the **Samoborska Pivnica** serves up all the local specialities, and a particularly generous portion of *štrukli*, even if their terrace is actually part of a car park. There's also, at the west end of town, the **Bistro Oleander**, a hugely popular barbecue place, and the **Medved**, which is just a whisper more upmarket than the others, and does especially good sausages.

WHAT TO SEE AND DO If you can tempt yourself away from the cakes, the most obvious thing to see is Samobor's **Town Museum** (*open Tue–Fri 09.00–15.00, Sat & Sun 09.00–13.00; entry 8kn*), spread out over both floors of local composer Ferdo Livadić's solid town house. Downstairs there are two interesting 1:100 scale models, both by local model-maker Marijan Majdak: one of the castle above the town, as it was in 1776, and the other of the whole of Samobor in 1764 – with the only two things you'll recognise being the church and the Livadić house itself. Also check out the 'Samobor Chicken' (a possible rival to the Vučedol Partridge in Zagreb – see page 192), a small local collection of Roman coins, and a well-intentioned palaeontological display featuring everything from plastic dinosaurs right up to present-day objects. Upstairs, highlights include an 1877 penny-farthing, a 1920 Puch motorbike, and – if our notes are to be believed – an 1830 portrait of Scooby-Doo.

Samobor's other main museum is, if anything, even more eclectic. The **Marton Museum** (*open Sat & Sun 10.00–13.00; entry 20kn*) is housed in a fine building from 1841, just above the church, and comprises a private collection of furniture, paintings, glass and china, skilfully put together by local businessman Veljko Marton.

Up to the west of the town is Samobor's 13th-century castle, **Stari Grad**, and the 25-minute walk up to inspect the ruins will help get you in shape for the next culinary delight. Follow the path along the stream, then veer left when you see the tennis courts off to the right, and zigzag your way fairly steeply uphill to the overgrown, agreeable ruins of the fortress. Coming back, take the wider, flatter path that leads through the woods to the little Church of St Anne, where you can turn left past a wooden gazebo onto the road which brings you back into Samobor, or head uphill through the woods to another chapel, higher up.

More ambitious hiking – but not much more ambitious – is available in the **Samobrsko Gorje Mountains** further to the west of town. Increasingly popular at weekends (it's some of the nearest hiking to Zagreb, and not too demanding), you'll find the well-marked trails almost empty out of season, especially if you're here midweek – get a map from the tourist office.

The tourist office also has an excellent **cycle route** marked out, and a free map with English instructions on it. The circuit's only 24km long, but the first nine of these are all steeply uphill, gaining 450m – unless you're pretty fit, you may want to do the route in reverse, which makes the climb at a gentler gradient. The only sad thing is that (at the time of writing) there wasn't anywhere to rent a bike in Samobor.

As if the salami festival wasn't enough, Samobor also hosts a huge pre-Lent **carnival**. It's one of the most popular in Croatia, attracting hundreds of thousands of visitors, which makes it enormous fun – but no joke at all if you happen to be looking for a room.

Finally, Samobor is a great place to pick up **souvenirs**. On Stražnička, the street heading north out of the main square (to the left of the Hotel Livadić), you can find bead necklaces, *bermet* and other curiosities at the first shop, and paintings, metalwork and wood next door. At the top of the same street is the Filipec family shop, which is reckoned to be the best place locally for *muštarda*, while on the next street east (to the right of the hotel), you'll find Samoborska Delicije, the most upmarket shop in town, which does nice *licitar* hearts, homemade patés, local olive oil, wine and *rakija*, beautifully presented in attractive packaging and gift boxes.

THE ŽUMBERAK

Southwest of Zagreb, and tucked up against the Slovenian border, is the Žumberak region, a designated Nature Park (*www.ppzsg.hr*) which comprises a sparsely populated expanse of dense forests, steep hills and sleepy villages. You can't get to most places using public transport – indeed, lots of the smaller hamlets and villages don't even have metalled roads to them – but if you do have your own wheels it makes for a lovely region to explore at leisure (especially if you're cycling – see page 96).

The northern part of the Žumberak is mountainous and forested, while further to the south are the beautiful steep vineyards of the Plešivica region (see page 263). The obvious gateway is Samobor, though you can also access it from Karlovac or Jastrebarsko.

There's not much to do or see in the Žumberak itself – beyond enjoying the fine scenery and splendid vistas, and perhaps hiking or biking through the hills – but if you have wheels there's a good circuit you can do anticlockwise through the region, starting at Samobor, heading round to Karlovac and coming back via Jastrebarsko and the Plešivica vineyards. You'd need to allow at least two days to see everything, or skip various parts of the itinerary, as it's a minimum 200km circuit, with quite long sections on gravel roads. (The circuit works just as well starting in Karlovac, if that's where you're based.)

Start by heading due north to Bregana, but turn left before you get whisked into Slovenia. The road then follows the river (the Slovenian border) for about 10km, until you reach **Divlje Vode**, which becomes something of a minor recreation area at weekends. The restaurant here serves excellent local trout.

ŽUMBERAČKO EKO SELO Shortly after Divlje Vode, the road divides – take the left-hand fork, heading up to Žumberačko Eko Selo. After a short while the tarmac runs out, and you're on about 8km of gravel all the way up to the camp, a collection of wooden buildings centred on a biggish restaurant in a valley with a pretty stream running through it (it's just off to the right of the main gravel road, when you get as high up as you're going to go).

You can stay up here, in one of the wooden huts (€25 a head) – call Ivana ahead of time (she speaks English) for more detailed information on ☏ 095 905 4198 or ☏ 01 338 7472. You can also book yourself in for horseriding – there's a stable, which only adds to the thoroughly American-cowboy atmosphere. Even if you don't stay, do consider eating here – not only is the restaurant first-rate, it's also the last place for a long time ahead.

There's no question that the easiest way onwards is to head back the way you came, but if you're feeling adventurous then press on – at a number of points the network of gravel roads rejoins the tarred road which winds its way around the northern and western sides of the Žumberak. A good sense of direction and the best maps available will help, but are unlikely to prevent you from getting lost. Essentially you want to keep heading west and/or south, and don't be afraid to ask smallholders the way to towns on the main road – Kostanjevac, Pribić and Krašić are all good names to ask for.

Up here you'll find life going on the way it has for centuries, with tiny villages far, far from the rest of the world, and almost all the work in the small fields still being done by hand. On your way down towards Pribić and Krašić, it's worth briefly stopping at **Medven Draga**, where you'll find a couple of lovely old watermills.

PRIBIĆ The next place you come to after Medven Draga is Pribić – it's easy to overshoot, so keep your eyes peeled for a Byzantine-looking church on the right-hand side of the main road, and park here.

You'd certainly never know it now, but Pribić was once an important Greek Catholic centre. In the face of Turkish expansion, Orthodox Slavs were brought into the region and protected by the Austro-Hungarians, as long as they agreed to recognise the Pope – hence Greek Catholics. Today all there's left to see is the outside of the church and the doomed 'castle' next door, which is gradually losing its battle with the encroaching vegetation (though there did seem to be some restorative efforts going on – maybe – in the summer of 2006).

The church itself sits on a tiny islet, reached over a diminutive bridge. The mosaics on the front are still lovely, kneeling angels flanking a Madonna and Child amongst stylised lilies. Over the doorway is a fine carved coat of arms bracketed by fanciful ropes and tassels. Look more closely and you'll also see some fine sardonic architectural flourishes, in the form of nightmare gargoyles and a couple of cheesed-off parrots.

KRAŠIĆ From Pribić it's a short, straight run down to Krašić, the home town of Cardinal Stepinac (see page 178), and the place where he was kept under house arrest during the final years of his life, after being released from Lepoglava. In front of the church there's a statue of the cardinal, while behind it, in the parish priest's house, his two-room flat has been preserved the way he left it. To visit, ring the bell and wait for a nun to let you in. There isn't much to see – the bed he died in, his writing desk, and quite a few photos of the cardinal (looking worryingly like Vladimir Putin in some shots) – but it's a poignant place all the same. It would be churlish not to make a donation as you leave.

The church itself was rebuilt in 1913, and first impressions of the plain exterior can be misleading – look out for the dramatic Jugendstil touches, with stern female friezes built into the walls. Inside, there's not a whole lot to comment on, though the vaulting is attractive enough, and the altar is positively understated – by Zagorje Baroque standards, anyway.

OZALJ From Krašić it's a 10km dog-leg west to Ozalj (another turning that's easy to miss – the main road to Karlovac, which you don't want, goes southeast), where you'll find the best of the region's castles.

In a perfect situation, high up above the River Kupa, the medieval settlement here was owned by the Frankopans from 1398, and taken over by the Zrinskis in 1550 – the impressive entrance tower was commissioned by Juraj Zrinski in 1599. During the 18th century, the medieval village was converted into a defensive castle, with the only access being across the drawbridge; the stone bridge you walk across today was built in 1821. It's being restored, but is already a wonder, and has everything you'd want in a castle – towers, solid bastions, ramparts, and great views down to the river.

There's not much else to see in Ozalj, but down in the town, by the bridge across the Kupa, have a look at the neo-Gothic building by the water – it's actually a hydro-electric plant, built in 1908 and still operational today.

From Ozalj it's only about 15km to Karlovac (see page 265), which is a great place to stop and spend the night. And from Karlovac, it's 20km northeast to the one-street town of Jastrebarsko, which is the access point for the Plešivica Wine Road (which gets you back to Samobor, if you're on the circuit), as well as the fish lakes and bird reserve at Crna Mlaka.

PLEŠIVICA WINE ROAD

The 25km road from Jastrebarsko to Samobor is among the most beautiful in Croatia, winding its way up into the Plešivica wine-growing region and then down a long, pretty valley through the village of Rude. It's well worth stopping in at one of the dozen or so vineyards for a tasting if you have time, and can persuade your designated driver it's a good thing – or indeed stay over (see listings below).

Make a special effort to sample the local speciality, Portugizac Plešivica, a claret-like red, though personally we're much keener on the crisp white Rajnski Rizling which is also made here. The Samobor or Karlovac tourist offices should be able to furnish you with a copy of the useful 'Plešivička Vinska Cesta' (Plešivica Wine Road) leaflet, which helps with navigation (though you also need a good road map as well – the best one by far, if you can find it, is the map issued by the Jastrebarsko Tourist Board).

The Plešivica countryside is delightful. Apart from the vineyards, there are lots of fruit trees in the steep fields, and in summer every village has hay drying picturesquely on the charming Slovenian-style latticed hayricks – designed surely with aesthetics rather than practicality in mind. Wagons and trailers full of brightly coloured beehives are strategically placed to allow the bees access to the best of the local nectar, and romantic hilltop churches crest every horizon.

WHERE TO STAY AND EAT

✘ Restoran Ivančić Plešivica 45; ☎ 01 629 3303

Housed in a large green building that's easy to spot from below, & with a view to die for from the terrace, this local favourite has been serving up its own homemade specialities like *pršut*, dried sausage & cheese since 1999. Famous for its goulash, meat stews & hearty soups, it's also vegetarian-friendly. Relatively expensive, & extremely popular at weekends – booking strongly recommended. *Open 12.00–15.00 & 18.00–21.00 daily.*

⌂ Krešimir Režek Plešivica 39; ☎ 01 629 4836; ☏ 01 629 4387

Down below Ivančić, this winery not only does tastings but has a handful of nice rooms, some with the same wonderful views you get from the restaurant above. Krešimir himself is friendly & helpful, but doesn't have much in the way of English; fortunately his excellent Rajnski Rizling does a great job of breaking down language barriers. *Dbl rooms €40 with b/fast, €60 HB. Open by appointment.*

✘ Velimir Korak, Plešivica 34; ☎ 01 629 3094

Above Režek, near the church, this place also has a stunning view out over the neighbouring vineyards, & is one of the nicest places to try wines or their locally made *rakija*, including a fabulous *oskoruša* liqueur, made from the fruit of their service tree (*Sorbus domestica*). A tasting area is set out in the garden under the shade of the lime trees, & there's also a family-run restaurant serving up tasty local specialities for groups (book in advance). *Open Fri 12.00–21.00, Sat 09.00–21.00.*

⌂ Klet Jana Prodin Dol; ☎ 01 628 7372; ☏ 01 628 7337

If the setting isn't as picturesque as the other places listed above, the welcome is just as warm, & you can stay in one of the newly refurbished rooms upstairs. It's a bit hard to find: from Prodin Dol go 2.1km south on a gravel track

264

marked 'Klet Jana', then turn hard right at the tatty wooden sign 'Vinsko Kuća Jana' & continue up a few hundred metres. If you're coming from the south, look for a sign that says 'Klet Jana' to the right, then follow the gravel road uphill for 1.7km to the junction & turn left at the same tatty wooden sign. *Open by appointment.*

♀ **Mladina** Lokošin Dol; ✆ 01 627 9030
Although it's easily the largest & probably best-known winery in the area, there's nothing much to see, it's located opposite a quad racing track & the owners don't speak English. Apart from that, it's great. *Open by appointment.*

KARLOVAC

Most people never see more of Karlovac than the big town suburbs and housing blocks on the outskirts as they speed past on the motorway, but dig a little deeper and you'll find a wonderful provincial old town and somewhere great to stay.

Karlovac (originally Carlstadt) was created from nothing, by the Austro-Hungarians, as a defence against the Turks, with the foundations being laid on 13 July 1579. A Renaissance six-pointed star defined the limits of the town, and its moats were kept well supplied with water by the citadel's situation, between the Kupa and Korana rivers.

As the Turkish threat receded, Karlovac grew in size and importance – notwithstanding a catastrophic fire in 1692 which razed it to the ground – and became a wealthy and influential provincial capital. Baroque houses and palaces sprang up, and the town walls were pulled down. The shape of the old town is still clearly defined, however, with the moats and earthworks now forming a near-continuous circuit of lovely parks and gardens around the former citadel, or Zvijezda (star).

Karlovac's great modern claim to fame is its local brewery, one of Croatia's first, which produces the excellent, and deservedly popular beer, Karlovačko Pivo, which you'll see all over the country.

GETTING THERE AND AROUND Getting to Karlovac is easy – it's under an hour from Zagreb, and both buses and trains run pretty much every half-hour. There are also good onward connections to Rijeka and Zadar.

The bus station is less than ten minutes southwest of the old town – head up the main north–south axis, Prilaz Vjećeslava Holjevca, and then turn right along Kralja Tomislava, which takes you all the way in. The train station is on the other side of the River Kupa, a kilometre north, also on Prilaz Vjećeslava Holjevca. Just east of the main bridge is the central district where you'll find the Hotel Carlstadt and the tourist office, on Petra Zrinskog, which is also known as Korzo, with the old town just behind it, away from the Kupa, to the southeast.

The **tourist office** (047 600 606; f 047 642 612; www.karlovac-touristinfo.hr) has good maps and can help you find a private room. They also have an excellent set of maps aimed at cyclists who want to pedal around Karlovac County, and are keen participants in the 'Bike & Bed' initiative (www.bicikl.hr/bike-bed).

 WHERE TO STAY AND EAT Karlovac has a handful of places to stay, and with such good connections to Zagreb it's a viable alternative to staying in the capital. Smartest is the **Korana Sraković** (047 609 090; f 047 609 091; www.hotelkorana.hr; dbls

€116–125), an excellent four-star establishment in a gracious building right on the banks of the River Korana. The hotel has tastefully furnished rooms and there's a nice restaurant which serves up excellent local specialities such as quail and venison (though there's plenty for vegetarians too) with a wonderful terrace overlooking the river.

A good alternative is the **Carlstadt** (\f *047 611 111; www.carlstadt.hr; dbl* €60), situated handily right across the street from the tourist office. With a substantial buffet breakfast, it's exceptionally good value.

Karlovac has plenty of places to eat and drink, though fewer within the 'star' than you'd expect. That's because when the old town was bombed out in the homeland war, all the action moved up onto the Korzo, and it largely remains there – though there's a sense that things are creeping back into the quieter old town.

The three cafés next door to one another opposite the tourist office – **Pivnica Carlstadt**, **Mozart** and **Otto** – are the busiest places, which is a bit of a shame as they're on the main road through town, though there is a lovely new fountain with a pair of mermaids attractively sitting in it between you and the traffic. The ritziest place to drink is **Papa's Bar**, a shameless copy of Hemingway (in Zagreb or Dubrovnik) without the pretension. Formerly the Gradska Kavana, it's in a perfect location with nice teak furniture and a big terrace overlooking the park. It's not cheap, but it's groovy, cheerful and well worth paying for.

The swankiest place to eat is the **Hotel Korana** (see above), but our absolute favourite is **Tiffany** (which doesn't, curiously, do breakfast), a busy, cheap and cheerful pizzeria with a wood-fired oven that's recently expanded its menu to include grills and barbecue dishes. The *mala* pizza is a good size, the *velika* is what it says (large) and the *monster* is really a meal for six. Don't be put off by the surroundings – it's located down an alley to the left-hand side of the supermarket, which is itself down the street to the left of the Hotel Carlstadt.

Finally, there's Karlovac's annual **beer festival**, which takes place on the last Friday of August (and goes on well into Saturday, as you'd expect). This used to happen in the main square, with the central fountain converted into a beer pump for the occasion, which was loads of fun, but the festival is now held on the Korana River, with international folklore performances and – of course – lots of drinking. If you're in the area it's absolutely not to be missed.

WHAT TO SEE AND DO The old town is centred on the big main square, Trg Bana Jelačića, which is still rather forlorn and abandoned, following the damage sustained in the 1990s war. There's talk of one of the big buildings here being turned into a hotel, which would liven the place up – even a café terrace would help – but for the time being it's still only talk.

Check out the **Plague Column** on the west side of the square, dating from 1691, and then move smartly on to the **Franciscan Monastery and Holy Trinity Church**, on the corner. Here you'll find fine Baroque altars and a series of dramatic, neck-cricking, 18th-century frescoes across the ceiling – why they were painted alternately upside down and the right way up?

Heading north out of the square towards the Kupa River you'll see an old **pharmacy**, called Crnom Orla (the black eagle), which is worth stopping in at as it retains most of its original 1726 fittings. The street leads through to the elegant Trg Strossmayer, where you'll find some vestigial ruins from Karlovac's first ever church, as well as the **Town Museum** (Gradski Muzej; *open Tue–Fri 09.00–15.00, Sat & Sun 10.00–12.00; entry 10kn*), housed in a former Frankopan summer residence.

The museum is a fascinating collection of everything from fossils to Roman fragments to local art to peasant costumes to civic souvenirs – it's only a pity that the captions are in Croatian only, which make it a bit hard to follow.

Look out for works by the local artist Vjekoslav Karas (1821–58). Some of them are way ahead of their time, wonderfully insightful portraits which are practically modernist, while others are embarrassingly amateurish, perhaps reflecting Karas's poor state of mental health. After a failed suicide attempt in Đakovo, where he was the guest of Bishop Strossmayer (a keen art collector), Karas successfully drowned himself in the Korana River at Karlovac, aged just 37.

The last room of the museum features an excellent collection of peasant costumes and crafts, from pottery and weaving to embroidery and basket work.

Continuing north, towards the Korzo and the Korana River, it's well worth taking a turn around the parks which were formerly the **walls and moats** of the old citadel – allow a half-hour or so for the full circuit.

Heading anticlockwise, the first thing you'll see is a small pink *glorietta*, primarily dedicated to Croatia's fallen in World War I, and the vast neoclassical façade of the

Karlovac Bank. Heading west, you'll see a large, graffiti-strewn, concrete plinth, which – until its destruction by the locals in the homeland war – was the base of a huge anti-fascist monument. A little further on you'll see **Kino Edison**, which was Croatia's first cinema. It's still operational, though rather damp and run down; the present owner bought it for the well-situated café terrace, rather than cinematographic entertainment.

Beyond the cinema is Karlovac's theatre, the endearing **Zorin Dom**, which was opened in 1892, and has a small version of the Ivan Meštrović masterpiece, the *History of the Croats* (see page 172), sitting in front of it.

If you have time, it's also well worth visiting **Dubovac Castle** (*open Tue–Sun 10.00–18.00; entry 10kn*), up on the hill 2km west of town (it's a short drive or a half-hour walk). The castle dates from 1339 (or possibly even earlier), and was a Frankopan and then Zrinski stronghold right through to the beginning of the 19th century, when it was taken over by the French, who added crenellations to make it look more appealingly medieval (there's a picture in the town museum of what this looked like). Fortunately, it recovered its genuinely medieval look in the 20th century, and you get a great view out over the town from the top of the tower – check out the excellent relief map of the whole area, which shows all the different castles and rivers in the region. And if you're here in May, don't miss out on the annual medieval fair which takes place here.

Finally, if you're hot and bothered – and it certainly can be baking – head down to the Korana River to the wonderful **beach**, just ten minutes from the old town centre; you can bathe in the weir here, which is excellent, or head out to less busy beaches on the Mrežnica River, 3km south of town.

SOUTH OF KARLOVAC – SLUNJ AND THE RASTOKE MILLS

Heading south out of Karlovac, towards the Plitvice Lakes, brings you (after about 50km, and 20km short of the lakes) to the former Austro-Hungarian garrison town of **Slunj**. Badly damaged during the war of the 1990s, the town's churches at least have now been fully restored, along with the main reason for coming here, the **Rastoke Mills**.

Built to take advantage of the waterfalls where the Slunjčica River drops into the Korana, some of the watermills are now back in working order and a stroll around them is a delight. If you want to swim make sure you choose the Korana, not the Slunjčica – the former warms up to a balmy 28°C in summer, while the latter never rises above a chilly 14°C. If its 'first-class trouts' you're fishing for, however, then the Slunjčica is your man.

PLITVICE LAKES NATIONAL PARK

Croatia's best-known and most-visited natural attraction – and a UNESCO World Heritage Site since 1979 – is the Plitvice Lakes National Park (☎ 053 751 015; www.np-plitvicka-jezera.hr; open every day of the year, from 09.00–17.00 in winter &

08.00–19.00 *in summer*). Covering a total of nearly 300km², the prize here is 16 lakes, falling from one to the next in a series of gushing waterfalls. The lakes are set in deep forests still populated by bears, wolves and wild boar, and are all the more unusual for being found in the middle of a typically dry *karst* region, where surface water is extremely rare.

The national park has been very carefully exploited, and although it can get busy – 600,000 people come annually, averaging around 4,000 people a day in the summer months – the crowds are rarely intolerable. Traffic is encouraged round one-way systems to avoid congestion, and the routes are often carried along attractive wooden walkways serving the dual purpose of avoiding erosion and allowing people to walk over, under, across and alongside the waterfalls, and around the lakes.

The whole park ranges in altitude from 380m to 1,280m, but the lakes are all situated between 502m and 637m, with the largest single waterfall (Veliki Slap) being nearly 70m tall. The combination of running water and altitude makes the park wonderfully refreshing almost all through the summer, although it can be cold and gloomy – not to mention frozen solid – in winter. April and October are the best times to visit – the former with the water flow increased by melting snows, and the latter with the deciduous woods enriched with fabulous autumn colours.

GETTING THERE AND AWAY Plitvice is situated a little over halfway down the main road from Zagreb to Zadar. Regular buses run from both, and also up from Split. The park has two entrances, wittily called Ulaz 1 and Ulaz 2.

In theory Ulaz 1 (the northern entrance) serves the lower lakes, while Ulaz 2 (the southern entrance) is the access point for the upper ones, but for most people Ulaz 2 is the more useful. It's here that you'll find most of the infrastructure, including the three hotels, the tourist office with access to private accommodation, a post office, a shop and a self-service restaurant – and it's in fact within easy reach of both the upper and lower lakes.

If you don't have your own transport, then leaving the park may be more difficult than arriving. Regular buses pass through on their way to Zadar, Zagreb and Split, but if these are full, or the driver doesn't like the cut of your jib, they have a habit of cruising right on past.

Entry to the national park costs a fairly hefty 100kn in summer (55kn in winter), though the money is well spent, going towards the park's upkeep and protection. On the ticket is a wonderful series of hieroglyphs explaining the park rules, most of which go without saying: don't pick flowers, make fires, engrave trees, steal nests or break stalactites. Some of the others aren't so obvious: don't leave the paths, sleep rough, go paddling in the lakes or dance wildly around to the sound of your boom-box.

WHERE TO STAY AND EAT There are three hotels in the park, the **Bellevue**, the **Plitvice** and the **Jezero** (*central reservations for all three, as well as tourist information and private rooms on* ☏ *053 751 015;* f *053 751 001*), with prices rising slightly and quality rising significantly as you move up the scale – book way, way ahead, if you want to stay.

For eating, your options are fairly limited. There's a good-value self-service restaurant at Ulaz 2, though it's not always open in the evening, while at Ulaz 1 there's the capacious **Lička Kuća Restaurant**, serving meaty local specialities. Otherwise the hotels all have restaurants but they may be full with their own residents. If you do get in at the Jezero's restaurant, downstairs from reception, the tagliatelle with truffles is truly excellent. Alternatively, you can pick up picnic food at the mini-market at Ulaz 2.

WHAT TO SEE AND DO The lakes were created and are maintained by their unusual vegetation – the mosses, algae and other freshwater plants absorb the calcium in the water and then deposit it as calciferous mud. This can be seen clearly as a white coating on submerged tree trunks and roots in the smaller lakes. The water flow causes this calciferous mud to be carried to the lips of the lakes, and deposited there, eventually solidifying as travertine (*tufa*), with the long-term effect that the whole lake system is gradually gaining altitude.

In the short term, the effect is that lots of people are keen to come and see Plitvice, and life has been organised so that this is as easy as possible – to the extent that there's a panoramic train ride, a couple of boats on one of the largest lakes, and a series of itineraries from one to ten hours' long which take in the most scenic parts of the park.

After the initial impression of being almost too looked after has worn off, it tends to be replaced by something akin to euphoria – the lakes really are beautiful, after all, and you'd have to be very determined not to be impressed by that much moving water. You can even begin to see why people who live in these conditions start believing in water gods.

Each of the lakes seems to be a different colour, ranging from turquoise to emerald through every blue and green you could imagine. In places the lakes seem as still and reflective as a cathedral, elsewhere they run away fast, frothing through steep gullies and shooting out from fissures in the rock. The magical noise of falling water drowns out even the shrillest of small children. On the less-frequented paths it's easy to imagine the bears and wolves, as you walk across a deeply shaded bed of leaves, crunching underfoot.

In a perfect world you'd have at least two full days (ie: three nights) to explore the whole park, but you can get a good impression of it all in a single day. Even if you're on an excursion, up from the coast or down from Zagreb, and you have only a couple of hours here, you won't regret it.

Apart from the marked itineraries, which lead you round the best-known sights, there are many other paths open to the public in the national park, though access to them is quietly discouraged by the park management, as there have been incidents of people despoiling nature off the beaten track. If you are wandering away from the marked trails, be ecologically friendly, and stay on the paths.

If you're doing any serious walking – or even if you're just interested – the park publishes an excellent 1:50,000 scale map of the area, including all the footpaths, with a 1:25,000 scale bird's-eye view of the lakes themselves on the reverse, along with all sorts of useful information about the lakes' relative altitudes etc. With the aid of this you can easily find a couple of days' walking in the area, none of which is too strenuous.

It's inadvisable, however, to be in the wilds after nightfall – the bears and wolves avoid the main paths and the crowds, but they do patrol at night. The wolves are normally seen only in winter, but a hungry bear, or one which thinks you're too close to its cubs, may be inquisitive. Walk in the daytime and stay on the paths marked on the maps and you'll be quite safe. There are absolutely no wild animals round here which would attack in the daytime unless seriously provoked.

If you're in Plitvice on the last Sunday of May there's a folk wedding held by Veliki Slap. This was once no doubt a highly traditional affair, but now has the air of being staged for the tourists. Nonetheless, even the most cynical visitor should be impressed by the traditional dress, the falling water all but drowning out the songs, and the folk dancing and festivities held afterwards.

THE TUROPOLJE

The Turopolje is the region southeast of Zagreb, characterised by old villages and wooden houses and churches, bordered by the meandering Sava to the east, and bracketed by Zagreb to the northwest and Sisak to the southeast. Exploring the region is not really possible without your own transport, although you can get to Velika Mlaka and Velika Gorica on Zagreb bus route #268. If you're planning on exploring the region in any detail, get maps and information ahead of time from the friendly and helpful Zagreb County Tourist Office (see page 69 for details).

In **Velika Gorica**, the de facto capital of the region, it's well worth stopping in at the **Museum of the Turopolje** (*Muzej Turopolje; open Tue–Fri 09.00–16.00, Sat & Sun 10.00–13.00; entry 8kn*). The museum is situated in a nice pastel building on the main street – because of Velika Gorica's one-way system, this is actually the road back towards Zagreb – and contains a small art gallery downstairs and the main museum upstairs. The collection is the usual hotchpotch of everything from ethnographic exhibits to artefacts and images which are historically important to the region. Check out the mammoth tusks and molar, and a small room of naïve art, and in particular the bitter 1977 work by Dragutin Tombetaš, entitled *Gastarbeiter in öl* (immigrant workers in a sardine can).

The Turopolje is most famous for its old **wooden churches**, of which more than a dozen remain – though some of them are spectacularly hard to find. If you see only one, make it **St Barbara's**, which is incongruous amongst the suburban houses of **Velika Mlaka**, off to the left, just before you get to Pleso Airport. The all-wooden church was originally built in 1642, and the decorative work inside covers every available surface. Most interesting of all is the double altarpiece, which folds out to reveal further religious scenes behind. If the church is closed – which it is, usually – ask for Ljubica Lacković, who has a key (and will expect you to make a donation to the church's upkeep for her trouble). Another wooden church which is easy to see is the **Chapel of the Wounded Jesus** which you'll have noticed if you took a shuttle bus or taxi on arrival, as it's right by Pleso Airport.

The southeastern end of the Turopolje – marked by the first bridge across the Sava since Zagreb – is dominated by the industrial town of **Sisak**. The solid **medieval castle** on the river doesn't entirely compensate for the huge oil refinery here, or the complete absence of road directions. Sisak is however the northern gateway to the Lonjsko Polje.

LONJSKO POLJE

Downstream from Sisak, the River Sava meanders slowly through the great marshy swamplands of the Lonjsko Polje. Prone to frequent flooding (the Sava can rise by up to 10m) and full of fish, the area is hugely popular with migrating birds, and especially with storks. The reedy shores of the ox-bow lakes also make for excellent nesting grounds for wading birds such as white egrets, grey herons and spoonbills.

Spotted Turopolje pigs root through the flooded oak forests, while dark, chunky Posavina horses – protected, and seen only in this region – graze in the summer pastures. Rustic villages preserve traditional oak houses, with barns on the ground floor and external wooden stairs leading to the living accommodation upstairs. It's a rare chance to see a landscape which was once common across central Europe.

On top of many of the houses in the area, and sometimes on platforms on telegraph poles, you'll see big, tatty storks' nests, and (if you're here between April and August) plenty of big, tatty storks too. They're most endearing. The storks arrive here in spring, and ship out during August and September.

Lonjsko Polje (*www.pp-lonjsko-polje.hr*) was declared a Nature Park in 1990, but you wouldn't necessarily know it – apart from the uninformative signs at the park's borders. The park headquarters claims to be in Jasenovac, but it most definitely isn't, and though there's an information point of sorts in the main stork village, Čigoć, at number 26, on both occasions we visited it was firmly closed. The problem seems to be one of understaffing, but you should be able to speak to someone on the phone (\/f *044 715 115*). The office is officially open daily from 08.00–16.00, but if you find it closed then call Davor Anzil on his mobile (m *098 222 085*).

Fortunately, most visitors will be content enough to drive along the pretty 70km road, most of which is now tarred, which runs through the park from Sisak to Jasenovac – public transport's not really an option. The villages along here are among the prettiest in the region, and all have storks in greater or fewer numbers, along with yards full of ducks, chickens, bantams and the occasional turkey. Many of the older houses are collapsing in on themselves, but a good number have been restored as weekenders. If it weren't for the total lack of accommodation, it would make for the perfect cycle ride.

From Sisak it's 30km to Čigoć, via the single-street villages of Topolovac, Prelošćica, Lukavec Posavski and Gušće. After Čigoć it's another 40km on to Jasenovac, passing through Kratečko, Možilovčica, Suvoj, Lonja, Trebez, Puška, Krapje and Drenov Bok on the way. There is a handful of places where you can sometimes eat, though you definitely shouldn't count on it.

More serious birdwatchers should contact the park office in advance (if they can

– the staff are even more elusive than the black stork), as there are several special ornithological reserves, protecting some 236 species of bird.

If you're in the area (or just driving along the *autocesta* east of Zagreb) it's well worth stopping in at the 18th-century **Church of Our Lady of the Snows**, in the otherwise unremarkable town of **Kutina**.

The plain, simple exterior of the church hides a plain, simple interior. No, of course it doesn't. Inside, it's wildly over-decorated, with stucco, *putti*, plaster saints, carved pilasters, gilt, medallions, *trompe l'oeil*, the whole gamut. The main altar, entirely filling the sanctuary, is practically unwatchable.

13 Language

The official language is Croatian, written using a Latin alphabet. For 98.5% of the population this is their mother tongue.

Croatian is a tough language to learn, but words are nothing like as difficult to pronounce as you'd think, since every letter always has a unique pronunciation – albeit often not the same as in English. Although you're unlikely to have time to learn much Croatian, grab at least a handful of words and phrases to take with you – the effort will be richly rewarded.

The Croatian language comes from the group described by linguists as Serbo-Croat, meaning that Serbs, Croats and Bosnians can readily understand each other – not that you'd necessarily know this, judging by the strife of the past 20 (or even 2,000) years. Within Croatia itself there are also regional variations and dialects, with the ones you'll most likely notice being the three different ways Croats have of saying 'What?'. The official version – used in the media – is the Slavonian 'Što?', but in Zagreb you'll hear 'kaj?' and along the coast it's invariably 'ča?'.

The use of the Latin alphabet is largely to do with religion, and the east–west division of the Roman Empire – it was in Croatia in the 9th century that Sts Cyril and Methodius invented the Glagolitic alphabet, which was converted by St

Clement, in Ohrid (now in the Former Yugoslav Republic of Macedonia), into the Cyrillic alphabet, variants of which are now used throughout the Orthodox world. You won't see Cyrillic – unless you happen into an Orthodox or Greek Catholic church.

Most people speak at least one foreign language, and English is widely understood and spoken – and especially so by the under-40s.

PRONUNCIATION

Croatian words aren't anything like as hard to pronounce as you might expect them to be – just concentrate on pronouncing each letter the same way every time, and you won't go far wrong.

A	as in party	E	as in pet
B	as in bed	F	as in free
C	as in fats, bats	G	as in goat
Č, č	as in nurture, culture	H	as in hat
Ć, ć	as in chew, chump	I	as in feet, pizza
D	as in dote	J	as in yet
Đ, đ	as in George, jam (sometimes written Dj, dj, to help non-natives)	K	as in kept
		L	as in leg
		M	as in mother

N	as in **n**o	T	as in **t**oo
O	as in h**o**t	U	as in l**oo**k
P	as in **p**ie	V	as in **v**ery
R	as in ai**r**	Z	as in **z**oo
S	as in **s**and	Ž, ž	as in trea**s**ure
Š, š	as in **sh**ovel, **ch**ampagne		

USEFUL WORDS AND PHRASES

COURTESIES

hello/bye (informal)	*bok* (familiarly *bok bok*)
cheers!	*živjeli!* [zhi-vel-ee]
good morning	*dobro jutro* [dob-ro you-tro]
good day	*dobar dan* [dobber dan]
good evening	*dobro večer* [dob-ro vetch-air]
good night (on leaving)	*laku noć* [lakoo notch]
good luck (as a salutation)	*sretno* (old miners' greeting) [sret-no]
how are you?	*kako ste?* [ka-ko stay]
I'm fine, thank you	*dobro, hvala* [dob-ro, hfar-la]
please/thank you	*molim/hvala* [mo-leem/hfar-la]
thank you very much	*hvala lijepo* [hfar-la lee-yepo]
excuse me	*izvinite/sori* [iz-vin-iter/sorry]

| goodbye | *doviđenja* [<u>doe</u>-vee <u>jen</u>-ya] |

BASIC WORDS

yes/no	*da/ne* [dar/nay] (*nema* = emphatic no) [<u>nay</u>-ma]
that's right	*tako je* [ta-ko yay]
OK	*OK* [okay]
maybe	*možda* [mozh-da]
large/small	*veliko/malo* [veli-ko/mar-lo]
	(*velika/mala* are feminine forms)
more/less	*više/manje* [vee-sh/man-ye]
good/bad	*dobro/loše* [<u>dob</u>-ro/lo-sh]
hot/cold	*toplo/hladno* [top-lo/hlad-no]
toilet	*zahod* [zar-hod] (also *toalet* [toe-a-let], WC [vay-say])
men/women	*muški/ženski* [moosh-kee/zhen-skee]

NUMBERS

zero	*nula* [<u>noo</u>-la]	five	*pet* [pet]
one	*jedan* [<u>yeh</u>-dan]	six	*šest* [shest]
two	*dva* [dvar]	seven	*sedam* [<u>seh</u>-dam]
three	*tri* [tree]	eight	*osam* [<u>o</u>-sam]
four	*četiri* [<u>tchet</u>-ree]	nine	*devet* [<u>dev</u>-et]

284

ten	*deset* [<u>deh</u>-set]	fifty	*pedeset* [<u>ped</u>-deh-set]
twelve	*dvanaest* [<u>dvar</u>-na-est]	one hundred	*stotina* [<u>sto</u>-teena]
fifteen	*petnaest* [<u>pet</u>-na-est]	one thousand	*hiljada* [<u>hill</u>-yarda]
twenty	*dvadeset* [<u>dvar</u>-deh-set]		

QUESTIONS

how?	*kako?* [ka-ko]
how much?	*koliko?* [ko-lee-ko]
what's your name?	*kako se zovete?* [ka-ko say zov-et-e]
when?	*kada?* [ka-da]
where?	*gdje?* [gud-ee-ya]
who?	*tko?* [teko]
why?	*zašto?* [<u>za</u>-shto]
do you speak English?	*govorite li engleski?* [gov-<u>or</u>-itay lee en-gleski]
how do you say in Croatian?	*kako se to kaže na hrvatskom?* [ka-ko say toe ka-zhay na hair-vat-skom]
can you tell me the way to ...?	*možete mi reći put do ... ?* [mo-<u>zhet</u>-e mee retchi put doe]
how do I get to ...?	*kako mogu doći do ... ?* [ka-ko moe-goo <u>do</u>-tchi doe]
is this the right way to ...?	*je li ovo pravi put do ... ?* [yay lee ovo <u>prar</u>-vee put doe]

is it far to walk?	*je li daleko pješice…?*
	[yay lee dal-ecko <u>pyay</u>-shee-tzay]
can you show me on the map?	*možete mi pokazati na karti?*
	[mo-zhet-ay mee pocka-zarti na <u>kar</u>-tee]

SHOPPING

bank	*banka* [banka]	market	*dućan/tržnica/market*
bookshop	*knjižara* [ke-<u>nyee</u>-zhara]		[<u>doo</u>-tchan/
chemist	*ljekarna/apoteka*		terzh-neetza/market]
	[lee-<u>ye</u>-karna/apo-tecka]	money	*novac* [<u>no</u>-vatz]
shop	*dućan* [<u>doo</u>-tchan]		

POST

post office	*pošta* [<u>posh</u>-ta]	paper	*papir* [pap-<u>eer</u>]
letter	*pismo* [<u>piz</u>-mo]	stamp	*poštanska marka* (or
envelope	*omotnica* [omot-<u>nitza</u>]		*just marka*)
postcard	*razglednica*		[<u>posh</u>-tanska mar-ka]
	[raz-gled-<u>nitza</u>]		

GETTING AROUND

| bus/bus station | *autobus/autobusni kolodvor* |
| | [out-o-<u>boos</u>/out-o-<u>boosnee</u> kolo-dvor |

train/express train	*vlak/brzi vlak* [vlack/berzee vlack]
main train station/	*glavni kolodvor/željeznički kolodvor*
railway station	[glav-nee kolo-dvor/zhel-<u>yez</u>-neetchki kolo-dvor]
plane/airport	*avion/zračna luka* or *aerodrom*
	[av-ion/zratch-na <u>loo</u>-ka or air-o-drom]
car/taxi	*auto/taxi* [out-o/taksi]
petrol/petrol station	*benzin/benzinska postaja* or *stanica*
	[ben-zin/ben-zinska <u>pos</u>-taya or <u>stan</u>-itza]
entrance/exit	*ulaz/izlaz* [oo-laz/iz-laz]
arrival/departure	*dolazak/odlazak* [do-<u>laz</u>-ak/odd-<u>laz</u>-ak]
open/closed	*otvoreno/zatvoreno* [otvo-<u>ren</u>-o/zatvo-<u>ren</u>-o]
here/there	*ovdje/tamo* [ov-<u>dee</u>-ye/<u>tar</u>-mo]
near/far	*blizu/daleko* [bleezu/dal-ecko]
left/right	*lijevo/desno* [lee-<u>yeh</u>-vo/des-no]
straight on	*ravno* [rav-no]
ahead/behind	*naprijed/iza* [nap-ree-<u>yed</u>/eeza]
up/down	*gore/dolje* [go-reh/dol-yeh]
under/over	*ispod/preko* [iz-pod/precko]
north/south	*sjever/jug* [syeh-vair/yoog]
east/west	*istok/zapad* [iz-tok/zap-ad]
road/bridge	*cesta/most* [tzesta/most]

hill/mountain	*brežuljak/planina* [breh-zhul-yak/plan-eena]
village/town	*selo/grad* [seh-lo/grad]
waterfall	*slap* [slap]

ACCOMMODATION

reservation	*rezervacija* [rez-air-vatz-eeya]
passport	*putovnica* [put-ov-nitza]
bed	*krevet* [krev-et]
room	*soba* [so-ba]
key	*ključ* [kl-youtch]
shower/bath	*tuš/kada* [toosh/ka-da]
hot water/cold water	*topla voda/hladna voda* [top-la vo-da/hlad-na vo-da]

MISCELLANEOUS

tourist office	*turistički ured* [tooris-titch-kee u-red]
consulate	*konzularni ured* [kon-zoo-larnee u-red]
doctor	*liječnik/doctor* [lee-yetch-nik / doktor]
dentist	*zubar* [zoo-bar]
hospital/clinic	*bolnica/klinika* [bol-nitza/klin-icka]
police	*policija* [pol-itz-ee-yah]

TIME

hour/minute	*sat/minuta* [sat/min-<u>oota</u>]
week/day	*tjedan/dan* [<u>tjeh</u>-dan/dan]
year/month	*godina/mjesec* [god-eena/mee-<u>yeh</u>-setz]
now/soon	*sada/uskoro* [sa-da/oos-koro]
today/tomorrow	*danas/sutra* [da-nas/<u>soo</u>-tra]
yesterday	*jučer* [<u>you</u>-tchair]
this week/next week	*ovaj tjedan/slijedeći tjedan* [ov-eye <u>tyeh</u>-dan/sli-<u>yeh</u>-detchi <u>tyeh</u>-dan]
morning/afternoon	*jutro/poslije podne* [<u>you</u>-tro/poz-<u>lee</u>-yeh pod-nay]
evening/night	*večer/noć* [<u>vetch</u>-air/notch)

Monday	*ponedjeljak* [pon-ed-<u>yeh</u>-lee-yak]
Tuesday	*utorak* [<u>oot</u>-or-ak]
Wednesday	*srijeda* [sree-<u>yeh</u>-da]
Thursday	*četvrtak* [<u>tchet</u>-ver-tak]
Friday	*petak* [<u>pet</u>-ak]
Saturday	*subota* [<u>soo</u>-bo-ta]
Sunday	*nedjela* [ned-yeh-la]

January	*siječanj* [<u>si</u>-yeh-tchan-yeh]
February	*veljača* [<u>vel</u>-ya-tcha]

March	*ožujak* [o-zhu-yak]
April	*travanj* [trav-anya]
May	*svibanj* [svee-banya]
June	*lipanj* [lip-anya]
July	*srpanj* [ser-panya]
August	*kolovoz* [kolo-voz]
September	*rujan* [<u>roo</u>-yan]
October	*listopad* [lis-toe-pad]
November	*studeni* [<u>stoo</u>-den-ee]
December	*prosinac* [pro-seen-atz]

spring	*proljeće* [pro-<u>lyeh</u>-tcheh]
summer	*ljeto* [<u>lyeh</u>-toe]
autumn	*jesen* [<u>yeh</u>-sen]
winter	*zima* [zeema]

FOOD AND DRINK
| bon appetit! | *dobar tek!* [<u>dob</u>-bar-tek] |

Essentials
| breakfast | *doručak* [do<u>roo</u>-tchak] |
| lunch | *ručak* [<u>roo</u>-tchak] |

dinner	*večera* [vetch-air-a]
water	*voda* [vo-da]
beer	*pivo* [pee-vo]
draught beer	*točeno pivo* [totch-ay-no pee-vo]
wine	*vino* [vee-no]
white wine	*bijelo vino* [bee-yello vee-no]
white wine and soda	*špricer* (0.1l)/*gemišt* (0.2l) [spritzer/gem-isht]
red wine	*crno vino* [tzair-noe vee-noe]
rosé wine	*roze vino* [rozay vee-no]
house wine	*domaće vino* [dom-atch-ay vee-no]
spirit (generic)	*rakija* [rak-ee-ya]
spirit (from herbs)	*travarica* [trav-are-itza]
brandy	*lozovača* [lozov-atch-ka]
pear spirit	*kruškovača* [kroosh-kov-atch-a]
cold	*hladno* [hlad-no]
hot	*vruće* [vroo-tchay]
bread/bakery	*kruh/pekarnica* [kroo/pek-are-nitza]
jam	*džem* [d-zhem] (some say *pekmez* [peck-mez])
coffee	*kava* [ka-va]
tea	*čaj* [tchai – rhymes with 'try']
tea with milk	*crni čaj su mlijekom* [tzair-nee tchai soo mil-yeh-kom (ask for black, otherwise you get fruit tea with milk)

tea with lemon	*čaj su limunom* [tchai soo lee-<u>moon</u>-om]
sugar	*šećer* [<u>shetch</u>-air]
salt	*slan* [slun]
cheese	*sir* [seer]
soup	*juha* [<u>you</u>-ha]
thick soup/bean soup	*ragu/grah* [ra-<u>goo</u>/grar] (not a vegetarian dish!)
egg (eggs)	*jaje* (jaja) [<u>ya</u>-yay/(ya-ya)]
ham	*šunka* [<u>shoo</u>nka]
air-dried ham	*pršut* [per-<u>shoot</u>]
fish	*riba* [<u>ree</u>ba]
chips	*pomfrit* [pom-<u>freet</u>]
meat	*meso* [<u>may</u>-so]
vegetables	*povrće* [pov-air-tchay]
fruits	*voće* [<u>vo</u>-tchay]
homemade	*domaće* [dom-<u>a</u>-tchay]
grilled	*sa roštilja* [sar rosh-til-ya]
baked	*pečeno* [petch-<u>ay</u>no]
fried	*prženo* [per-<u>zay</u>no]
boiled	*kuhano* [<u>koo</u>-hano]
stuffed	*punjeno* [<u>poon</u>-yayno]

Fish

bass	*luben* [<u>loo</u>-ben]
bream	*zubatac* [<u>zoo</u>-ba-tatz]
catfish	*som* [som]
crab	*rak* [rak]
grey mullet	*cipal* [tzi-pal]
lobster	*jastog* [yah-stog]
mackerel	*skuša* [<u>skoo</u>-sha]
mussels	*dagnje/školjka* [dag-<u>nyeh</u>/shkol-<u>yeka</u>]
	(in general – there are other variants)
oysters	*oštrige/kamenice* [osh-<u>trig</u>-eh/kam-en-itz-eh]
perch	*grgeč* [gerg-etch]
pike	*štuka* [sh<u>too</u>ka]
prawns/crayfish	*šcampi* [shkampi]
red mullet	*barbun* [bar-<u>boon</u>]
salmon trout	*losos* [loss-oss]
sardines	*sardina* [sar-<u>deena</u>]
squid	*lignje* [lig-<u>nyeh</u>]
trout	*pastrva* [pas-<u>ter</u>-va]
tuna	*tuna* [<u>too</u>na]
zander/pike-perch	*smuđ* [smoodge]

Meat

beef	*govedina* [goved-<u>eena</u>]
chicken	*piletina* [pil-et-<u>eena</u>]
lamb	*janjetina* [yan-yet-<u>eena</u>]
mutton	*ovčetina* [ov-tchet-<u>eena</u>]
pork	*svinjetina* [svin-yet-<u>eena</u>]
veal	*teletina* [tel-et-<u>eena</u>]

Vegetables and side dishes

asparagus	*šparoge* [shpar-o-gay]
garlic	*češnjak* [tchesh-nyak]
green peppers	*paprika* [pap-<u>reeka</u>]
onion	*luk* [look]
potatoes	*krumpir* [krum-<u>peer</u>]
rice	*riža* [<u>ree</u>-zha]

Salads

salad	*salata* [sal-ata]
green salad	*zelena salata* [<u>zel</u>-ena sal-ata]
cucumber	*krastavac* [krasta-vatz]
cabbage	*kupus* [koo-poos]
tomato	*rajčica* [rai-tch-itza] (*paradajz* [para-dize] is sometimes used)

mixed	*miješana* [me-<u>yeh</u>-sha-na]
with chillies and cheese	*grčka* [<u>gertch</u>-ka]
with tomatoes and cheese	*šopska* [<u>shop</u>-ska] (many also use name *grčka*)

Fruit

apples	*jabuke* [ya-boo-keh]
bananas	*banane* [ba-na-neh]
cherries	*trešnje* [tresh-nee-yeh]
lemons	*limun* [lee-<u>moon</u>]
melon	*dinja* [<u>din</u>-ya]
orange	*narandža* [na-<u>rand</u>-zha] (or *naranča* [na-ran-tcha])
peaches	*breskve* [<u>bresk</u>-vay]
pears	*kruške* [<u>kroosh</u>-kay]
plums	*šljive* [<u>shlyee</u>-vay]
strawberries	*jagode* [yag-o-deh]

14 Further Information

BOOKS

Some of the books listed here are well out of print, but most can be found secondhand – either by trawling through old bookshops, or online at places like AbeBooks (*www.abebooks.com*).

Crnković, Vladimir *The Art of the Hlebine School* Croatian Museum of Naïve Art, 2005. Definitive snapshot of Croatia's naïve art scene and the people and places behind it, by the curator of the museum himself.

Goldstein, Ivo *Croatia: A History* C Hurst & Co, 1999 (2nd edition). Well-balanced Croat historian's view of Croatian history from Roman times to the present day. Hard to find, however, in spite of its relatively recent publication.

Kaplan, Robert *Balkan Ghosts* Picador, 1994 (out of print). The author uses his 1990 odyssey through the Balkans to explain the conflictual politics across the region in depth. Relatively easily available secondhand.

Letcher, Piers *Croatia: The Bradt Travel Guide* Bradt Travel Guides, 2007 (3rd edition). Just the guide you need if you're going beyond the confines of this particular book.

Murphy, Dervla *Through the Embers of Chaos: Balkan Journeys* John Murray, 2002. Brilliant account of a long cycle tour through the Balkans, including Zagreb. Truly a wonderful, inspirational book.

Pavičić, Liliana and Pirker-Mosher, Gordana *The Best of Croatian Cooking* Hippocrene, 2000. You're back home and missing those Croatian dishes? This is the book for you.

Radovčić, Jakov *Gorjanović-Kramberger and Krapina Early Man* Školska Knjiga Zagreb, 1988. Fascinating biography of the man who discovered and created the Krapina Man collection, by the current curator and the man responsible for the new museum opening in Krapina.

Silber, Laura et al *The Death of Yugoslavia* Penguin, 1996. Tie-in with the BBC series, and while it's not wholly successful without having seen the programmes, it's still a frightening blow-by-blow account of the events of the war.

Susnjar, Ante *Croatian–English/English–Croatian Dictionary and Phrasebook* Hippocrene, 2000. Good, helpful reference guide to the language.

Tanner, Marcus *Croatia: A Nation Forged in War* Yale University Press, 1997. An excellent and detailed history of Croatia, by *The Independent's* correspondent during the conflict – one of the best histories currently available.

West, Rebecca *Black Lamb and Grey Falcon* Canongate Books, 1993. Without question the most comprehensive (1,200pp) and best-written account of Yugoslavia in the 1930s. Rebecca West travelled widely in Croatia (and the other republics of the former Yugoslavia) in 1936 and 1937, and spent five years researching and writing this book. Fatally flawed in places, and naïve in its conclusion, it's nonetheless by turns funny, passionate and tragic – and always brilliantly opinionated. If you come across the original two-volume hardback from the 1940s, go for it; there are excellent black-and-white photographs.

Zagreb Tourist Board *Zagreb: An Old Town – Young At Heart* Zagreb, 1973. If you want to know what Zagreb was like in the 1970s, this is for you.

WEB RESOURCES

As you'd expect there's a mountain of information and a wealth of resources about both Zagreb and Croatia on the web. Here is just a handful of useful links:

ZAGREB

www.zagreb-touristinfo.hr The official site of the Zagreb Tourist Board. Excellent, detailed information about just about everything you'd want to know.

www.zagreb.hr City of Zagreb website. A few pages in English; most in Croatian.

www.zagreb.com News portal site in English.

GENERAL

www.tportal.hr/imenik/default.asp?lang=en Croatia's online phone directory (the English-language option). Just what you need when it turns out the phone number listed in this guide has already changed.

www.meteo.hr (and mirror site at **www.tel.hr/dhmz**) Croatian Meteorological Service. Click on the flag for English and find out everything you ever wanted to know about Croatia's weather, including forecasts.

www.croatia.hr The National Tourist Board's exemplary website, with a huge amount of practical information and the phone numbers of most hotels, travel agencies and campsites across the country.

www.hr The so-called 'Croatian Homepage', an English-language site featuring 7,500 links in hundreds of categories, all about Croatia. You can spend many hours here.

www.hr/wwwhr/useful.en.html In the same site, features especially useful categorised links.

www.uhpa.hr Association of Croatian Travel Agencies. A good way of finding out what can be organised for you.

TRANSPORT

www.zagreb-airport.hr Official website for Pleso Airport; usefully includes live flight arrivals and departures.

www.akz.hr Zagreb bus station website, with English options and comprehensive timetables.

www.hznet.hr Zagreb railway station, with excellent information available in English.

www.zet.hr Zagreb trams and buses (in Croatian only).

www.hak.hr Hrvatski Autoklub (Croatian Automobile Club). In Croatian only, though it does have an interactive traffic snarl-up area in English.

www.ina.hr The state-owned oil company. Complete with fuel prices and the locations and opening hours of every petrol station in the country.

GOVERNMENT, MEDIA, ETC

www.dzs.hr Croatian Bureau of Statistics. Everything you ever wanted to know.
www.dzs.hr/Eng/censuses/Census2001/Popis/Edefault.html That census, in full.
www.hic.hr/english/index.htm Another news portal (also available in Croatian and Spanish).
www.hrt.hr Croatian national TV and radio (in Croatian).
www.mint.hr Ministry of Tourism. More statistics and all the forms you'll need if you're planning on starting business in the Croatian tourist industry.
www.mvp.hr Ministry of Foreign Affairs. Everything you need to know about visa requirements etc.

LANGUAGE

www.eudict.com With excellent English–Croatian and Croatian–English dictionaries, though you need to have some idea of context as the responses are provided without separate definitions (the word 'set' gives you 41 different responses, for example).

Index

Page numbers in bold indicate major entries

303

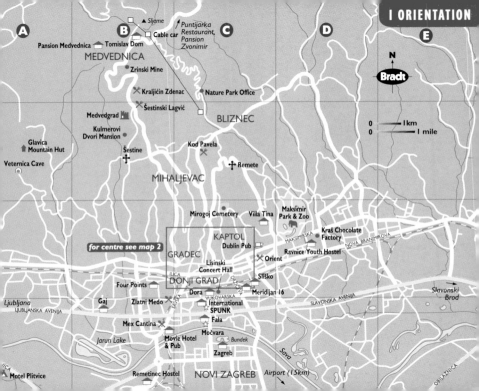

A   B   C   D   E

▲ Sljeme
Pansion Medvednica   ⌂ Tomislav Dom
Puntijarka
Restaurant,
Pansion
Zvonimir
Cable car

MEDVEDNICA

● Zrinski Mine

✕ Kraljičin Zdenac   ■ Nature Park Office

Medvedgrad ■   ✕ Šestinski Lagvić

Kulmerovi
Dvori Mansion ●

BLIZNEC

Glavica
⌂ Mountain Hut

Veternica Cave

† Šestine

● Kod Pavela

MIHALJEVAC

† Remete

Bradt

N

0 ────── 1km
0 ────── 1 mile

Mirogoj Cemetery   Villa Tina ⌂   Maksimir
Park & Zoo

MAKSIMIRSKA   Kraš Chocolate
Factory

for centre see map 2

KAPTOL
Dublin Pub ☕

GRADEC

Lisinski
Concert Hall

DONJI GRAD

Four Points ⌂

Gaj ✕   Zlatni Medo ✕

Ljubljana
LJUBLJANSKA AVENIJA

Orient ✕   Ravnice Youth Hostel

Slisko ✕   NOVA BRANIMIROVA

Dora ✕

International   Meridijan 16 ✕

SPUNK ★   VUKOVARSKA

Fala ✕   SLAVONSKA AVENIJA

Mex Cantina ✕

Močvara ♫

Movie Hotel
& Pub   Bundek

Zagreb ▲

Jarun Lake

Slavonski
Brod

Sava

Motel Plitvice

Remetinec Hostel   NOVI ZAGREB   Airport (15km)

OBILAZNICA

ŽELJEZNICA

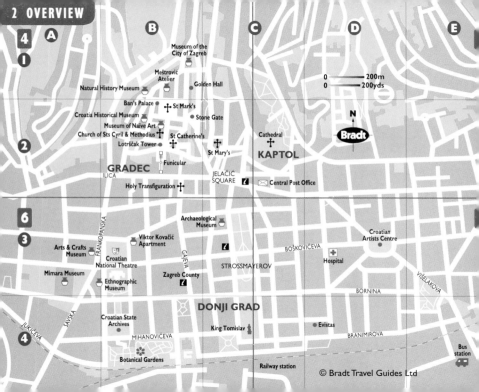

Museum of the
City of Zagreb

Meštrović
Atelier

Natural History Museum

Golden Hall

Ban's Palace

St Mark's

Croatia Historical Museum

Stone Gate

Museum of Naive Art

Church of Sts Cyril & Methodius

St Catherine's

Lotrščak Tower

St Mary's

Cathedral

KAPTOL

GRADEC

Funicular

ILICA

JELAČIĆ
SQUARE

Central Post Office

Holy Transfiguration

0   200m
0   200yds

N

Bradt

Archaeological
Museum

Croatian
Artists Centre

FRANKOPANSKA

Viktor Kovačić
Apartment

GAJEVA

BOŠKOVIĆEVA

Hospital

Arts & Crafts
Museum

Croatian
National Theatre

STROSSMAYEROV

Mimara Museum

Zagreb County

VIŠESLAKOVA

Ethnographic
Museum

BORNINA

DONJI GRAD

SAVSKA

Croatian State
Archives

King Tomislav

Evistas

BRANIMIROVA

JUKIĆEVA

MIHANOVIĆEVA

Botanical Gardens

Railway station

Bus
station

© Bradt Travel Guides Ltd

© Bradt Travel Guides Ltd

Museum of the
City of Zagreb

Meštrović
Atelier

Natural History Museum

Golden Hall

Ban's Palace

St Mark's

Croatia Historical Museum

Stone Gate

Museum of Naïve Art

Church of Sts Cyril & Methodius

St Catherine's

St Mary's

Cathedral

Lotrščak Tower

KAPTOL

GRADEC

Funicular

START

ILICA

Holy Transfiguration

Central Post Office

Centar

Zagreb

Archaeological
Museum

Viktor Kovačić
Apartment

Croatian
Artists Centre

Arts & Crafts Museum

Croatian
National Theatre

Hospital

Mimara Museum

Ethnographic
Museum

Zagreb County

DONJI GRAD

Croatian State
Archives

King Tomislav

Botanical Gardens

Regent Esplanade

Railway station

Bus
station

N

Bradt

Route of walk 1
Route of walk 2

0   200m
0   200yds

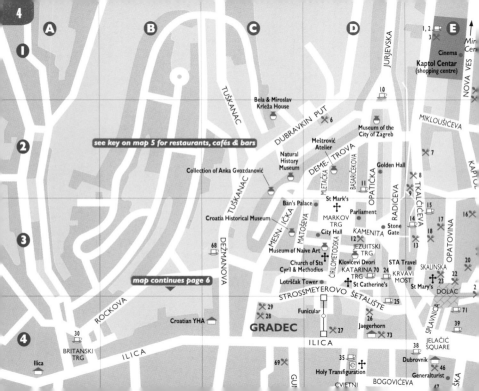

4

Ⓐ Ⓑ Ⓒ Ⓓ Ⓔ

1

TUŠKANAC

DUBRAVKIN PUT

Bela & Miroslav
Krleža House

6

Museum of the
City of Zagreb

JUREVSKA

Min
Cen

1, 2
3

Cinema
Kaptol Centar
(shopping centre)

NOVA VES

MIKLOUŠIĆEVA

KAPTO

2

see key on map 5 for restaurants, cafés & bars

Natural
History
Museum

Meštrović
Atelier

DEMETROVA

METAČKA

BASARIČEKOVA

Golden Hall

× 7

× 8

TKALČIĆEVA

RADIĆEVA

OPATIČKA

9

Collection of Anka Gvozdanović

× 11

St Mark's
†

Parliament

15

16 ×

TUŠKANAC

MESN-IČKA

Ban's Palace

Croatia Historical Museum

MATOŠEVA

**MARKOV
TRG**

City Hall

68

Museum of Naive Art

KAMENITA

Stone
Gate

14

17

18

13

OPATOVINA

DEŽMANOVA

ĆIRILOMETODSKA

Church of Sts
Cyril & Methodius

JEZUITSKI
TRG

12

Klovićevi Dvori

KATARINA 70 24

STA Travel

SKALINSKA

20

map continues page 6

Lotrščak Tower

St Catherine's

KRVAVI
MOST

St Mary's
†

22

23

DOLAC

2

ROCKOVA

STROSSMEYEROVO ŠETALIŠTE

25

SPLAVNICA

71

× 29

× 28

Croatian YHA

Funicular

GRADEC

ILICA

× 27

26

Jaegerhorn

× 73

39

JELAČIĆ SQUARE

30

BRITANSKI
TRG

ILICA

GUI

35

Holy Transfiguration

†

69 ×

38

Dubrovnik

Generalturist

46

ŠKA

Ilica

CVIETNI

BOGOVIĆEVA

4

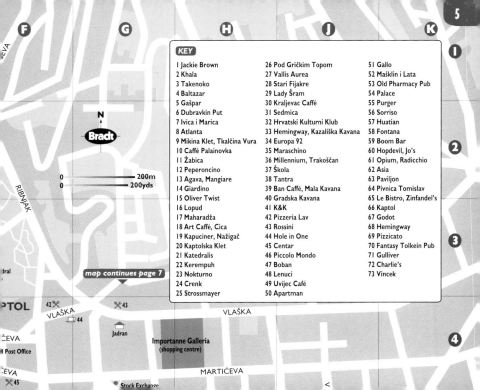

F   **G**   **H**   **J**   **K**

5

I

KEY

1 Jackie Brown	26 Pod Gričkim Topom	51 Gallo
2 Khala	27 Vallis Aurea	52 Mašklin i Lata
3 Takenoko	28 Stari Fijakre	53 Old Pharmacy Pub
4 Baltazar	29 Lady Šram	54 Palace
5 Gašpar	30 Kraljevac Caffé	55 Purger
6 Dubravkin Put	31 Sedmica	56 Sorriso
7 Ivica i Marica	32 Hrvatski Kulturni Klub	57 Huatian
8 Atlanta	33 Hemingway, Kazališka Kavana	58 Fontana
9 Mikina Klet, Tkalčina Vura	34 Europa 92	59 Boom Bar
10 Caffé Palainovka	35 Maraschino	60 Hopdevil, Jo's
11 Žabica	36 Millennium, Trakošćan	61 Opium, Radicchio
12 Peperoncino	37 Škola	62 Asia
13 Agava, Mangiare	38 Tantra	63 Paviljon
14 Giardino	39 Ban Caffé, Mala Kavana	64 Pivnica Tomislav
15 Oliver Twist	40 Gradska Kavana	65 Le Bistro, Zinfandel's
16 Lopud	41 K&K	66 Kaptol
17 Maharadža	42 Pizzeria Lav	67 Godot
18 Art Caffé, Cica	43 Rossini	68 Hemingway
19 Kapuciner, Nažigač	44 Hole in One	69 Pizzicato
20 Kaptolska Klet	45 Centar	70 Fantasy Tolkein Pub
21 Katedralis	46 Piccolo Mondo	71 Gulliver
22 Kerempuh	47 Boban	72 Charlie's
23 Nokturno	48 Lenuci	73 Vincek
24 Crenk	49 Uvijec Café	
25 Strossmayer	50 Apartman	

N

Bradt

0   200m
0   200yds

RIBNJAK

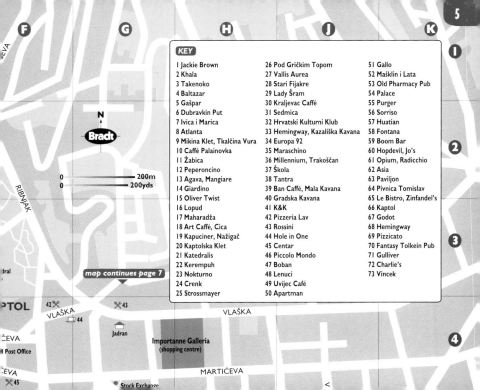map continues page 7

2

3

dral

PTOL

VLAŠKA   42   43   VLAŠKA

44

ČEVA

Post Office

Jadran

Importanne Galleria
(shopping centre)

4

EVA

45

MARTIĆEVA

Stock Exchange

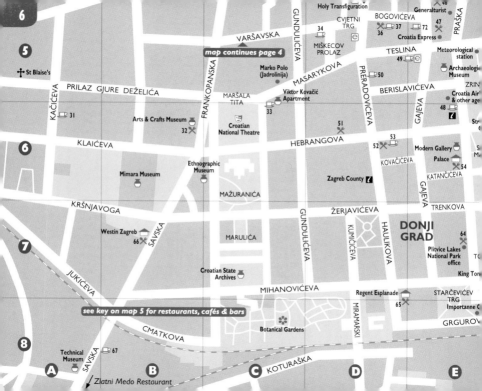

6

5

✝ St Blaise's

PRILAZ GJURE DEŽELIĆA

VARŠAVSKA

GUNDULIĆEVA

Holy Transfiguration

CVJETNI TRG

34

MIŠKECOV PROLAZ

BOGOVIĆEVA

37

36

72

Croatia Express

Generalturist

47

PRAŠKA

TESLINA

49

Meteorological station

Archaeological Museum

ZRIN

Croatia Air & other age

FRANKOPANSKA

MARŠALA TITA

Marko Polo (Jadrolinija)

Viktor Kovačić Apartment

33

MASARYKOVA

PRERADOVIĆEVA

50

BERISLAVIĆEVA

48

KAČIĆEVA

31

Arts & Crafts Museum

32

GAJEVA

Str

6

KLAIĆEVA

Croatian National Theatre

HEBRANGOVA

51

52

53

KOVAČIĆEVA

Modern Gallery

Palace

54

Mo

Mimara Museum

Ethnographic Museum

MAŽURANIĆA

Zagreb County

KATANČIĆEVA

GAJEVA

KRŠNJAVOGA

ŽERJAVIĆEVA

TRENKOVA

SAVSKA

Westin Zagreb

66

MARULIĆA

GUNDULIĆEVA

KUMIČIĆEVA

HAULIKOVA

DONJI GRAD

64

7

JUKIĆEVA

Croatian State Archives

MIHANOVIĆEVA

Plitvice Lakes National Park office

TO

King Tom

Regent Esplanade

65

STARČEVIĆEV TRG

Importanne C

MIRAMARSKI

see key on map 5 for restaurants, cafés & bars

CMATKOVA

Botanical Gardens

GRGUROV

8

Technical Museum

67

SAVSKA

A

Zlatni Medo Restaurant

KOTURAŠKA

B

C

D

E

map continues page 4

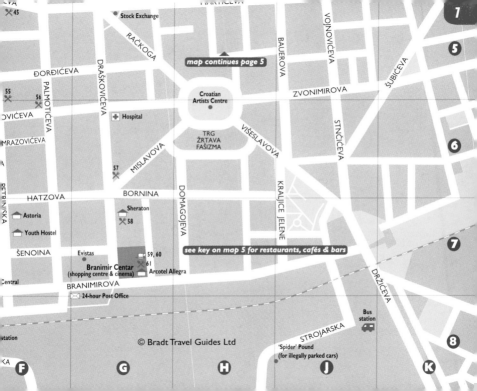

1

5

6

7

8

Stock Exchange

RAČKOGA

map continues page 5

ĐORĐIĆEVA

DRAŠKOVIĆEVA

PALMOTIĆEVA

55

56

...OVIĆEVA

...MRAZOVIĆEVA

PETRINISKA

Croatian
Artists Centre

BAUEROVA

VOJNOVIĆEVA

SUBIĆEVA

ZVONIMIROVA

Hospital

TRG
ŽRTAVA
FAŠIZMA

VIŠESLAVOVA

STNČIĆEVA

57

MISLAVOVA

HATZOVA

BORNINA

DOMAGOJEVA

KRALJICE JELENE

Astoria

Youth Hostel

Sheraton

58

ŠENOINA

Evistas

Branimir Centar
(shopping centre & cinema)

59, 60

61

Arcotel Allegra

see key on map 5 for restaurants, cafés & bars

DRŽIĆEVA

Central

BRANIMIROVA

24-hour Post Office

STROJARSKA

Bus
station

© Bradt Travel Guides Ltd

'Spider' Pound
(for illegally parked cars)

...station

...KA

F

G

H

J

K

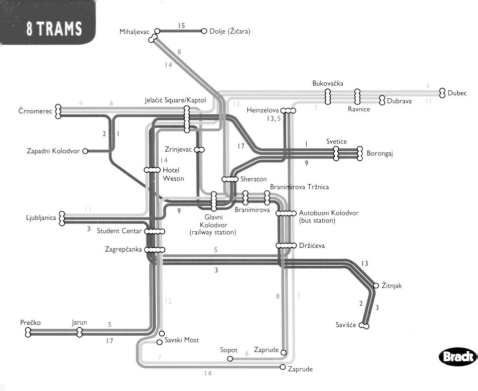

8 TRAMS

Mihaljevac

15 — Dolje (Žičara)

8
14

Bukovačka
Dubec
Ravnice
Dubrava

Jelačić Square/Kaptol
Heinzelova
13, 5

Črnomerec
4   6
12
7

2   1
17
Svetice
Borongaj
9

Zapadni Kolodvor
Zrinjevac
14
Hotel
Westin
1

Sheraton
Branimirova Tržnica
9
Branimirova

Ljubljanica
11
Glavni
Kolodvor
(railway station)
Autobusni Kolodvor
(bus station)

3   Student Centar
Zagrepčanka
Držićeva
5
13
Žitnjak

3
2   3

12
8   7
Savišće

Prečko   Jarun   5
Savski Most
17
Sopot   Zaprude

7
6

14
Zaprude

Bradt